Claiming the Constitution

Perspectives, 2000-2007

Clarence Hightower

President/CEO Minneapolis Urban League

W9-BDL-970

Published by the Minneapolis Urban League

Claiming the Constitution

Copyright 2007

Minneapolis Urban League

Contents

Acknowledgments

As President and CEO, I wish to thank the members of the Minneapolis Urban League Board of Directors for always supporting and believing in the vision that we've collectively crafted. This work would not have been possible without their support. I credit staff members of the Minneapolis Urban League, who carry out their work in step with the League's mission, as being the motivation behind these writings. I also acknowledge the unbending resolve of the Minneapolis community--- its residents, its neighborhoods, and its grassroots organizers--- for providing inspiration. I thank Al McFarlane, Editor in Chief for *Insight News*, for providing space in the publication that served as the venue for most of the articles that form this book. Finally, I thank Gary Marvin Davison for arranging these writings in a manner that makes the message this book was intended to convey so clear.

Chapter One

Introduction: Claiming the Constitution

> We the People of the United States, in order to form a more perfect Union, establish Justice, insure domestic Tranquility, provide for the common defence, promote, the general Welfare, and secure the Blessings of Liberty to ourselves and our Posterity, do ordain and establish this Constitution for the United States of America.

The great preamble to the United States Constitution contains the essence of the social contract that joins the government of the United States to the people. I believe fervently in this social contract. I grieve because neither governmental leaders nor the people themselves have lived up to the obligations that they assumed in establishing the Constitution. The history of the United States is for African Americans and other people of color largely a narrative of rightful citizenship denied or abused. But having moved closer to citizenship in the aftermath of the civil rights movement of the 1950s and 1960s, the people themselves have fallen short of the standards that active citizenship demands. My consternation over the failures on the part of both the government and the people drove me to write a number of articles over a period encompassing the years from 2000 to 2005. Most of these articles were published in *Insight News*, a newspaper targeted especially to an African American readership in Minneapolis. In this book I present these articles as an appeal to the parties joined in the social contract to better fulfill their obligations.

In chapter three of this book, I put forward a number of ideas for promoting positive values and community advancement. One of the articles in that chapter directly raises the matter of the social contract. Toward the end of that article I write,

> Society cannot function when the basic premises that we live by--- the belief that we will be safe, that our children will grow to adulthood, that our home is our castle--- are undermined and thus the social contract is not observed. Somehow, many young people have come to believe that their own lives have no value and, therefore, that the lives of others aren't worth anything either. There are neither enough police officers nor enough jail cells to combat that belief.

Law enforcement is, by nature, after the fact. The police do not enforce laws; rather, they arrest people who have allegedly broken the law. If the violence that occurs everywhere, every day, is to be stopped, it will come from society. Somehow society must convince young people who have rejected the parameters of the social contract that every life has value, that conflict can be resolved without violence, and that they will benefit from peace.

In that chapter three I reveal my deep and abiding belief in the importance of values, and I suggest numerous ways in which the African American community, other communities of color, and the community at large can act in ways more supportive of the social contract. In the articles that form chapter three, I ask people to pause during major holidays to remember those who are less fortunate, lest we forget that not everyone enjoys the security and abundance allowing so many of us to celebrate with such untrammeled joy. I express my belief that we are indeed our brother's keeper, and that at the dawn of each New Year we would do well to remember that good intentions and ethical deeds sustain perpetual sibling relationships within the family of humanity. I offer an appreciation for the Honorable Elijah Muhammad's metaphorical comment, "Don't throw away any bricks," and for upholding the idea that all people are valuable, deserve their dignity as human beings, and have potential to contribute to the human enterprise. I argue that we in the African American community should, in the spirit of a BET special report, conduct an honest examination of the black family, building on its considerable strengths while addressing frequently witnessed flaws that keep that venerable institution from reaching its full potential. Very specifically, I argue that a 70% rate of unwed parentage among African Americans is not acceptable and should never be tolerated as acceptable. I plead for unity between young and veteran African American leaders, lest we fall prey to the classical strategy of divide and conquer; I do, in fact, advance the notion of a think tank conducive to the transfer of wisdom from the elderly to the young. I call upon people to observe such homespun, tried and true values as saying "thanks" to those who have made life easier along the way, and dedicate one of my articles to my own expression of gratitude to those who have rendered such help to me: my stepdad, my elder brother Ed, my wife Beverly, and my wonderful Urban League family.

Throughout that chapter I call on the African American community to develop active and alert citizens who will understand and support such initiatives as the African American Agenda, honor black history not only in the designated month of February but with

3

knowledge and action throughout each year, and build on a proud past to create an even better tomorrow. Elsewhere in the book I call for the wonderful people who reside in North Minneapolis and other areas of the city to work persistently for better schools, to take advantage of programs that educate people on how to build wealth and acquire property, and to be active in forming the lead component of the approach to better neighborhood security known as "community policing." I urge people to be the first guardians of their own health, observing routines of diet and exercise conducive to robust lives and longer lifespans; to develop those attitudes and habits likely to cut the high rate of pregnancy among African American teens; and to do such common-sense things as wearing seat belts in order to ensure that no one's life ends due to an avoidable circumstance.

These sorts of exhortations provide the ongoing message of Part One of this book: "The Need for Community Action." There is in all of these messages more than a hint of my unavoidable optimism. One article argues for seeing the glass half full even during a time of horrific state government deficit. Another article calls for expressions of gratitude, and gives my own such sentiments, even as we approached the Thanksgiving following the 9-11 bombing of the World Trade Center with the knowledge that life would never be quite the same. The articles that form this book continually ask people to vote, to educate themselves on issues of historic and current relevance, and to cultivate the talents of a great community so as to produce both effective grassroots workers and strong leaders. I believe in the future and want people maximally to prepare themselves for the years and generations to come.

But in an excerpt from the introduction to another Minneapolis Urban League publication, *The State of African Americans in Minnesota 2004*, I also recall the words of Dr. Martin Luther King, Jr.:

> The majority of... white Americans believe that American society is essentially hospitable to fair play and steady growth toward middle-class Utopia embodying racial harmony. But unfortunately this is a fantasy of self-deception and comfortable vanity. Overwhelmingly America is still struggling with irresolution and contradictions. It has been sincere and even ardent in welcoming some change. But too quickly apathy and disinterest rise to the surface when the next logical steps are to be taken.

In that chapter we offer the follow-up comment that

4

In the best tradition established by Dr. Martin Luther King, Jr., the Minneapolis Urban League recognizes the high ideals that in large measure accord with the reality of life for Minnesota's white citizens. It seeks to hold Minnesotans to their own best values and to make these a reality for African Americans and other people of color in the state.

This is the theme that suffuses Part Two of this book: "The Need for Institutional Response." This section of the book features chapters that hold the institutions of society and government accountable for their responses to the needs of African Americans and other communities of color. In the articles that form Part Two, I point out that the problem of racial profiling by police officers is real and abiding, despite efforts of municipal leaders and the white majority to deny or minimize its existence. I raise reality's specter again when I cite the daunting fact that more African American men are housed in prisons than in institutions of higher learning. I hold our systems of social welfare accountable for a rate of out-of-home placements for African American children far beyond that of the white community and lamentably disproportionate relative to the percentage of African Americans in the general population. I take the city of Minneapolis to task for failing to cultivate the leadership talents of African Americans, so that too often when time comes to fill a position we hear the familiar refrain, "We tried, but there was just no one qualified from among the communities of color." Similarly, I note that the University of Minnesota has a chronic problem of institutional racism; ever too slow to promote African Americans of talent, the University also has held individuals such as Clem Haskins and McKinley Boston to standards and subjected them to processes different from those witnessed for their white counterparts. More generally in the world of sports, I note that the white community is far faster to exploit the talents of the black athlete than to promote African Americans to positions of managerial responsibility. And in many other arenas, as seen in the appointment procedures that attended the selection of Samuel Alito as Supreme Court Justice, the de facto process too often becomes, "Just hire a white man."

As I conceived the idea for this book and reviewed the articles that provide its content, I realized that two overarching messages pervade my writing:

1) There is more that African Americans and other communities of color can and should do in advancing the current and future prospects of those communities and of the general society. There is a need for much greater community action on the issues of significance that affect us all.

5

2) The institutions of public governance and private enterprise likewise have a long way to go in recognizing and advancing the right of African Americans and other people of color to participate equitably as citizens and economic actors. There is a need for a much more effective institutional response to conditions of life that too often discriminate between the white community and communities of color.

None of this should surprise us. This is the American, not just the Minnesotan, dilemma. At the time that the great preamble of the world's preeminent constitutional document was written, African Americans were assessed a value exactly three-fifths of their white counterparts for the purpose of counting state populations determining proportionate membership in the House of Representatives (Article I, Section 2). The institution of slavery was effectively recognized and upheld: Those who fled or otherwise for the moment escaped their condition of servitude were to be "delivered up on the Claim of the Party to whom such Service or Labour may be due" (Article IV, Section 2). Not until 1868 were African Americans freed from slavery by the 13th Amendment. Not until 1870 was the right of people to vote regardless of "race, color, or previous condition of servitude" recognized by the 15th Amendment. And in the interim, it was only in 1868, according to the 14th Amendment, that the great document of constitutional freedom contained the phrase, "All persons born or naturalized in the United States, and subject to the jurisdiction thereof, are citizens of the United States and the State wherein they reside."

Freedom had been too long coming, but it would be longer still. In the waning years of the 19th century, the Jim Crow system took root in the South, making mockery of the constitutional amendments that should have put all citizens of the United States on an equal footing. Jim Crow and the arduous exactions of the share cropping system impelled African Americans forward in the Great Northern Migration. A disappointing reception for African Americans in the North led to the founding of both the NAACP and our own beloved National Urban League and necessitated the continuing labor of W. E. B. Du Bois, Mary McLeod Bethune, Ida B. Wells Barnett, A. Philip Randolph, Thurgood Marshall, Malcolm X., Martin Luther King, Jr., and many others committed to the cause of civil rights. Because of the courage and exhausting effort of such eminent leaders, the United States would come closer to living the spirit of its great Constitution with the passage of the Civil Rights Act (1964), the Voting Rights Act (1965), and the Equal Opportunity (affirmative action) legislation of 1972.

Yet, as my articles in this book make clear, we have not yet arrived at our final destination on the road to freedom. None of the parties to the social contract have perfected their own roles in the agreement that binds all people in a society together. There are many things that the African American community, other communities of color, and the larger human community need to do in the quest for social betterment. And there remain many things in turn that the institutions created to serve these communities need to do to fulfill their part in the social contract: Public systems formed of police, courts, and correctional facilities are deeply flawed; both governmental and private bureaucracies are rife with discriminatory policies.

For all of their flaws, though, there is hope in the people and the institutions of our democracy. So declared Martin Luther King, Jr., when he was found guilty of putative criminal infractions in the aftermath of the Montgomery Bus Boycott of 1956:

> Let us not lose faith in our democracy. For with all of its
> weaknesses, there is ground and a basis of hope in our
> democratic creed.

And in the book, *Strive Toward Freedom* (1958), that chronicled the boycott, Dr. King suggested the consequences that would await this country if it failed to fulfill its democratic promise:

> The democratic ideal of freedom and equality will be fulfilled
> for all--- or all human beings will share in the resulting social
> and spiritual doom.

The Constitution was a flawed document. But in its vow to "secure the Blessings of Liberty to ourselves and our Posterity" it presented to the "People of the United States" a framework for governance that at its best can provide opportunity for all citizens now and in the generations to come. Part Three of this book embraces the ideal of uniting people and institutions so that the city of Minneapolis, the state of Minnesota, and indeed the United States live up to their own best ideals. The longest chapter in that section strongly suggests that the Minneapolis Urban League has striven to serve as a bridge between the community and the institutions that are justified by service to the community. Certainly, during my nine years as President and CEO of this great organization, I have been acutely aware of my duty to urge the community forward in constructive efforts on its own behalf, and to hold public institutions accountable for the quality of their service to the people of the community. I am deeply committed to the great goal of uniting people and institutions. I will retain and act

7

aggressively on this commitment for the remainder of my tenure as leader of the Minneapolis Urban League, and I will continue to promote the structures and programs that will allow this organization to serve as nexus between people and institutions long after my own period of service has ended.

Let this book, with its call for community action, institutional response, and unity between people and institutions make clear to all people, in every walk of life, the need to embrace the duty and revel in the privilege of "claiming the Constitution."

Part One

The Need for Community Action

Chapter Two

Education

1

Connecting Success in School to Regular Attendance

January 19, 2000

The three pillars on which success in school is built are attendance, behavior and achievement. They are inextricably linked. If you don't go to school consistently, you won't learn the material. If you disrupt the class, you will be removed from the classroom and you won't learn the material. If you don't know the material, you won't pass the test. If you're not succeeding in school, you begin to think there is no point in going anyway. That is the downward spiral that catches too many of our students.

Missing school creates problems beyond the particular day of absence; the consequences are cumulative. Research by Samuel Myers, Jr. of the Humphrey Institute indicated that school attendance was the most reliable predictor of success on test scores (Star Tribune, April 2, 1997). Larry Harris, a former teacher and now a very dedicated volunteer, has been crusading since 1993 for a community-wide program to get kids to school EVERY DAY. According to Harris, "A child who misses one day per week of school has missed a full year of school by the fifth grade."

Dr. Carol Johnson, Superintendent of Minneapolis Public Schools, has set a goal of 95% attendance for every student. To meet the goal, a child can miss only eight days of school. But the reality is that a child can miss 100 days of school before being held back for poor attendance. A child who is absent that much is held back anyway by his/her lack of knowledge.

I went to school every day because my mother would have killed me if I didn't. Today, not all mothers can see the importance of regular school attendance. They may come from a land where not everyone has the opportunity to go to school; they may come from a family where no one has been successful in school; they may be in an environment that is so chaotic that a child's school attendance is not a priority. A number of initiatives at both the city and county level have focused on this issue.

9

Hennepin County has a Truancy Work Coalition that has recommended a number of ways schools, businesses, and government can increase attendance. The North Area Community Conversation, which took place in May, attracted nearly 300 people. Students, parents, community leaders, faith members and educators gathered together to begin identifying barriers and forming strategies to support good school attendance. The list of barriers and strategies is five pages long.

The Minneapolis Urban League is part of one demonstration project, with Hennepin County and Minneapolis Public Schools, to increase attendance. The hypothesis to be tested in the two-year project is that stable housing increases school attendance. The intent of the project is to determine whether housing stability adds significantly to the efforts of the county and the city in achieving 95% school attendance among high-risk, high-mobility children. It's a small project, with only thirty families, but enough to give us an understanding of the correlation between housing and attendance.

Until recently, most of the research and speculation has been focused on the question: What leads kids to miss school? Now folks are beginning to look at the other side of that question: what leads to better attendance? My mother had one answer. But without Daisie Hightower, what can be done to make kids WANT to go to school and then get there every day?

Incentives must be found to make attendance preferable to non-attendance. Young people need a reason to be in school. For students who are doing well academically, that's reason enough. For those who aren't succeeding, there has to be something else that gives them a sense of belonging. They need to know there is a place for them to fit in and they are welcome despite their struggles with academics. Two examples come to mind. The North High School Gospel Choir, which performed at the Urban League's Annual Dinner, plays many roles. Members learn to sing well and have a good time doing it, and the opportunity to sing in the choir in turn motivates these students to come to school. This summer, CLUB FED organized a Summer School Perfect Attendance Incentive Program that at the end of the summer session rewards students for being present every day. Thirteen Northside schools are participating this year.

The one thing everyone seems to agree on is that there is no easy solution. But everyone involved in this problem has come to believe that the whole Minneapolis community will have to work together, working every angle and every facet of our children's lives, to change a culture that has had a casual attitude about school attendance to one that places a premium on 95% attendance.

Vallejo, California, has conducted a massive community campaign to keep children in school. Every segment of the community and every location in the community became involved. Concerned community members used dozens of incentives and rewards for both parents and children. Movie theaters even had "You should be in school" messages on the screen during afternoon movie showings. The most effective strategy of all may have been home visits made by teacher's aides. In all, the aides made more than 8,500 brief visits to inquire if a child was okay and to deliver a flyer on the importance of being in school (*Times-Herald*, Vallejo, CA, June 29, 1999). I recognize that Minneapolis is not Vallejo, California, but we will need the same level of commitment that occurred in that city if we are to reestablish the standard for attendance that my mother took for granted.

The Excitement and Anticipation of the First Day of School

August 23, 2000

The first day of school. Those words conjure up images for all of us: the end of summer, the beginning of new possibilities or new anxieties, knowing that you're more grown up than last year. The first day of school brings new shoes, new school clothes, a book bag, pencils, a ruler. At the same time, it is fraught with worry: Will I miss the bus? Will I get on the wrong bus? How will I know when to get off the bus? Who else will be on the bus? The mixture of expectation and trepidation tantalizes even the most world-weary of students.

The first day of school. On September 5th, the day after Labor Day, over 35,000 students of all ages will be on the street corner, with their backpacks filled with must-have school supplies, wearing the must-have article of apparel. The day may be too hot or too cold for the carefully selected first-day outfit. No matter--- apprehensive, excited, terrified, bored--- they all wait for the bus. Four hundred buses, running three morning shifts, will roam the streets of Minneapolis collecting what we hope will be the right children for the right school at the right time. More than a quarter of the students will be at a different address from the one at which they lived when they last rode the bus in June. Only NASA has more intricate logistical issues.

There are 128 schools in Minneapolis. Some are traditional schools, like those I attended; some are highly specialized. When everyone is counted , about 50,000 students will be on the rolls. More than five thousand will be five years old or younger. Over seventy percent of the children riding those buses will be children of color, children of many races and ethnic groups. Ten thousand will study English as their second language.

When the students arrive at school, fifteen thousand will be served breakfast provided by the district's Nutrition Center. The cost is 95 cents if you're in elementary school. Later that day, 28,000 will have lunch. If you're in high school, the price of lunch is $1.60. Sixty-five percent of the students will get lunch free or at a reduced price.

The first day of school is important for more than the students. About 4,700 teachers and 3,000 support staff will report on that first day. For teachers, the questions are very similar. What will my class be like?

What will be there needs? How long before the children feel that they belong? Who will be the leaders, the bullies, the quiet ones? With the diversity in today's classroom, just being there is an education. Teaching there is more of a challenge.

The Minneapolis School District is a massive enterprise. Each of our children make up a small piece of the big picture. But they are our piece. As adults, as parents, grandparents, aunts or uncles, we anticipate the first day of school along with our children. We want it to be an important day for them because it was so important to us.

The first day of school. The chance to start over. This could be the year I make the honor roll, this could be the season I make the team, this could be the time I will be chosen, maybe this year she will like me. The first day of school marks a fresh start never again experienced after we leave school. As we get older, the chances to start over with a clean slate are rare. Wins and losses at an early age DO matter. They are important steps to success in the future. That is why we, as parents, must ensure that our children have every opportunity we can give them to succeed in all aspects of their lives.

Teaching Urban Students Effectively

October 18, 2007

Last week, the Minneapolis Urban League hosted a lively and informative discussion on a wide range of issues pertaining to urban education. Highly respected educators, college administrators, representatives of the Minneapolis Public Schools, education students and Urban League staff exchanged views on the existing approach to preparing teachers, the reality of urban classrooms, and how to integrate the two.

A disconnect has occurred between teacher training and classroom reality in urban areas. This is a problem, not just in Minnesota, but all across the nation. The academic process for graduating and licensing teachers for our schools is seriously flawed. Historically, the model has been based on the needs of children of two-parent, nuclear families of northern European descent; children who lived in small, homogeneous, probably rural, communities where they were likely to spend the rest of their lives doing what their parents did before them. This agrarian model, which required a summer vacation to allow students to work on the family farm, was outdated by the 1920's.

A teacher standing before an inner city class today faces rows of students who come from many different countries and speak dozens of different languages, whose heritage claims every race and ethnic group, and who may not stay long in the same school. Among older students, many are no longer living in a parent's home. The United States has changed and will continue to change in ways none of us can predict. The way we teach our children must change completely if it is to come into line with the world of today's students. A student who does not fit the old European model needs an adjusted approach, but she or he should not usually require "special" education.

Much attention is now paid to the concepts of standards, testing, accountability, benchmarks, educational alternatives, curriculum, choice, and class size. We blame school boards, tax policy, school administrators, teachers, parents and students for the poor performance of a high percentage of our children. Bill Gates is convinced that the sheer size of the modern high school is the prime fault in American education. We would all like to find the one thing that is wrong and fix it.

There is no one thing that will change the academic performance of our children. We have to work on many barriers at the same time. Re-examining the profiles of 21st century students is an obligation that is vital to the teaching of education in our colleges and universities. The only thing that today's urban student has in common with the old model is an eagerness to learn. Those who become teachers need to realize that pedagogy is no longer the art of mastering a subject and presenting one's knowledge to pupils. As Valerie Gaither of Metropolitan State University stated, "Today's model requires the teacher to empower students to answer the question, "What does it mean to be educated?"

Teachers graduating today must bring to their classroom many skills they did not learn in teacher training. They must command three or four teaching styles if they want to reach everyone in the classroom. They must overcome lifetime biases that may be the product of their own upbringing. They must learn how to listen to their students when they voice concerns that are far removed from the classroom, and they must learn to listen to parents even when a parent seems unresponsive.

Good teachers do all of these things either instinctively or through experience. They didn't learn them as an education major. That's why it's so important to change how we teach our teachers. Bringing parents and families into school life, bringing the community into school life, making curriculum work for students depends, to a great extent, on how teachers are perceived.

Some colleges and universities are making changes. Minneapolis Community Technical College is one. Their Urban Teaching Program there is dedicated to seeing students as they are, not as the textbooks portray them. The University of Minnesota offers a similar program. Metropolitan State University seeks prospective teachers who have attended public schools in Minneapolis and St. Paul and know the issues.

The long-term goal is to put more teachers of color into classrooms with students of color. That's a bigger task than these three programs can complete. But it is a beginning. If you ask teachers, most will say that a teacher of their own inspired them to join the profession. Bringing teachers of color into the classroom will inspire another generation of students.

What we must never forget is that children will learn if given the chance. It is the nature of children to be curious, to explore, to investigate. If given an opportunity for learning that plays to their strengths, tools for learning that they can use, and the expectation of success, they will surprise us all. Remember, the history of our race has proven that some will learn even if NEVER given the chance.

State Funding for Education

January 4, 2007

It's not easy to follow the workings of the Minnesota State Legislature. We know that it is the Governor's prerogative to establish the budget for the coming two years and it is the legislators' task to accept or make changes to the budget. If they do, the Governor could veto any legislation containing such changes.

It is the nature of the political process that trade-offs become necessary and deals must be made. Compromise is the coin of the realm in lawmakers land. When it comes to money, things get harder to follow. Is a surplus real money? Does a budget cut mean less than the last biennium or does it mean less than the increase that was proposed for the coming biennium? Is the state budget really a shell game in which money is moved around with lightening speed but it is always the same money?

While the Governor's budget shifts some education money around, there is NO new money for education in 2001-2002. Beyond that, when it comes to education funding, I can't begin to explain where it comes from or how it gets where it goes. I do feel confident in explaining that our K-12 schools are looking at a bad deal from the biennial budget this year. There are real sacrifices, not compromises, to be made under the present budget scenario.

Minneapolis, St. Paul, and Duluth now get the largest portions of a special fund that is targeted to students living in poverty. The fund comes under the designation, "compensatory" dollars, because the money has been set aside for services to compensate for the particular educational barriers faced by low-income students.

The problem stems from a desire to spread the money more evenly across the state. There is a bill afloat in the legislature that would take this compensatory pot of money and, using a different formula for distribution, spread it around to all of the schools in Minneapolis.

On the face of it, many of you might think that to be fair. But such a practice would have a devastating effect on inner city schools with the highest poverty rates. In those schools, budget cuts mean people cuts. Budget cuts mean that children who can be helped most by consistent, one-on-one instruction and attention from an adult who is dedicated to their success will be left to cope on their own.

Inner city communities would be further stripped of sorely needed revenues. These are the very communities that are just beginning to make progress. This is not the time to reduce their resources; rather, it is a time to increase them in every way possible.

While I don't doubt that every school has some poor students, the answer is not to spread assistance to those students more thinly. The answer is to increase the size of the pot so that all students in need will be nourished. The public K-12 schools don't have the resources to influence public opinion the way the University of Minnesota can. Some of our schools are in danger of truly dramatic disruption in the education of their students.

WE need to exercise our political power by contacting Minnesota legislators. They haven't made a final decision yet.

There is still time to persuade them to keep full funding for our elementary and secondary schools. That's really all you have to say.

Tell your legislator to support full funding to our public schools (K-12) and to oppose the bills that "rob Peter to pay Paul." Tell them to cut out the shell game that is being played with the education of our children. The State of Minnesota should provide the money for what the state expects school districts to deliver, which is what students and families deserve.

Considering Education, Pre-K to UM, as an Organic Whole

January 8, 2001

I have been following the budget battle between University of Minnesota President Mark Yudof and Governor Jesse Ventura. Two of the most powerful men in the state are going toe-to-toe over what's right for this state.

This is an interesting situation.

Yudof has at his command probably as much fire-power and troops to get his budget passed as the Governor has to prevent it. The personal dynamic is something to watch.

I think both the University President and the Governor have lost sight of what is at stake here. I think they have forgotten why we educate people in the state of Minnesota. We do it to create productive citizens who can, in turn, make the state stronger.

The University Charter, drawn up even before Minnesota became a state, says, "The object of the University shall be to provide the inhabitants of this Territory with the means of acquiring a thorough knowledge of the various branches of Literature, Science and the Arts."

Both Yudof and Ventura need to consider what that means. They should be asking themselves how we want a child in Minnesota to be educated from pre-school through graduate school.

Nobody is talking about that.

Institutions from local school districts to MNSCU to the U of M itself want what will benefit them and are willing to have another institution get less if they will get more.

Where does that leave our children?

There are 59,000 students enrolled in the University of Minnesota at all levels. About 1,500 of them are African American. Only about a quarter of those will graduate.

In fact, less than half of all the students who enroll at the U will graduate, even after six years, which is now the standard timetable for completion.

Statistics like that call into question how well the University is fulfilling its mission. In recent times, the University has seen its mission as a dual mandate to educate the citizens of the state and to pursue top-quality research. Admittedly, it is hard to do both.

High-tech businesses need the research to produce new products. Young students need a place to complete their education.

Only a handful will ever experience both sides of the university's mission by becoming members of the elite research world. The rest seek the knowledge and skills that will enable them to adequately support themselves and their families and to participate fully in the life of this state.

Surely, then, education is all of a piece. If we don't do it right when a child is very young, poor education cannot be corrected at the university level.

President Mark Yudof ought to be concerned with the continuum of education in Minnesota. It is the pre-school teachers of today who are preparing his freshman class of 2016. Both the University of Minnesota and MNSCU have a huge stake in the education of our state's youngest residents. But they don't seem to get the connection.

As African Americans, we should be particularly attuned to the allocation of money for education. Since 1989, the number of African Americans enrolled in public schools in Minnesota has nearly doubled. After completing an elementary and secondary public school education, less than a quarter of the "college-ready" African Americans attend the University of Minnesota.

In fact, fewer than 600 even take the ACT.

Even in a state with a substantial projected budget surplus, there is a finite amount of money for the state to spend. It would be spent more wisely if education in Minnesota were regarded as an organic whole rather than a series of competing interests.

Carol Johnson, MPS, and the Meaning of Educational Success

June 28, 2001

Dr. Carol Johnson, Superintendent of the Minneapolis Public Schools, will remain in Minneapolis after all. After nearly two weeks of speculation, news leaks, offers, counteroffers, and a tidal wave of pleas, Carol Johnson will not be going to Nashville.

It must have been a difficult decision. Nashville is home for Carol or close to it. The prospect of going home, back to family, back to where she went to college, back to her origins –who wouldn't want that chance?

On the professional side, Nashville is a larger district with a bigger budget and fewer of its students living in poverty. Nashville appears to be a school district that has enjoyed relative stability over the years, a district ready for success. This was a very attractive offer from any standpoint--- personal, professional, or financial. Carol Johnson gave up a lot to stay in Minneapolis.

Right now, the situation she faces in Minneapolis seems bleak compared to Nashville. The budget increase for the Minneapolis Public Schools in the coming biennium is down to two percent. A two percent increase translates into the elimination of 126 teachers and 130 educational assistants from our classrooms and 75 administrators from the system. If money is one key to success for the district, as Dr. Johnson has argued before the state legislature, Minneapolis will be less ready to succeed.

Why would Carol Johnson turn down the chance to head up the Nashville school district? I can only speculate. Perhaps it's the personal challenge to finish a job she started. Her work here may never be done but there are initiatives in the Minneapolis Public Schools that she has developed that have not had time to germinate, much less flower.

With last year's referendum, Dr. Johnson instituted the 12-Point Plan to raise the level of achievement of students of color. This year, she has asked high schools to design a way to reduce the size of the community in which students learn. Carol Johnson sincerely wants all students, students of color and white students, to perform on a higher and equal learning plane.

Typically, consideration of a job change is a private deliberation undertaken with family and close friends. By placing herself at the center of a very public Go/Don't Go debate, Carol Johnson has made her record a subject of public discussion. She has opened herself and her performance to public scrutiny. This may be more than she bargained for when she responded to the call from Nashville.

There is nobody better at building consensus than Carol Johnson, nobody better at forming partnerships that work, nobody better at involving community. They could use her at the legislature. At some point, however, consensus, partnership, and community engagement have to produce results. At some point, you have to be able to say, success has been achieved or it has not.

A problem for me, and I suspect for many members of the African American community, is that I'm not sure what a successful school district is. We have been so concentrated on failure (the failure of our children, the failure of teachers, the failure of administrators, the failure of testing mechanisms, the seeming failure of every reform that has come before us) that we may not be able to recognize success.

Today, 38% of the young people who enroll as 9th graders in the Minneapolis Public Schools are no longer in school for what should be their senior years. That is failure. Would success be the completion of high school by all students? If not, how many dropouts are acceptable to us? Countless students perform below grade level on standardized tests. Is success performance by all students at grade level or above? How many students are we willing to pass on to the next grade despite a demonstration of failure?

Those of us who seek to lead in the African American community must wrestle with these questions and come to agreement on what we will accept as the standard for success. We are as accountable as Carol Johnson is to our children. We need to agree on what our community wants for our children and we must become unrelenting in our pursuit of what we want.

Carol Johnson probably has the toughest job in the state. Maybe she deserves to be paid more than Governor Ventura. While we wish for her success, it is not our job to make her job easier. We do her no favors if we fail to offer constructive criticism from our community, if we fail to hold her administration accountable to our community. The time has come to identify the road on which we can all travel in both directions carrying genuine support and sincere criticism.

Welcome back, Carol. Now, let's all of us get this education thing DONE!

21

A Final Grade for School Completion

August 29, 2001

A few weeks ago, the Citizens League released, *A Final Grade for School Completion*, a study of high school dropouts overseen by Gary Cunningham and George Latimer, former mayor of St. Paul. The study was prompted by the fact that, each year in St. Paul and Minneapolis, three thousand young people do NOT graduate from high school. That is right, 3000 students who should graduate, DO NOT graduate.

In 1999, of the 3016 students who should have graduated from Minneapolis Public Schools, only 1425 received a diploma. About five hundred seniors were not yet ready to graduate but over one thousand had dropped out of school. That's a thousand youth per year condemned to a life of flipping burgers, waiting on tables, making beds, cleaning toilets, or stocking shelves--- if they are employed at all.

Too many of the dropouts are our children. Two white students graduate for every black student. It wasn't always this way. Thirty years ago, the difference in graduation rates was fairly small. Twenty years ago, 68% of the black population in Minneapolis consisted of high school graduates, relatively close to the 76% for the white population.

Why is the ratio two-to-one today? I don't know. There doesn't seem to be any single reason we can point to. Yes, poverty hits us harder. But if growing up in poverty were the controlling factor, many of among us who have risen to jobs of prestige would be relegated to low-wage labor.

The Citizens League study takes a comprehensive view of the failure to graduate. The League describes "dropping out" as a multifaceted phenomenon occurring over time. It most certainly is not a single event that takes place at a clearly defined point in a young person's life. It is more accurately described as a gradual process of detaching from school and community. The process begins many years before the label "dropout" is applied.

The typical approach to issues of school failure is to line up the risk-factors--- low-income, poor attendance, disrupted family, high mobility, pregnancy, and the like---and target each factor with an intervention by a social service agency. According to the Citizens League, this approach doesn't work very well. For example, if you take the accepted top predictor--- absenteeism--- it turned out to be the major factor in individual cases only 16% of the time. In fact, many students with multiple risk factors never drop out at all. Many of us can attest to that.

The study considers a very different approach. It concentrated on the role of schools in decreasing the huge drop-out rate. It concludes that school districts are in the wrong business. Instead of being in the business of running schools, they should be in the business of giving children the education they need. That's a very different matter.

If tests can now predict as early as the first grade whether a child will eventually drop out or graduate, why do schools continue to operate an assembly line of instruction? If we know that a third-grader who reads below grade level is unlikely to graduate, why do schools continue to conduct "business as usual"?

There is plenty of responsibility and accountability to go around. The public, the legislature, executive branch, parents, teachers, administrators, and students have not demanded that schools operate as businesses that offer a product that education consumers can use. None of us has demanded that school districts respond to the needs of students. Instead, we have tried to mold students to meet the needs of school districts. We HAVE demanded better test scores. But test scores only measure the performance of the students who are there.

As the Citizens League study states, schools must, ". . .despite external factors, ...do better at engaging students and become more responsive to their needs in order to keep them in school."

Source: *A Failing Grade for School Completion*: *We Must Increase School Completion in Minneapolis and St. Paul*, final report of the Citizens League Committee on School Completion (www.citizensleague.net/reports).

23

in their tracks. Overnight, the goal of education became the production of more scientists. The curriculum had to expand to offer courses needed by potential engineers, mathematicians and physicists. Policy makers believed that schools could accomplish the goal only by introducing efficiencies brought on by greater size and standardization.

Compliance with school desegregation and special entitlement programs in the 1960s put additional pressure on schools and school districts to consolidate. The argument was made that large schools are more cost-effective. What really happened is that power and decision making were consolidated in fewer and fewer large districts. While it is true that there are some efficiencies initially, the cost of managing and controlling large numbers of students drives costs up.

The report by Kathleen Cotton takes each factor in academic performance and analyzes the research point by point. Every factor shows the same conclusion. Minority and low-income students sustain a greater negative impact in large schools than other students.

The level of participation in extracurricular activities by minority students is especially significant.   It is the best-supported finding in the research. A correlation has been established between student participation and student attitudes and social behavior that makes this aspect of small schools a very important consideration.

Small schools NEED every student to fill positions in student government, school yearbook, class officers, sports teams, and academic clubs. Small schools NEED every parent to support those activities. In a small school, nearly every student gets the chance to excel sometime and be recognized. In a large school, a far smaller percentage of the enrollment has that opportunity.

If we accept studies like this, we will have to change the way we think about high school. Bill Gates certainly has. But even Bill Gates is not suggesting that we tear down all of our high-schools and build educational venues for only 400 students. Those who believe in the benefits of small schools envision creating several separate, independent schools within existing buildings.

"Independent" is the operative word. Advocates call for complete control over budget, staffing, scheduling, and the specifics of curriculum and assessment. The ability to develop an educational environment that is psychologically, if not physically, "close to home" can change both the performance and the behavior of students as well as parents.

The dilemma is that today minority and low-income students are concentrated in large schools in large school districts, as they are in Minneapolis. Size works to the benefit of the district rather than to the benefit of students.   R. S. Jewell, in a study done twelve years ago, summed up the difficulty, " . . . **if minority students must struggle more to achieve a solid public education and if large districts and large schools find it increasingly difficult to achieve solid educational results for their students, we may be acting contrary to the interests of all concerned by organizing our public education system in a manner which assigns high proportions of minority youngsters to large schools within very large schools districts."**

Why does Bill Gates know that and we don't?

Source: Kathleen Cotton, "School Size, School Climate, and Student Performance," Norwest Regional Educational Laboratory, School Improvement Research, Series, Close-Up #20.

Measuring Up:
Troubling Statistics on African American School Attendance

October 24, 2001

Today a new report on the Minneapolis Public Schools was released. The report, *Measuring Up*, was developed by The Minneapolis Foundation and the Greater Minneapolis Chamber of Commerce in partnership with the Minneapolis Public Schools. The district has a set of goals to be achieved by 2005. This report describes the progress to date in the areas of test scores, attendance, suspensions, graduation rates, placement in special education, and the achievement gap between students of color and white students.

While improvement is cited in every category for the district as a whole, the news for students of color is not good. Too many African American students are absent each day; not enough of our students stay in the same school throughout their elementary or secondary careers. Too many African American students are suspended; too few graduate. The most alarming finding is that African American students who DO have good attendance are NOT doing as well in school as other students of color, including those who speak English as a second language. How can this be? Children from other countries, struggling to speak English, are doing better than our children born in Minneapolis.

That is a very troubling fact. The correlation across the district between consistent attendance and test scores is undeniable. Why doesn't that correlation benefit our children? Forty-five percent of the students in the Minneapolis Public Schools are African American. Admittedly, many don't come to school every day. I'm talking about the students who do come to school regularly. They are not doing as well as other students of color with the same attendance rate. Why is that?

Are they changing schools? Don't they do their homework? Are they not paying attention even though they are present? Don't their parents value education? Don't their parents or caregivers value them? Somebody will try to attribute this discrepancy to one or all of those things. We should not let this one go by. We must insist on a thorough explanation.

Researchers have proclaimed that consistent attendance is the key to learning. Why isn't it the key for our children? *Measuring Up* covers dozens of points that compare the performance of students ranging from test scores to suspension rates to special education. It does not explain why a positive factor like attendance fails to produce a positive result for African American children.

Source: *Measuring Up, A Report on the Minneapolis Public Schools 2002,* Published by Minneapolis Public Schools, Greater Minneapolis Chamber of Commerce, and The Minneapolis Foundation, October 2001.

African American Graduation and College Attendance Rates

September 16, 2002

In many ways, early fall is the best of all seasons and the worst of all seasons. As I head for work each morning, little boys and girls are standing on nearly every corner waiting for the school bus. You can see in their faces the pride in new shoes, new backpacks, new school uniforms. They stand on the corner bright and eager for what the day will bring. It reminds me of a few years ago when my own daughter stood on a similar corner, never doubting that something good would happen that day.

Then reality--- the reality for many of these children--- slaps me dead in the face. I can see the future that they cannot see. If the children at the bus stop are African American, nearly three-quarters of the group will qualify for school lunch, one out three of them will drop out of high school, half of their families will be homeless at some point in their lives.

When these little ones are in sixth grade, 86% will say that they plan to attend college. Unfortunately, when they reach eighth grade, fewer than half will pass the Basic Standards Test. I know for a fact that many of these African American children will live less well than the kids waiting for the bus in a white neighborhood.

For those who do make it through to high school graduation, having survived stops by police and orders to move along on the street, I see them coming up against the grim reality of college. A recent study by the Pell Institute for the Study of Opportunity in Higher Education states that the rate of college-bound students has dropped 12%, a statistic that includes one of the largest declines in the country in enrollment by poor students. While Minnesota still has a higher number of students going to college than most states, that figure is only about one out of three high school graduates.

Here is the Catch-22 for poor families. When the state's economy is thriving, as it was in 1999-2000, there is a strong incentive for children from poor families to move right into current job openings. When the economy is bad and jobs are few, poor families don't have the means to support a child in college.

For families that are better off, there is a strong incentive for children to attend college when the economy is strong because the family is doing well. In an economic downturn, their children turn to college anyway because jobs are not available. According to Phil Lowenstein at the Minnesota Higher Education Services Office, ". . . those access gaps have not closed in the last 35 or 40 years."

A gap in access translates into a gap in future opportunity. The Pell Institute report pointed to studies that show that someone with a bachelor's degree will earn $1,000,000 more in a lifetime than a high school graduate. Although both the University of Minnesota and the MnSCU system can help students in need, often through Pell grants, there is not enough help for a young person from a poor family.

I have heard over and over again the proverb from my motherland: "It takes a village to raise a child." Would someone please tell me what it takes to educate one?

Source: "College Eludes the Poor," *Star Tribune,* September 9, 2002.

In Praise of Alternative Schools

January 20, 2003

Charles entered an alternative school after being kicked out of his high school. He was an angry young man who was seldom in school. His father was on drugs and his mother was in prison. Charles used marijuana heavily and was involved in gang activity.

Despite the long odds against his success, staff at the alternative school made a decision to stick by Charles. Charles moved in with the family of another student. In time, he began to value his education and the strict but caring family he found at the alternative school more than he valued the street and the drugs. He made a decision to stay in school. Charles got off marijuana and his grades and attendance began to improve.

In his senior year, Charles visited Dunwoody Institute and immediately felt a connection. With the help of an employer who paid part of his tuition, Charles enrolled in computer technology at Dunwoody. After graduation, his employer plans to move him into a computer technology position at the company.

I share this story with you to illustrate a point: Many more of our young people would be lost to the future if not for alternative schools. A significant number of African American children have never had the life experience or acquired the developmental skills to succeed when they enter the Minneapolis Public Schools. Inadequate preparation can start a child on the downward slope of continuing failure.

Too often, their school develops a subconscious perception that these students are unable to learn. As a result, they are not expected to learn, nor are they expected to graduate or become self-sufficient adults. No one should be surprised that such students perform well below their actual ability.

There are now 5,800 alternative schools in the U. S. performing a vital function for students who have been cast off by the traditional school system. Alternative schools have existed in Minneapolis for over 30 years. Most are community-based, culturally competent, and accredited by the North Central Association of Colleges and Schools. Typically, the more than 30 alternative schools across the state operate under contract with a school district.

The quality of alternative schools in Minneapolis has been cited in numerous local and national reports and studies, including citation of best practices in a Washington study. All reports recommend expansion of alternative schools to address various areas of public school inadequacies.

These days, test scores seem to be the only way of measuring a school. While standardized test scores in alternative schools are generally lower than in traditional schools, the rate of improvement in 2002 among schools that belong to the Federation of Alternative Schools was greater in both reading and math than the rate of improvement in non-Federation schools.

The strength of alternative schools lies in their teachers, their size, and their structure. Teachers and staff believe in the ability of their students to excel. Two important elements of the alternative school give them the power to reach young people against incredible odds. First, expectations are high. The curriculum provides a structured environment that is safe, nurturing, and conducive to gaining the skills necessary for achievement. Distractions are reduced as much as possible to allow students to concentrate on learning. Second, the number of students is low. Students acquire a sense of belonging to a family. Many find in the school what they were seeking when they became involved with a gang: love, acceptance, nurturing, and belonging. Some experience, for the first time, ongoing, stable relationships with caring adults.

In 2002, over 200 students graduated from alternative schools and many have gone on to post-secondary education. They have succeeded in spite of dismal past performance and past experience. They have succeeded in spite of little or no family support. They have succeeded because the overwhelming support from the people at their alternative school taught them to believe in success over failure.

Celebrating High School Graduates

June 16, 2003

By the time you read this, over 3,000 high school seniors will have graduated from the Minneapolis Public Schools. This is a time for honor, for celebration, and for anticipation of what the future will bring. For many students, high school is a progression that includes study, parties, tests, sports, a driver's license, extracurricular activities, a part-time job, prom, the SAT or ACT, and college applications. Graduation is the culmination of four years filled with hopes, dreams, friendships, fun, and accomplishment. The future stretches ahead with college, career, and more accomplishments.

As a community, we devote a lot of time and talk to the miserable performance of African American children in the Minneapolis Public Schools. This week, it is time to exalt in the success of students who graduate, whether with honors or by the skin of their teeth. One way or another, they have crossed the threshold into a wider world.

For hundreds of students, walking across that stage to receive a diploma is, in itself, the culmination of a dream. Children who have grown up in poverty, who have lived in chaotic households, who have never seen anyone from their family or social network graduate from high school, consider themselves blessed when they put on that cap and gown. The struggle to be at school every day, to gain the discipline to do homework and prepare for tests, to participate in school life is truly daunting for them. Many have no backup at home, no one to care whether they succeed or not. Some do not even live at home. There should be a special award for these graduates just for being there.

There are others who make it against enormous odds because they DO have someone at home who loves them and insists on success. Despite a 67% rate of low-income families in the Minneapolis Public Schools, children are making it. Despite schools where low achievement seems to be the norm, children are graduating. Their stories are as compelling as those of the scholarship winners, the sports heroes, and the school leaders.

I saw living proof of those stories at the Minneapolis Urban League's Street Academy graduation. Two dozen young men and women came forward in caps and gowns to be presented as people who had achieved success even though the traditional school system had given up on them. These students had struggled through failing grades, truancy, suspension, and expulsion; some had even dropped out before reenrolling. Some of the young women had become mothers as young teens. They had overcome disappointment, anger, fear, isolation, and feelings of helplessness to make it onto the graduation platform.

All of the graduates gave thanks to the people who stood behind them, confronted them, insisted on success, and picked them up when they failed. They named immediate family members, older and younger relatives, teachers, counselors, and friends who never stopped believing in them. On graduation day, the same hopes, dreams, and pride of accomplishment could be seen on their faces as seen at any other graduation exercise. The vision they see before them includes college, career, and making a contribution to society.

All too often, we concentrate on the many negative things that happen in our community. Today is a time to highlight the many young folks who made it – despite the odds.

13

Calling for Community Participation
at the Dawn of a New School Year

September 12, 2003

One of the most exciting and rewarding times of the year for me is the time just after Labor Day. Most see this time as a chance to visit the State Fair. Others are excited because the weather is beginning to change. For me, it's exciting because it marks the start of a new school year. As I drive my route from home to work, I am rejuvenated by the sight of our babies standing on school bus stops with their backpacks and eager smiles. Smiles that say they are ready to learn. If I had one wish for them as they embark upon a brand new school year it would be that they keep that same enthusiasm throughout the year.

In fact, it would be great if all of us--- families, schools, neighbors, churches, area businesses and corporations, community centers, and various organizations located in our communities--- would unite in an effort to maintain the enthusiasm we see in our babies on that first day of school. Parents who attend school board meetings and parent conferences can encourage another parent to attend. They can get involved with school through the extra-curricular activities in which their children are participants. But aside from the things that parents can do, all of us can create a nurturing environment that extends beyond home and demonstrates to our children that the entire community is interested and invested in their educational success.

I know it's a difficult time right now for our public schools. They've already been severely affected by budget cuts that determine most of what they can or cannot do, and they're operating with the knowledge that more cuts are coming. At the same time they are required to meet new standards set by the Bush Administration's "No Child Left Behind" Act. Worst of all, they're losing a great superintendent at the end of this month! With so much at stake, we must all become active in support of our schools. We should feel a sense of obligation to do so. Find time to volunteer at a school in your area. Think of the boost it would give our children if some of us who are usually busy in our offices showed up to work at a school carnival or a book fair--- or came to observe a school performance. Wouldn't it be great if when a child stopped to buy a drink or a snack at the local food market, they saw some kind of inspirational message on student achievement in the store window?

What we do as a community to involve ourselves in education - particularly early education - can have a lasting impact on those smiling faces we see at the bus stops. Our encouragement could arouse a new sense of purpose for some children. We can inspire our babies to keep making progress and to persevere through any obstacles to complete their K-12 educational experience. All we have to do is get involved. And when those that we have inspired go on to the next level of education, whether it be some kind of technical training or a college degree program, we--- as a community--- will be rewarded.

From the Minneapolis Urban League to each parent who works so hard to get our babies ready for school, we extend to you a heartfelt, "Thank you."

Hard Questions about School Closings

February 12, 2004

One of the most difficult questions facing the community today is this: How do we advocate for the education of African American students, who are disproportionately the victims of the failure of schools to educate? About 10 years ago, education + money was supposed to be the answer; however, our children continued to fall behind. Then it was education + money + smaller class sizes, along with maintaining a 90% attendance rate. Still our children fell behind. Drastic budget cuts over the past two years have only served to further complicate an already complex problem. Last week, Interim Superintendent of Minneapolis Public Schools David Jennings injected yet another complexity into the equation. Jennings proposes closing nine inner city Minneapolis schools.

I believe that the issue of closing schools is much broader than it appears on the surface. The issue starts and ends with the following question: How is it that you best serve low-income students of color, many of whom are already struggling? Is it best to take the limited resources currently available to the district and spread them over a large number of schools, thus maintaining smaller class sizes, community familiarity, and family proximity? Or do you take those same limited resources and spread them out over fewer schools, gaining potential efficiencies while at the same time concentrating students and increasing class sizes? These are tremendously difficult questions, over which many of us will argue and find ourselves on different sides.

But there are, at minimum, three specific questions that need to be asked we discuss closing inner city schools. The first question: How do we calculate the loss of a school to the fabric of a community? In other words, how do we calculate the value of having after-school activities available to children where they can walk home after the activities have ended? And how do we calculate the value of having community facilities available in close proximity to school and home for recreational use and for parent/community meetings? How do we quantify these values?

The second question has to do with the notion of busing. If there are going to be fewer schools in the inner city, this suggests to me that there will, of necessity, be more busing. How do we figure the increase in busing into the efficiencies gained through school closings? Also around the question of busing, how is it that the busing will flow? In my hometown of Alton, Illinois, officials made the decision to use busing as a way to integrate the schools. But what actually happened is the low-income students of color were bused to more affluent areas. Affluent white students were left untouched. We must be exercise foresight with questions concerning an equitable transportation scheme, lest we find low-income students of color disproportionately designated for busing. The flow then only runs one way.

The third, and most important, question about closing inner city schools has to do with the quality of education. In this discussion, when have we talked about the product itself--- about enhancing the educational product so that more and more parents feel good about what is going on in the public school system? One of the reasons that we are facing school closings is because approximately 3,000 fewer students are expected to enroll in Minneapolis public schools over the next two or three years. I would venture to say that a large portion of the parents of those 3,000 students made the decision to place their students elsewhere because they are unsatisfied with the product. I'm not sure that anything matters until we get the product right.

There are two public hearings scheduled for February 18th and 19th to discuss the proposal of Interim Superintendent Jennings to close nine schools. These hearings come after his discussion with the Board of Education and in the midst of a fast track to a Board decision slated for the 24th of February. We, the community, have to ask the questions I've outlined above, and they must be answered--- or at least addressed--- in the context of the rationale for the Jennings proposal. If not, that proposal could be viewed as offering nothing more than budgetary expediency, with only an outside chance of improving the education of African American students.

15

Questions about the Jennings Plan: Will it Close the Achievement Gap? Why the Fast Track?

February 20, 2004

In my most recent "Urban Views" column, I raised three questions that I felt needed to be answered by Interim Superintendent David Jennings in light of the proposal to close and consolidate a number of schools for the 2004-2005 academic year. Well, on Tuesday, February 17, I attended a School Board meeting at which Interim Superintendent David Jennings, on behalf of the staff of the Minneapolis Public Schools, presented his plan. I, the members of the School Board, and others in the room listened intently to what was being presented. However, to my chagrin, only the seven elected members of the School Board were allowed to speak in response to the presentation.

Because I wasn't allowed to speak out, I wasn't able to ask two crucial questions that I felt needed to be answered. So, I'll ask those questions now.

The first question that I would have asked in response to the proposed plan to close and consolidate schools is this: What does closing schools have to do with closing the achievement gap between white students and students of color? The most apparent causes for such a wide gap are so well-documented that it would be redundant for me to repeat them. However, many would argue that the "gap" is a resource issue. Others would contend that the resources were, and are, available to make improvements, but they have been distributed in a manner that didn't address the "gap" in a meaningful way.

How many people remember the late Gary Sudduth's "Show Me the Money" speech to the Minneapolis School Board in 1997? He pointed out back then that more than $500 million had been spent in the previous six years to improve the achievement of poor and minority students in Minneapolis; despite that massive infusion of funds, though, the learning gap had not narrowed and disadvantaged students in Minneapolis were worse off than they had been. Do the math, folks: Thirteen years have now elapsed since Sudduth's speech and we're still in the same holding pattern! Maybe the Minneapolis Urban League should repeat our former leader's demand to the School Board that "funding for compensatory education, Title I, desegregation, and Special Education be used as intended and that the Minneapolis Public Schools document every dollar it receives and spends for poor and disadvantaged students." The bottom line is, as long as achievement levels for students of color continue to fall behind, and the gap between students of color and white students continues to widen, neither closing schools nor finding a better use for limited resources will accomplish any meaningful purpose.

So again the question is the following: What are you going to do to close this achievement gap, and how will closing schools help achieve that objective?

The other question I would have asked should I have been allowed to respond to the Minneapolis Public School's presentation this one: What is so magical about March 2? Does it not make sense to allow time for deliberation to ensure that you get it right? What I heard at the meeting was that if the plan were delayed, parents would have limited ability to make a choice about where to send their child to school this coming fall. But is that not exactly what the plan would do if it eliminates existing schools and school programming?

This plan is definitely on a fast track, and it's now up to the School Board to slow the train down. The two public hearings scheduled right in the middle of the presentation to the Board on the 17th, and a request for the Board to make a decision on the 24th, could not have been meant to do anything more than fuel debate about the plan, which is unfortunate. I'm not saying the plan is right or wrong. What I am saying is that it's wrong to put such an important decision on a fast track! I believe, like many others, that there are too many questions that need to be answered before anybody votes the plan up or down.

16

Moving Forward in the Spirit of *Brown v. Board*

May 20, 2004

As we celebrate the 50th anniversary and great civil rights victory of the *Brown v. Board of Education*, I think it's important to reflect on two other major Supreme Court decisions that mark history. According to basic principles established by the United States Constitution, the decisions I refer to should have prevented the faulty doctrine of "separate but equal" many years before *Brown*.

Way back in 1868, the 14th Amendment of the Constitution was passed, giving Blacks the right to vote, to own property, and decreeing that Blacks be treated equally to whites in the application of federal and state laws. Congress stated at the time that racial segregation in schools was unconstitutional. That was 136 years ago.

Then there was the case of *Plessy v. Ferguson* (1896), which introduced the concept of "separate but equal" as a sacred doctrine. Its application to law seemed to turn the 14th Amendment on its head. It asserted that "separate" facilities for blacks and whites were constitutional as long as they were "equal," an invidious ruling that carried over into other areas of public life, including public schools. That was 108 years ago.

Even though the "separate but equal" doctrine was challenged time and again in the courts, it wasn't until the Supreme Court decided the case of *Brown v. Board of Education* in 1954 that it was finally struck down. What was particularly remarkable about the *Brown* decision is that it did not rely on a comparison of mere tangible factors that purported to equalize black schools and white schools, such as buildings, curriculum, or teacher qualifications. Instead it took an honest look at the effect of segregation itself on public education and its propensity to deprive African Americans of equal educational opportunities. The case of *Brown v. Board* of education was indeed believed to be a stunning victory for civil rights activists and advocates of the day. That was 50 years ago.

So in my mind, this focus on the Supreme Court's 1954 decision in the case of *Brown v. Board of Education* is both timely and telling. Timely in that it's always wise to remind ourselves at some prescribed interval of the trials and tribulations that have marked our progress as a nation. What is telling is that even today, 50 years after that landmark decision, we're compelled to ask the question, how victorious are we?

In Minneapolis, this question is particularly important. How victorious are we when just 47% of all Minneapolis 9th graders graduate from high school within four years? How victorious are we when ten Minneapolis schools were tagged as "underperforming" for the third year in a row for failing to meet standards set by the current administration's No Child Left Behind Act? How victorious are we when thousands of students leave Minneapolis schools for the suburbs, for charter, private and alternative schools, or to be home-schooled? And how victorious are we when state budget cuts disproportionately affect schools in a district where African Americans make up 42% of the student population, and where the African American child poverty rate is almost 50%, while the white child poverty rate is barely 10%?

Therefore in celebrating Brown v. The Board of Education, we have to do more--- as parents, as educators, and as a community--- than reminisce about the times when academic achievement was the greatest status symbol for the black family. It's okay to stoke the embers that remind us of past struggles and the victories that they brought about--- as long as we intend to ignite a fire. Let's reignite the fire that was started in Topeka, Kansas by Oliver Brown and the NAACP, who took on the Board of Education's policy of segregation and won the right for his daughter to attend elementary school in her own neighborhood.

17

In Praise of the Superintendent Selection Process

June 6, 2004

Public opinion of the Minneapolis School Board has, for some time now, been less than favorable. When David Jennings's interim role as Superintendent was unexpectedly announced as being made permanent by the School Board, public outcry was enormous. Then, in early February of this year, the School Board's consideration of the Interim Superintendent's proposal to close 8 public schools by next school year caused the community further consternation.

As a community, we have been appropriately critical of the School Board, particularly on those occasions when its members have shown an apparent lack of judgment in matters critical to the largest student population represented in the public schools system. When they have fumbled the ball, so to speak. So I want to be one of the first to say that they have finally picked up the ball in a way that deserves to be acknowledged.

On June 7, the School Board announced the three finalists in the search for a permanent Superintendent of Schools. The Board's so-called "4-3-2-1 Process" to engage the community at every interval has clearly been instrumental in bringing these three candidates forward. I commend the school board for being inclusive of the community in establishing the criteria by which applicants would be reviewed, and for consistently keeping the community updated on the national search process from the time it began to its conclusion. In sum, the School Board has responded very professionally and magnanimously to our concerns about a fair and open search process, a fact that is reflected in the opportunity for the community to meet the three final candidates on
June 9.

Now that the final three candidates have been brought forward, it will be the sole responsibility of the School Board to decide which one of the three will be our new Superintendent of Minneapolis Public Schools. Although not a litmus test for racial or gender balance, the fact that two of the final candidates are female and two are people of color says something about a commitment to diversity that the search process must have insisted on. But I don't believe the School Board's final decision will rest on race or gender. I am confident that School Board Chair Sharon Henry Blythe will continue to insist on the same fairness and sound judgment that brought the board to this important point.

As head of an organization that has persistently advocated for reforms within the school system, I've been asked any number of times what kind of superintendent the Minneapolis Urban League would prefer. Our preference has not changed. Fundamentally, we believe that person must be properly accredited and skilled in the field of education, specifically experienced in urban education, and must be prepared to deal directly with the community on a regular basis. Most importantly though, we believe the new superintendent must already have a plan and a priority for advancing the academic achievement of students of color within the public school system. It appears that each of the three candidates is prepared to meet our criteria, and I look forward to working with that individual in the very near future.

Welcoming Thandiwe Peebles

June 18, 2004

Last week I congratulated the school board on an open and inclusive process for selecting a new superintendent. Now I want to congratulate its members on their final selection. From all indications, Ms. Thandiwe Peebles brings with her the awareness, the understanding, and the capability to construct solutions to the major issues confronting the Minneapolis Public Schools.

I look forward to welcoming Ms. Peebles to the city of Minneapolis, and to sharing with her my thoughts on some of the pressing problems facing African Americans in public education. I also look forward to hearing, in a community setting, her own observations on our school system. We all know the story of how poorly African American students are performing; it has been submitted as a referendum for reform by this community on any number of occasions. We even have a name for it: "Closing the Achievement Gap." I'd like to know what her 40 years of experience in school districts in New York and Cleveland can tell us about the dynamics of this issue in comparison with other school districts, based on our size and demographic makeup.

I realize Ms. Peebles will have many mandates to which she will have to respond as she prepares to lead this school system, but there's some untold business that I'm not sure she knows the extent of. I'm talking about the lack of human capital needed to work with low income students and students of color. Statistics will show that fewer and fewer teachers of color are emerging from the qualified pool of teachers for the State of Minnesota. From 2001 through 2003, a total of 7,998 teachers passed the state test to teach mathematics. Of that total, only 124 were African American, and only 46 were Native American. In that same period, a total of 8,141 teachers passed the state test to teach reading. Of that total, only 110 were African American, and only 48 were Native American. During that same period, 8,256 teachers passed the state test for writing; following a pattern similar to other totals, only 120 of those passing were African American, and only 46 were Native American.

My point is not that we lack qualified teachers in Minnesota. What I am arguing, though, is that there is a disconnect between the number of students of color in the public schools and the number of qualified teachers of color at the school system's disposal. I believe that as the new superintendent settles into a new educational environment, she should look at this growing problem sooner rather than later. I wish her Godspeed.

Thandiwe Peebles: Tough Job, Right Person

August 20, 2004

By any stretch of the imagination, the job of Superintendent of Minneapolis Public Schools is tough. In a drama stretching back to 1993 with the departure of Robert Ferrara, through the tenure of Peter Hutchinson & Company and that of the well-regarded Carol Johnson, the job of the superintendent has been pretty close to impossible. The job has if anything gotten harder.

First of all, the current economic climate for education in Minnesota is tough. Schools throughout all school districts, including Minneapolis, are facing budget cuts that escalate with each coming school year. And with the 'No Child Left Behind' Act looming over their heads, school administrators are faced with the daunting task of doing more with less. Then consider the precarious position of those schools that now have fewer students because of the current decline in enrollment. Anybody in the position of superintendent will have to talk about even more school closings, and that's going to be tough.

These elements alone would lead any objective person to believe that the leader of the Minneapolis Public Schools will need the ability to walk on water to be remotely successful. Yet there are even more issues that the superintendent will have to deal with sooner rather than later. She'll have to deal with teacher lay-offs and families leaving the district for charter and private schools, as well as responding to the concerns of the community. Addressing these issues with even a modicum of success is going to be tough.

Let me just say that in my short life I've been high and low, and I've met some bad (I mean good) folk along the way, but I have yet to meet anybody who can walk on water. But having said that, I do believe that the school board, given that it has a hard job of its own overseeing the district's budget, curriculum, personnel, and facilities, has found the right person in Thandiwe Peebles.

I can say that because Ms. Peebles and I have met now on a couple of occasions; first in a very professional setting where I had an opportunity to hear her perspectives on education. I left that meeting absolutely convinced that she knows what it will take to move our community forward and to lead all students on a successful path that truly leaves no child behind. The other chance I had to be in Ms. Peeble's presence was on a float in the Urban League's Annual Family Day Parade. The environment was totally informal, and believe me, education was not the topic of conversation. I left that experience impressed with her ability to mingle with the "folks," as well as with every single individual who approached her.

My only concern as this transplanted Clevelander begins to lead our school district is that we will spend too much time comparing her to her predecessors and not enough time comparing her skills to her job. I have had the opportunity to do that, and I will leave you with this summation: Tough job, right person.

20

Nine Principles Toward Better Education

September 3, 2004

Please forgive me for mixing two of the most important things in my life with this article, but for me they are hard to separate. They involve my spiritual faith and my love for children.

This morning as I was driving to work, I noticed on almost every street corner young kids of every race, ethnicity, and possibly several religions, anxiously and excitedly waiting to start their first day of the 2004-2005 school year.

Now, I'm not an educator in the academic sense, but on most Sundays, I take a shot at helping people to better understand their responsibilities as Christians. This leads me to suggest an idea that calls on all of us to be thoughtful--- and faithful. I suggest that we as a community pledge adopt a sort of "Ten Commandments" approach to educating our children and ensuring their academic success. Reducing the biblical number by one, I offer the following "Nine Commandments" as suggested principles toward better education, simply to initiate your input as to the highest priorities needed to achieve success. To the degree that you respond with your own suggestions, I will already have done what I intended to do.

First:　　We as a community pledge to provide an environment free of violence and disorder, an atmosphere in which each child can learn and thrive;

Second:　We as a community pledge to put the education of our children first before recreation, before television, and before expensive shoes and clothes;

Third:　　We as a community pledge to invest in the educational process of our children;

Fourth:　We as a community pledge to seek an understanding of the best methods of teaching for each individual student. We will no longer accept the cookie cutter approach to teaching;

Fifth:　　We as a community pledge to support families as they go through the many life struggles that often interfere with a child's ability to cope with the learning process;

47

Sixth: We as a community pledge to examine every optional teaching model to ensure that the one being used is absolutely the best to bring out the most from our children;

Seventh: We as a community pledge to seek the brightest and the most enthusiastic educators to serve as both teachers and mentors for our children;

Eighth: We as a community pledge to be inquisitive about what each child learns and will engage a child each and every day in talking about what he or she learned and how they interpret what they learned;

Ninth: Finally, we as members of the community will hold each other accountable for any and every lost opportunity to educate a single child.

Realizing that the Holy Bible talks about Ten Commandments, I thought it might seem blasphemous to suggest ten commandments for educating our children, so I instead settled for nine. Again, perhaps you can suggest more, or perhaps you will wish to reduce the list to those that you feel to be the very most important. But more important than the numbers, perhaps even more important than the precise principles, is that we talk about the education of our young, and that we do so in earnest.

21

Minnesota-Educated: Two Planes of Progress

September 17, 2004

I am highly upset about something I just read, so forgive me if my ire is apparent in my remarks. This morning, as I opened the *Star Tribune* to the "Metro" section, I was jolted by an article that pronounced Minnesota as being rated Number 2 amongst all of the states in the nation in terms of getting students ready for college and then getting them graduated. On the surface, being rated Number 2 amongst 50 states for accomplishing something that appears to be so positive gives the impression that you've absolutely done enough. However, from where I sit, Minnesota hasn't even come close.

As you read beyond the headlines, the report referred to in the *Star Tribune* article (prepared by the National Center for Public Policy and Higher Education) shines light on a number of very disturbing trends. It reveals Minnesota as a state that educates its students on two very different planes. Sure enough, on one plane, white students are fairing quite well; but on the other, students of color are continuing to fall behind and the achievement gap continues to widen.

Let me outline a couple of points.

First, the report indicates that 10 years ago, 37 out of every 100 adults of color were in college somewhere in Minnesota. Now that number is down to only 26. How can we as a state be doing so great when fewer and fewer of our students of color in high school are finding their way to institutes of higher learning?

Second, the state of Minnesota got a grade of "C-"as it relates to college affordability. In laymen's terms, that means that by and large most students can't afford to attend college. How do we think this is interpreted when you factor in the family income level of those students of color who are prepared to go to college but are at or below the poverty line? It makes college almost impossible to afford! A student who does manage to get into college is faced with a boatload of loans that could take a lifetime to repay when she or he gets out.

Third (and then I'm done), it bothers me that the governor's adviser on higher-education policy is pleased with the state's performance. How can any of us be pleased with our performance on higher education when more and more students of color in Minnesota are not even graduating from high school? Research indicates that the graduation rate for African American students is 43%, and for American Indian students, 41%. Hispanic students graduate at a slightly higher rate of 53%. The fact of the matter is that Minnesota has one of the lowest graduation rates among African American students in the nation, and one of the widest achievement gaps between white students and students of color. In my mind, you can't look at these kinds of dismal figures and say "we've done the best among the worst" and be satisfied.

I am concerned about a report that can rate the state of Minnesota so high when I know my brothers and sisters are doing so poorly. Before I can celebrate, I've got to see a reverse in the current trend for students of color. I've got to see all of Minnesota's students educated on the same plane. When Minnesota is leading the nation in getting students into college based on the performance of all of its students, then I'll be pleased.

22

Star Tribune Counterpoint:
In Defense of Thandiwe Peebles

January 2005

I have a pressing need to comment on an article written by Star Tribune columnist Steve Brandt. The article was headed　Peeble's Strong Ways Chafe Some." It appeared on January 5, 2005.

After reading the article twice I was left bewildered as to why the story was ever written. My more suspicious side leads me to believe that someone had a personal axe to grind, and that this person felt the need to do so in a public arena. This belief was strengthened the further I read, because it became more and more evident that fifty percent of the article was based on the thoughts and opinions of a former staff member. Not that former staff members don't have a voice, because clearly they do;　I disagree vehemently, though, when anyone's voice is used in this manner.

At issue here, it seems, is the culture in which employees within the Minneapolis Public Schools system operate. Every system in America, regardless of how large or how small, has its own corporate culture, highly influenced by leadership. Therefore, whenever new leadership is brought into any setting, the existing culture will absolutely change. The degree to which change is manifested is directly proportionate to the different styles of the outgoing and incoming leaders. Superintendent Peebles and Superintendent Johnson have two vastly different leadership styles. Neither is better---just different. I myself have had the experience of being the newly selected leader at three different organizations over the past twenty years. At each of those organizations, my leadership style differed from that of my predecessor.

But I am disappointed that so early in Dr. Peebles' tenure as superintendent we have resorted to evaluating her style. Style is not the most important issue, performance is! But as we look at her performance, we need to acknowledge the circumstances in which Superintendent Peebles inherited this job. If one were to seek to describe the Minneapolis Public Schools district the day Dr. Peebles became its superintendent, it could be described as having these three traits:　1) a district with a declining enrollment, 2) a district with a consistent low performance rate for students of color, and 3) a district with revenues that lag behind expenses. All three of these traits have created very difficult scenarios for the district, none of which were created by Dr. Peebles, but all of which she has been charged with improving.

Obviously, one cannot improve those kinds of very large issues without someone questioning how you go about getting it done. We must not, however, lose our focus. In a district within which only 47% of African American third graders score at or above grade level on the Minnesota Comprehensive Achievement Exam in reading compared to 82% of white students, we cannot afford to lose our focus. In a district wherein only 44% of that same population test at grade level on the Minnesota Comprehensive Math Exams compared to 81% white students, we cannot lose our focus. In a district in which one finds the four-year graduation rate for black students in 2003 to be only 39%, compared to 83% for white students, we cannot lose our focus. Someone is upset about how Dr. Peebles is asking the question; I am upset that the questions have remained unanswered for far too long.

Superintendent Peebles was brought to Minneapolis to educate every student in the Minneapolis Public Schools. She was given the particular charge to make measurable progress in closing the achievement gap between students of color and white students in the system. Unlike the writer, who said the reason she got the job was because she had less baggage than one finalist and more passion than another, I believe she got the job because she is uniquely qualified to focus the limited resources of the district on the most prominent areas with which it has struggled for the last decade.

23

On the Systemic Problems of the Minneapolis Public Schools

2005

If you've read any of the local newspapers, you might have noted that an extensive report has just been issued on the effectiveness of the Minneapolis Public Schools system. The report was just recently presented to the School Board by the Executive Director of the Council of Great City Schools, a coalition of the largest urban public schools systems in the nation. It acknowledges the historic reputation of Minneapolis's public school system as one of the best in the country, but warns that immediate action must be taken to impede recent evidence of decline. Those of us who have been concerned about the progress being made by public schools to educate our children are already aware of some of the issues the report revealed.

We know for instance that teachers have no real incentive to work in the neediest schools in the district. Our children often see a different face in the middle of their school year--- sometimes more than once. Obviously, that doesn't lend to the trust and respect that a teacher-student relationship needs in order to see progress. Something must be done to remedy this situation, as the report recommends.

We know that the Twelve Point Plan was instituted with a specific focus on improving the academic performance and graduation rates of students of color. The Minneapolis Urban League fully supported the plan as it was written, because we felt it provided a clear, easily adaptable road map for all schools to achieve success. This report reveals why, despite the good work that went into formulating the Twelve Point Plan, it didn't produce the results needed to demonstrate progress. The trend for African American children in public schools continues to be high representation in special education programs, lowest test scores in math and reading, highest suspension rates and highest dropout rates. These circumstances directly correlate with the widening achievement gap between white students and students of color; as the report recommends, reforms must be put in place to reverse those trends.

The report found that Title I and other compensatory allocations are inadequate for some of the neediest schools. As an organization that operates an alternative education program, we at the Minneapolis Urban League know that. The guidelines for how these funds can be used are complex enough. When the funding is inadequate, it's extremely difficult to be successful at achieving desired results for our unique population of students. More funding is needed, for instance, to respond to "special needs" students whose level of poverty, tendency for frequent housing moves, and family instability make them the most challenging student population with which to work.. It is recommended by the CGCS that, if it is going to boost academic performance for these students, the district needs to focus more Title 1 monies (particularly those funds that are carried over) on schools with larger numbers and percentages of poor students.

Superintendent Thandiwe Peebles has been quick to acknowledge that there are some exemplary educational programs out there. She talks about the need to spread "best practices" across the district. Her own Strategic Plan for improving district outcomes incorporates some of the practices already in place. But what has not been acknowledged--- or perhaps comprehended--- is the impact that site-based curricula and other individualized educational programs have had on the potential for any measurable progress. The authors of this report extensively discusses the need for the school system to become more uniform. The coalition of experts who examined our public schools system have found many schools are disjointed from district-wide efforts and have a tendency to "do their own thing." They recommend that more uniform instructional tools be used across the district. It strikes me, in reading some of their specific recommendations, that the CGCS is promoting a "get back to the basics" concept. I know that this phraseology is probably too simplistic, but it would seem that the experimentations in Profiles of Learning and Small Learning Communities that we've gone through over the years may not have been the answer, at least not for those students who are struggling the most.

I'm not an expert in education, and I don't claim to be competent enough to pinpoint the exact cause of the district's problems, provide answers to the problems, or to judge the competency of the district. But this report commissioned by Thandiwe Peebles should relinquish any doubt that the problems of our district are systemic. If you believe otherwise, as I'm sure some do, I encourage you to request a copy of the CGCS report for your own review. I think it will convince you of the urgency for reform. It will also convince you that Superintendent Peebles clearly has the best interests of our district at heart. Her actions since being selected to lead our public schools system have proven that she is willing to be held accountable, but it's clear that she expects others to be held accountable, as well.

It's time for the district and for the community to get fully behind her efforts. I truly believe that full cooperation with her leadership in establishing a Strategic Plan for the Minneapolis Public Schools district is not only advisable, it is essential.

24

Giving Superintendent Peebles the Benefit of the Doubt

The latest issue involving Superintendent Thandiwe Peebles deserves a response from this column. I'll say from the outset that I am personally skeptical of the charges being made against her. Nonetheless, a number of things came to mind as I thought about the stir an "anonymous" letter writer has caused throughout this city.

My first thought was that for the first time in a long time, I can say that the school board has, in general, behaved appropriately. Many people would not know for instance that this issue has been on their table for a month. They'd already begun an independent investigation into the matter without making a big deal out of it. They conducted their work as it should be conducted, in private consultation, which protects the right of Dr. Peebles to a fair hearing and also lends credibility to the school board itself. For that, board members should be commended.

But another thought came to my mind that quickly dispels the notion that the school board will be able to continue to move forward in a commendable manner. That is the apparent inability of the school board to rein in the behavior of one or two of its members. It's troubling to me--- and it should trouble the board as well--- that a member of the school board feels compelled to make very public statements about an issue so controversial, knowing that her remarks could so easily be interpreted as being the position of the school board. I would think that the School Board of the Minneapolis Public Schools would be no different than other boards, in which one can have her or his own independent viewpoint, but that person can't run around shouting it from the mountain top out of personal frustration with a person or situation. That kind of behavior is messy; it's inappropriate in this case and should be unacceptable to the school board.

My final thought has to do with the *Star Tribune*'s obvious intention to sensationalize this issue. I have no way of knowing whether any of the allegations against Superintendent Peebles are true or even deserve attention. The bottom line now is that they've been made, and made in a manner that frankly, in my mind, makes everybody involved look bad. I understand that newspapers like to whet the appetites of their readers when there's an apparent controversy to report, but front page coverage one day with follow up coverage before any type of investigation can reveal true facts is a disservice to the public. The *Star Tribune*'s handling of this particular issue causes me to believe that this is much more than a news story for the reporter. In fact, it appears to be a determined effort to undermine the leadership of Dr. Peebles.

Again, I am in no position to state with either personal knowledge or authority that none of the allegations made against Dr. Thandiwe Peebles are true. I will say, however, that based on what has been reported, it should not be beyond the realm of possibility that members of her staff--- the people that were her first and most frequent points of contact in a new city--- would extend a helping hand to her as someone new to this city. It should also not be beyond the realm of expectation that Dr. Peebles would to some degree accept that help.

Let's just wait, folks. Let's allow the investigation being carried out by the school board to take its proper course. In a relatively short period of time Dr. Peebles has done some tremendous work on behalf of our children, so let's give her the benefit of our doubt. She deserves it from us, and I'm sure she would appreciate it.

Chapter Three

Values and Community Advancement

1

Remembering Those in Despair during the Holidays

December 13, 2000

In the coming weeks, people around the world will experience the hope and the expectation that surrounds the observance of religious and cultural rites both ancient and new. December marks the convergence of the profound religious, cultural, and spiritual longing for a better time and a better world.

Christmas, Ramadan, Kwanza, and Hanukkah will all overlap in the coming days. Each has its own rituals of hope and promise; each carries deep significance for the participants.

There are as many ways of preparing for this holy and joyous season as there are families in Minneapolis. We all have traditions--- things we always do, food we always serve, relatives we always tolerate. When Christmas comes we tend to close ranks and spend time with those closest to us. For children, it is all about expectation and hope. For adults, it is often about the past rather than the present--- remembering other moments when we were together with those who are gone. Home, family, heritage and religion are all concepts intimately bound to the month of December.

The season of birth, of renewal, of hope does not carry the same message if you don't have a home, or a job or enough to eat. Poverty is always harder when it is cold and dark. The story of Bethlehem paints that picture very clearly: a young man and woman expecting their first child alone in a strange town with no one to call on and nowhere to turn.

On any given night in Minnesota, over 700 young people are alone on the streets without a permanent place to live. Nearly a thousand families in Hennepin County are homeless. The ideal of home and family becomes a burden rather than a blessing for them at this time of year. People who have no place to live are often employed. If a person is making $5.15 per hour, even if she or he works two jobs, such a person can't pay the rent in Minneapolis. Nor can one pay the cost to keep warm in the frigid temperatures of last week.

The Bible tells us, "For ye have the poor always with you; but me ye have not always." (Matthew 26:11). As we prepare for a joyous time warmed by friends and family, we cannot forget those for whom the season of hope is hopeless, the period of joy is despair, the time of peace is chaos.

2

New Year's Resolution: "Being My Brother's Keeper"

January 10, 2001

By mid-January, a certain percentage of New Year's resolutions have already been broken. By the end of 2001, very few will have survived intact. The practice of making resolutions for the New Year is a curious exercise. With such a low success rate, why does the practice persist?

Many people use the beginning of the year to examine their own behavior, identify their shortcomings, and set a goal for the coming twelve months. We've all made these kinds of promises to ourselves: I'm going to lose ten pounds... I'm going to quit smoking... I'm going to get a new job... I'll get more exercise... I'll watch less TV... I'll make time for myself. How many of us persevere beyond a few months?

When we analyze our good intentions, we find out that it's all about us. We, ourselves, are the center of our good intentions. We resolve to make things better for ourselves. We want to change who we are or how we are. There's nothing wrong with that. At the same time, the concentration on self may be one reason that New Year's resolutions are so hard to keep.

I suggest that directing our good intentions outside ourselves may reap greater benefits. We might be better served throughout the coming year if we direct our energies of mind and body toward the goal of "being my brother's keeper."

That's not a popular position to take. That's not the message we get from 21st century culture. The worlds of politics, sports, movies, television, music, and magazines continually show us how public figures and fictional characters get what they want, how they keep things for themselves. The behaviors of wanting and getting are before us all the time.

We may all accomplish more, with less stress, if we concentrate on what we can give to life. As we celebrate the birthday of Martin Luther King, we might consider a belated New Year's resolution that says:

>	**I will act on my concern for the poor.**
>	**I will be quick to seek reconciliation.**
>	**I will give others the benefit of the doubt.**
>	**I will go out of my way to say positive things about my neighbor, and I will learn to forgive.**

In response to the question, "How many times should I forgive my brother, seven times?," the Bible says "seventy times seven."

By December of 2001, we may be more satisfied with our efforts to keep this resolution than any other.

Giving Thanks at Thanksgiving, Despite a World Changed by 9-11

November 26, 2001

Our concept of time has changed. We begin sentences with "Before September 11 . . . " or "Since the World Trade Center . . . " The events of that day distort our frame of reference. Nothing has really changed. The economy continues its nosedive, 17 million American children are still hungry, Minneapolis remains the city with the greatest income disparity between whites and people of color, housing costs are causing homelessness, our children still fail in school at the same rate.

Our perception, though, is that everything has changed. We have fears we can neither name nor understand. We have had to confront two realities. On September 11, we came face to face with evil. We know and understand human weakness, human failings, lapses in judgment, and temptation. We are not well schooled in evil. We watched those videotapes hundreds of times in the first week and it never seemed real.

I don't know anyone who died at the World Trade Center or the Pentagon. In fact, I don't even know anyone who lives in New York City. Why, then, did I need to know that my family was safe that day? We have the sense that we can no longer be sure of things. We accept that auto accidents, fires, train wrecks, even plane crashes occur. But we want them to be accidental.

I feel sorrow for our children who should be looking forward to a life full of possibilities but who now must live with possibilities we never considered. Despite the uninterrupted presence of racism and discrimination, my daughter will not view the future with the freedom that I did at her age.

The celebration of Thanksgiving comes as irony. In the face of such horror, what are we thankful for? Some who read this will say, "There is nothing to be thankful for." They will not be the majority. This Thanksgiving, I think most of us have a heightened sense of what we treasure. Knowing full well that family can sometimes engender conflict, jealousy, or humiliation, we choose to honor family as a mysterious and wonderful source of comfort, love, and joy. We choose to give thanks for our blessings.

Many in our community have very little to count when it comes to blessings. We have missed out on so much of the American dream. Yet, we do give thanks. We bless the Lord who has given us those we love and those who love us. Despite our burdens and our sorrows, we head home to honor the bond that, this season, seems more important than ever.

4

"Don't Throw Away Any Bricks"

December 3, 2001

A few days ago, I was in a meeting with Tyronne Terrell, Director of the Civil Rights Department for the City of St. Paul. During our conversation, Tyronne quoted The Honorable Elijah Muhammad, leader of the Nation of Islam from 1934 to 1975. He used the phrase, "Don't throw away any bricks". When I pressed Tyronne for an explanation, he pointed to the brick clock tower outside my office and said, "You don't know which one of those bricks – if you took it out – would cause that tower to topple."

I was profoundly struck by that thought, so much so that I offer the same analogy to our community. Our community, the black community of inner city Minneapolis, is like that tower. It is a tower that depends on every one of our members to achieve its strength. Each day, we see this tower of strength besieged by forces that threaten to destroy it: rampant, deadly disease, babies born to children, young men in jail, homeless families, children failing in school. We need every brick in the tower just to withstand the onslaught.

As our community braces for the year 2002, we need a unified vision of who we want to be and where we want to go. A clear, common strategy and a collective effort are the only things that will get us through the coming years of an economy in recession.

The leader of the new administration for the City of Minneapolis, R. T. Rybak, has said that his tent is big enough to be inclusive. The question is, what will we do once we are inside the tent? I'm convinced that now is the time for all of us to set aside our differences and to map out a common strategy that will work to the advantage of African Americans in this city.

Sometimes our community finds it difficult to stick to a common strategy because we associate our long-term goals with short-term leadership. I'd like to make two quick points about leaders and leadership. First, regardless of who is in charge of a city, a committee, a task force, or whatever, there is still room for each of us to contribute. We have to . . . we must.

Second, we must remember that leadership is fleeting. No one person remains in a position of leadership forever. I often reflect on my tenure at the Minneapolis Urban League. I look toward the future through a lens that shows me that, one day, I will wake up and not be the president of this organization. Therefore, I have an obligation to do the best that I can in the time I am given.

One of the things that I can do is to remind our community of our long-term goals. We want strong families; we want our children to achieve in school; we want our young men in jobs, not in jail; we want good health and longevity; we want to live in decent places; we want to be recognized for our contributions. We cannot lose sight of what we want in the fog of a changing environment. We need to be able to count on every member of our community to sustain our tower. It will not stand if anyone is left out. Equally, it will not stand if anyone chooses not to carry their load.

I agree with The Honorable Elijah Muhammad, "We can't afford to throw away any bricks."

Thoughts on BET's "Under One Roof"

December 17, 2001

Have you heard about the news feature on BET called "Under One Roof"? Each week BET presents news, research, and personal stories about things that are reshaping the lives of African Americans, their relationships, and their households. After the weekly report, viewers can log on to the Bet website to become part of the "Under One Roof" project to participate in chats, polls and forums.

BET wants the national African American community to explore and evaluate, together, the forces that affect our families and, using this national communication, to develop a plan of action and set priorities that individual families and the community at large can use to challenge politicians and policymakers.

Other news shows have used their website to monitor public reaction. CNN and CNBC do it every day. But this is new to the African American community. BET has invited ALL of us to participate in a common discussion of subjects that we seldom discuss outside our own homes or a close circle of friends.

A recent poll undertaken by "Under One Roof" asked a series of questions about parenthood and children. The respondents were sometimes harshly critical of the family situation for African American children today. In the most decisive result of this poll, 56% of the respondents, all of whom were black, answered yes to the question, "Have Black Men Failed Their Families?"

This public response was so unusual, not because of the answer but because it WAS public, it prompted Leonard Pitts, a syndicated columnist, to write an article about it. His premise is that the African American community needs to bring discussion of the issues that hit us the hardest out from behind closed doors and into a public forum. After centuries of never airing our dirty laundry in public, this sounds like betrayal. The truth is Leonard Pitts is probably right.

We need to have frank and open discussion as a means of confronting the enormous problems that we face as a community. We've always been afraid of public discussion of our problems. We worry that acknowledgement of a problem will give white people the chance to claim that there is some inherent failing in people with dark skin. So we remain silent.

As a people, we are reluctant to go beyond those closest to us to get help. If a family has a problem, the family determines to solve it within the family. The fear that we will be found inadequate prevents many from acknowledging the need for help. Evidence of waiting too long to seek help is all around us.

Besides the disastrous consequences this can bring to health, economic status, and relationships, there is another serious consequence. We don't know very much about what those outside our immediate circle really think. We don't know what our neighbors or colleagues believe about the value of marriage, the role of fathers, the responsibility for children.

While an Internet poll is part entertainment and part research, it opens the door for discussion. If we do not put an issue squarely on the table and openly discuss its pros, its cons, its ramifications, and its consequences, we are left with supporting or not supporting the people who are already involved in the issue. The result is a popularity contest. If we do not put forth our own views, we end up choosing sides according to the views of others. This method greatly narrows the range of opinions and the voices that are heard within our community.

It's time to learn how to have open discussion that does not disintegrate into mean-spirited accusations. If we can do that, we can honestly acknowledge community problems in a way that allows meaningful discussion to take place.

Source: www.bet.com Search for "Under One Roof."

The program airs on Tuesdays at 10 PM CST.

R. T. Rybak and the African American Agenda

December 24, 2001

A very important meeting occurred at the Urban League's Glover-Sudduth Center on Monday, December 17. The mayor-elect of Minneapolis, R. T. Rybak, came out to North Minneapolis to meet with fifty people representing every facet of the African American community.

The group presented Mr. Rybak with a five-point agenda that African Americans consider a priority for his administration. The agenda laid out for the mayor-elect is based on the following premise: Concentrated, persistent poverty among African Americans in the Twin Cities area (particularly Minneapolis) is the worst among the top 25 cities in the entire United States. The new Mayor of Minneapolis must develop an immediate, comprehensive, and focused plan for elimination of this problem.

The plan must include elimination of the disparities that exist between the black and white populations in the incidence of:

> Disease and ill health
> Removal of children from the home
> Participation in projects using government financing
> Home ownership
> Rental housing opportunities
> Police stops
> Enforcement of civil rights and equal justice statutes
> Inclusion in the political process

Speakers also addressed the need for the Mayor's support for efforts already underway:

> The Twelve Point Plan advanced by Superintendent Carol
  Johnson to correct inequities in the education of African
  American children

> Culturally –based programs offered in Minneapolis schools

> Affordable housing initiatives

> Utilization of alternative sites as emergency homeless shelters

> Reparations ordinance in support of national legislation

The first level of this multi-tiered agenda calls attention to the disparities that we, as African Americans, face in every aspect of our lives. In health, recent data suggest that people of color suffer from poor health and remain underserved by the traditional health care community.

In family stability, statistics show that out-of-home placement of African American children has reached epidemic proportions. In Minneapolis and Hennepin County, more than 50% of the children removed from their homes in the past decade have been black. The police have played a major role as the main source of referral. Racial profiling of children and African American families are a major source of the problem. Dr. Nancy Rottenberg, at a Minnesota Senate hearing in early December, called it "a family liability to be black in Minnesota."

In matters of civil rights and equal justice, the question of racial profiling continues to be a serious problem for blacks in Minneapolis. While some serious efforts have begun, action in this area has not been substantial.

There were several things about the December 17 meeting that impressed me. First, during his campaign, Mayor-elect R. T. Rybak expressed interest in meeting with members of African American leadership in Minneapolis to hear the issues that are most important to the African American community. Second, Mr. Rybak came into our community to hear our views. Furthermore, his visit occurred before he took office and not on the heels of a community crisis. Third, Mayor-elect Rybak listened to our call that he provide leadership and advocacy on behalf of the agenda of the African American community.

To me, it looked like an important first step in creating ongoing dialogue between the Mayor's office and the African American community using regularly scheduled, open meetings.

Over the next few weeks, I will expand upon the African American agenda for Minneapolis in the areas of health, employment, housing, education, civil rights enforcement, and reparations. I hope to give our community a better understanding of these problems and to prepare the way for future discussions with the Mayor.

Next week, I will focus on how the African American agenda suggests we deal with reparations.

African American Agenda: Reparations

December 31, 2004

In last week's column, I gave an overview of the African American Agenda for the City of Minneapolis. The first part of the Agenda addresses the disparity between black and white populations in health, housing, education, employment, criminal justice, income, police stops, and out-of-home placement.

The second part of the Agenda addresses the question of reparations for African Americans. It calls for "city support for and passage of a Reparations Ordinance in support of national legislation." It says further, "The city should implement aggressive local actions to address local profits from slavery."

The concept of reparations, or payment for an injury or to redress a wrong, is not new. Jews after the Holocaust, Japanese Americans after World War II, American Indians in Connecticut, as well as African Americans, have sought reparations. It is only African Americans who haven't received any.

Talk of compensation for the labor of slaves began in the early nineteenth century. In the weeks before the end of the Civil War, a Freedman's Bureau was created by Congress. The Freedman's Bureau had the authority to assign not more than 40 acres of abandoned land in the South to the slaves in the Confederate states who had been freed. Within a year, all of the *abandoned* land was reclaimed by white plantation owners.

The idea of compensation in the form of "40 acres and a mule" hung on and carries over to this day. Determination of what promises were or were not made impedes discussion of the real issue. Beyond the discrimination, humiliation, and exploitation inflicted upon us for four hundred years, the greatest wrong to our people was the loss of opportunity to create wealth. A freed slave was still deprived of all assets--- no land to farm, no stock to raise, no crops to sell or barter, no collateral to show the bank--- and deprived of the ability to acquire assets. Nothing existed to pass on to one's children. The progeny of slaveholders retained the assets to build new fortunes; the descendents of slaves had no more to build on than their parents or grandparents did.

Such a loss cannot be redressed. But other measures can be applied. In 1963, Dr. Martin Luther King, Jr., proposed a Bill of Rights for the Disadvantaged that called for the restitution of unpaid slave wages. Dr. King stressed that such compensation would bring about a "psychological and motivational transformation of the Negro."

In 1989, U.S. Representative John Conyers introduced a bill to establish The Commission to Study Reparations Proposals for African Americans. He reintroduced the bill in 2001. While the Conyers bill would not directly provide for compensation, it would establish the first federally chartered commission to study the impact of slavery on African Americans and recommend a range of appropriate remedies.

As you can imagine, there is tremendous opposition to reparations. Rep. Conyers's position--- and the position to support--- is that, just as white Americans have benefited from education, life experiences, and wealth that were handed down to them by their ancestors, so too have African Americans been harmed by the institution of slavery imposed upon their ancestors.

Mayor-Elect R. T. Rybak agreed to support local initiatives for national legislation. Rybak thought it best to talk about reparations as a way to broaden the discussion and create a learning environment for all Minnesotans. I am pleased that there is a local group that has spent both time and energy organizing our efforts. When the mayor-elect and others are ready to get on board, there should be little standing in their way!

Calling on Mayor Rybak to Support the African American Agenda's 12-Point Plan for Education

January 7, 2002

For the past two weeks, I have written about the African American Agenda for the City of Minneapolis presented to Mayor R.T. Rybak on December 17, 2001. This week, I want to examine another component of the African American Agenda.

What role will our community play in achieving the goals of our agenda for the City of Minneapolis? At our meeting with then Mayor-Elect Rybak, community leaders pointed out that African Americans bear a far greater burden of poverty, unemployment, disease, incarceration, and school failure than similarly situated whites. Racial disparities in Minneapolis exceed other major cities in a number of categories.

The poor educational performance of our children is reflected in their future unemployment, economic disadvantage, incarceration, or drug and alcohol abuse. The failure to graduate is one of the most glaring disparities. Despite the fact that African American children make up 45% of the student population in Minneapolis, two white students graduate for every black student. Even though tests in the early grades can accurately predict school success, many students continue through the system without intervention.

Our community must partner with the Minneapolis School District to begin to remedy this situation. Together, we must develop and implement strategies to remove racial disparities and improve the quality of education for our children. The *Twelve Point Plan*, advanced by Superintendent Carol Johnson in the summer of 2000, provides a good road map for us to follow. In fact, it encompasses many of the strategies recommended in the NAACP's *Call for Action in Education*.

Our community leaders must play a lead role in developing community support systems that will enhance and reinforce the district's Twelve Point Plan. Agencies such as Phyllis Wheatley, Sabathani, Turning Point, The City, Inc., Summit Academy, Oak Park, Pilot City, the Urban League, and others, are the building blocks of our community. Their programs provide a culturally-based foundation to give young people and their families the tools and the capacity to overcome the barriers that keep them in ignorance and poverty. Countless hours, boundless energy, and continual attention are required to make that happen. All of us must require the city to support this work.

We call on Mayor Rybak to provide the leadership to enable us to provide support to our own community and the advocacy needed to guarantee its success.

For more on the Minneapolis School District's Twelve Point Plan, see www.mpls.k12.mn.us/about/twelve_point_plan.shtml.

African American Agenda: Housing

January 14, 2007

In a continuation of our discussion of the African American Agenda for the City of Minneapolis, this week I want to focus on housing. People who need a place to live in Minneapolis range from the homeless to the aspiring homeowner. Mayor R. T. Rybak pledged to address affordable housing as a major plank in his election platform. Leaders of the African American community support his commitment.

At the same time, we must be on record as posing the question, "Affordable for whom?" Seventy-one percent of whites are homeowners, while only 28% of blacks own their own homes.

Minneapolis Public Housing Authority controls 20,000 places to live in Minneapolis but they are 99% occupied. Over the past five years, the Greater Metropolitan Housing Corporation has developed or rehabilitated over 3,000 units, but the demand is greater than the supply. While we are seeing growing public/private collaboration to expand the housing stock and make it accessible to people below the city's median income, there are not enough units available at a truly affordable price.

The problem is that we have more people who need a roof over their head--- or a bigger or better roof--- than we have habitable units. Since below the median income is where many in our community dwell, it is important to all of us to be vigilant in holding Mayor Rybak to his campaign promises.

As a community, Mayor Rybak should know that we support:

> elimination of institutional racism across the housing industry (rentals, mortgages, insurance, etc.)

> lifting of restrictions to allow community centers, schools, or churches to provide shelter for the homeless if needed

> implementation of the Hollman Way Housing Plan to allow for maximum housing opportunities for former residents

> creation of affordable, multi-unit housing stock in EVERY ward in the city

> preservation of existing housing stock in Minneapolis

> 50/30 homeowner initiatives (50% of blacks owning a home by age 30

As a community, it is incumbent upon us to monitor the progress that this administration makes in every one of these areas.

African American Agenda: Accountability

January 21, 2002

Over the past month, I have written a series of columns laying out the African American Agenda for Minneapolis as formulated on December 17, 2001, by a group of fifty community leaders.   You will recall that the agenda addresses the great differences in the quality of life for whites and nonwhites in this city. It speaks to the following issues:

- Disease and ill health
- Academic performance
- Removal of children from the home
- Home ownership and rental housing opportunities
- Police stops
- Enforcement of civil rights and equal justice statutes
- Participation in projects using government financing
- Inclusion in the political process

As I review the list above, it's clear that the December 17th agenda is not new. These issues have been around a long time. We have had countless meetings, workshops, conferences, campaigns and dialogues around these questions. The energy devoted to discussion of health disparities, affordable housing, equity in education, or racial profiling would propel your car around the world.

After all of the talk, all of the promises, all of the compromises, the problems remain. In most cases, they are getting worse.

It is important that WE keep the great disparities in health, employment, housing, education, and civil rights enforcement before the public, because no one else will. Disparities come from a comparison of behavior of the white population with populations of color. We are the ones with more disease, failing children, sons in prison, and unlawful detainers.   We are the ones with fewer homeowners or high-income workers. If we don't keep these issues in front of the new mayor and city council, who will?

We need to make a commitment as to what our community will do over the next four years. Endless promises and pledges were made during last fall's election campaigns.   Our elected officials need to know that we are just as committed to seeing that those promises are kept.

Understanding that I can only speak for the Urban League, I believe that our organization, in collaboration with NAACP and others, is prepared to:

- Actively engage in the political process in an attempt to help shape public policy and influence the political dialogue
- Provide an open and welcoming feedback loop that both encourages and expects regular dialogue among constituent groups
- Develop a Score Card of Accountability that rates the sensitivity, concern and action on issues or problems that are pertinent to communities of color.

Our community can, for example, determine if the new political boundaries being drawn across our state, and particularly in the cities of Minneapolis and St. Paul, will be a benefit or a burden to the black community. We can assess where our elected officials stand on the question and publicly rate their position in terms of its effect upon African American interests.

Of course, such an assessment works both ways. We must also track how we, as a community, respond to a threat to our well-being. We must be willing to be publicly rated on the keeping of our own commitments.

At the end of each year and every four years, at the end of the term for mayor and city council, I invite each of you to look back and see what has been accomplished. I invite each of you to hold all of us accountable – the mayor, the city council, community organizations, and those that purport to speak out on behalf of our community. We are all responsible for the outcome.

All Kids Count (Children's Defense Fund): The Need to Evaluate Institutions That Affect Children of Color

January 28, 2002

African American and African children comprise thirty-six percent of all of the children of color in the State of Minnesota. That's why we should pay attention to a new study, All Kids Count!, that was released last week by the Children's Defense Fund. Never before has data about children of color in Minnesota been collected from so many different sources and combined together in a single report. The result is not good news. Children of color tend to face more difficulties than white children in every category in the report.

All Kids Count! does, however, report some findings that we don't often see:

- The majority of parents of all races work full-time
- Most families of color do not receive welfare benefits
- 86% of African American sixth graders plan to attend college
- average school attendance rate for African American eighth graders is 90%
- 71% of African American students felt their parents cared for them "very much"

Other results may not surprise you:

- The Minnesota Family Investment Program (MFIP) is not as successful in moving families of color to self-sufficiency as it is for white families
- 11% of African American children are not covered by any health insurance
- Average earnings per year of African American families are 40% that of white families
- 33% of African American families own their own homes compared to 87% of white families
- Over half of the homeless families with children are African American
- Five African American children are removed from their homes for every white child that is removed

- 70 out of every 1,000 African American girls will give birth as juveniles
- only 31% of African American eighth graders pass the math section of the Minnesota Basic Standards Test

Let us look at just one set of figures to try to understand what this report is telling us: *African American eighth graders in the state attend school 90% of the time, but they pass the math section of the Basic Standards Test only 31% of the time.*

Why? There is more to this than test scores. What is going on in Minnesota that would cause this result? Certainly there are individual family factors such as unemployment, poverty, unstable housing, or family disruption that contribute to the outcome. But can those factors account for a 31% pass rate for all African American eighth graders?

In any report, what we learn is dependent upon the data that is collected. Most statistics are collected about an individual's behavior such as school attendance, test scores, income levels, or homeownership. It is much more difficult to learn about the behavior of institutions. We all know that the statistics on Minnesota children reflect the pervasive, long-term racial bias in Minnesota institutions--- schools, government agencies, real estate and banking industry, businesses and social organizations--- but there are few, if any, official studies to support our knowledge.

The All Kids Count! report concludes, "Without adequate information and evaluation of our institutions, it is difficult to promote institutional change and solutions stay focused on individuals." Those of us in the African American community must continue to press for real examination of institutional policies and practices. But it is not solely our responsibility. Citizens of all races, politicians, policymakers, decision makers of all kinds must ask the question, "How do institutional practices and policy decisions contribute to the destructive reality that children of color face?

The complete All Kids Count! report can be found at www.cdf-mn.org.

Avoiding the Divide and Conquer Tactic

February 25, 2002

I read with interest the recent article by Hannah Allam in the March 18th edition of the Pioneer Press describing emerging leaders in our community. The story was part of a series that the Pioneer Press is doing for Black History Month. Members of this new generation of leadership ranged in age from a high school senior to a community organizer pushing fifty. Each of them displayed drive, commitment, and belief in their ideas. They have ambition; they want to change things; they want to run for public office. We need those qualities in the people who will lead our community in the future.

I was struck, though, by the way the article tried to pit young folk against old folk--- emerging leaders against those that have been out there for a while. That is the game that the media is renowned for playing! Well, the Civil Rights Movement is not a game.

The Civil Rights Movement is the collective voice of an oppressed people. Its strength comes from the universal recognition of a common struggle. It is the struggle that must never be forgotten. To forget it is to risk the repetition of racism, hatred, and discrimination; to ignore it is to risk the return of enslavement.

Youth will always believe in the future more than the past. Youth will always listen to itself rather than to history. That is a necessary ingredient of human progress. But the leaders among our youth have an additional obligation to remember where they came from. They have a mandate to learn about manipulation, double-dealing, and mendacity so that they will recognize it when it envelopes them.

I am reminded of the statements attributed to Willie Lynch, a slave owner from the West Indies, in the early 1700s. Willie Lynch was brought to the colony of Virginia to advise plantation owners on how to control their slaves. He tells the gentlemen of Virginia that controlling slaves is very easy. You identify the differences among slaves and exploit those differences playing on fear, distrust, and envy. He cites everyday differences that can be magnified to cause distrust: age, skin color, body type, hair quality, sex, place of residence. He points out that slave-owners could make slaves on small plantations envy those enslaved on large plantations, and make house slaves believe that they are better than slaves who work in the fields. With these keys to control, there would be no need for beating, whipping, or hanging. This was valuable property after all. In closing, Willie Lynch admonishes the gathering, " I shall assure you that distrust is stronger than trust, and envy is stronger that adulation, respect or admiration. . . . Don't forget. You must pitch the old black vs. the young black."

Though the story is probably apocryphal, it serves as a word of caution to our emerging black leaders. Manipulation of our people into thinking they were lucky to be slaves worked for three hundred years. It can work again if we allow ourselves to look at each other as having greater or lesser value. We are all in this struggle together--- old, young, man, woman, light- skinned, dark-skinned, tall, short, strong, weak, suburban, urban, rich or poor. Whatever our individual statuses as to education, employment, achievement, or recognition, the daunting fact for African Americans is that we are all only four generations removed from the likes of Willie Lynch.

African American Agenda: Community Policing

April 22, 2002

On April 16, both the Star Tribune and the Pioneer Press carried reports of rumors that Mayor R. T. Rybak was about to oust Police Chief Olson. By the time you read this column, we will probably know if those rumors were true.

It's not my place to comment on the competence or incompetence of either man especially since I am not walking in either of their shoes. But I do think that the Minneapolis Urban League ought to express an opinion on what principles should guide law enforcement in our city.

The Urban League's interests are long term – longer than elected officials will serve, longer than the contracts of appointed leaders, longer than the promises that are made.   Our long-term interest is to make it possible for African Americans and other people of color to compete in this state on a par with all other residents. There is no room for permanent friends or foes. There is only the achievement of the goal.

In December of 2001, fifty community leaders formulated an African American Agenda for Minneapolis. Several points on that agenda touched on the relationship between the police and other government agencies and the people in our central city neighborhoods.

I suggest that there are four areas in which the Police Chief and the Mayor, whoever they are, can be a force for change:

- Recognition that people are different and that it is important to learn the differences
- Belief that community policing holds a solution to some of our most intractable problems
- Rejection of racial profiling as it is passed down from one generation of cops to another
- Adoption of a Civilian Review Authority that can enforce its findings

The Minneapolis population today is 35% non-white. Gone are the days when dark skin or almond eyes were a curiosity on our streets. We now have neighborhoods in which close to seventy percent of the residents are not white. The people policing those neighborhoods should look like the people at the bus stop, in the supermarket, in the schools, in the churches, or in the mosques. They must be seen as peers of the people they meet every day. Cops on the beat who know the shop owners, the school principal, even some of the kids by name are a strong influence on the flavor of a neighborhood.

Officers will not get the chance to become a part of the neighborhood if they themselves are perceived as a threat. The motto of the Minneapolis Police Department is "to protect and serve." In fact, most of the time, the police force can do neither. The police are not even called until a crime is in process or has been committed. One's property or person has already been violated before they show up. That is a long way from protection or service.

Community policing is a philosophy of integration of police officers into the fabric of a neighborhood to strengthen the bond between residents and the people sworn to protect them. Community policing can work both ways. Time after time, in tragic stories of the shooting of black men, police officers have perceived the black man as an immediate threat. Without question, in some cases they were. In other cases, the victims were perceived as black BEFORE they were perceived as a threat. Community policing can help to change the fear on both sides.

Neither a diverse police force nor the adoption of community policing can change the relationship between citizens and officers unless the public believes a balance of power exists. The establishment of a Civilian Review Authority that actually has some authority would be a good first step. Give the Civilian Review Authority subpoena power and the ability to conduct an independent investigation. Give it the clout to determine the consequences for an officer rather than just "recommend" a course of action.

In this first decade of the 21st century, our community and other communities of color have an opportunity to influence how these decisions are made. With growing populations, we should be listened to. We must learn how to make our voices heard. The City of Minneapolis deserves to have all of its people feel safe and all of its people believe that there is recourse when things go wrong. The City of Minneapolis deserves to have all of its citizens feel proud that they live here.

African Americans and Seat Belts

June 3, 2002

If you drive by the corner of Plymouth and Penn in North Minneapolis, you will see a large banner on the side of the Minneapolis Urban League building announcing the Buckle Up Northside campaign. The banner shows a thermometer that will be used to gauge the increase in seat belt use as measured at that intersection.

Here are some things about seat belts that I don't understand:

• Motor vehicle crashes are a leading cause of death for African American adults.
• African American males are nearly twice as likely to die in a crash as their white counterparts.
• Seat belts reduce the risk of serious injury and death by 50%, yet nearly half of African Americans do not use them.
• Near North residents, in particular, don't wear seat belts.

People have been telling us to "Buckle Up" for thirty years. Carmakers have installed irritating buzzers to remind us to fasten the seat belt. Why don't African Americans "hear" the message? Why don't we get it? Here is something that can make the difference between life and death and we fail to take advantage of it. It raises my concern over other messages many do not seem to hear like "Smoking may be hazardous to your health" or "Don't Drink and Drive." I worry that some people don't hear the message because they do not place a great value on their own lives. Such a thought is cause for greater concern than limited seat belt use.

I've heard folks say, "Seat belt laws are just another excuse for the cops to stop us." Even if that were true, which I don't believe, it is such an easy regulation to comply with, there ought to be no reason to be stopped. There are a lot of laws out there that have a greater impact on people of color, but this is not one of them. At least you will be alive when you are pulled over.

As the driver of a car, you have a responsibility for the safety of your passengers. That begins with the words, "Buckle Up." No one should be allowed to ride with you without fastening the safety belt. The only way children will learn this lesson is from a parent. School buses don't require seat belts, so we cannot put this responsibility on the schools. Seat belt use is a life-time habit that must be formed very early in life--- like brushing your teeth. In our community, we are at least one generation behind in forming that habit in ourselves and insisting upon it for our children. It is time to catch up and save lives.

The big thermometer on the corner of Plymouth and Penn is just one of the ways Buckle Up Northside will challenge community residents to use their seat belts. The buckle up campaign will be promoted via the media (KMOJ will sponsor a Buckle Up contest later this year), at community events such as Juneteenth, and through churches and local businesses.

"Buckle Up Northside." North Minneapolis residents, community organizations, businesses and the Hennepin County Community Health Department want to say it loud enough, clearly enough, and often enough to change the frightening statistics in our community.

Signing Young People Up for the Social Contract

July 22, 2002

Like many people, I am alarmed by the increasing level of violence among youth in Minneapolis. Shootings that involve young men under age 25 seem to occur every day. For awhile, it looked as though resorting to guns to settle every difference was on the decline. Now 2002 is beginning to look like 1995.

Population experts tell us that we have more crime and violence perpetrated by young men because we are experiencing a boomlet of males in the 15 to 25 age range. The experts would say they have expected this for about twenty years, since these children were born. In fact, they would say the population of young men was higher in the early to mid-1990s, too.

While this may be a plausible explanation by statisticians, I'm not sure I buy it. I think we are seeing the erosion of the social contract. The social contract represents the way our world operates for the common good. It is the reason we all drive on the right side of the road or stop at stop signs. It is the reason we presume that the money we deposit in the bank will be there when we return to withdraw it. It is the presumption by the video store owner that we will return the movie we rent.

Nobody signs the social contract; it is not written on paper. It is implicit in our relations with one another. We believe that we should be able to walk or drive down the street without being harmed or eat in a restaurant without it being blown up or let our children play in the front yard without being kidnapped. All of those assumptions seem to be in jeopardy.

In Minneapolis in 1999, the latest year for which cumulative police statistics are available, police officers answered 3356 calls involving shots fired, 1468 calls reporting a person with a gun, 954 reports of fights with weapons, and 300 calls saying someone had been shot. Beyond that, they responded to 27,319 calls that involved the taking of someone else's property. Keep in mind that these are just the incidents that were reported.

Society cannot function when the basic premises that we live by--- the belief that we will be safe, that our children will grow to adulthood, that our home is our castle--- are undermined and thus the social contract is not observed. Somehow, many young people have come to believe that their own lives have no value, and therefore, the lives of others aren't worth anything either. There are neither enough police officers nor enough jail cells to combat that belief.

Law enforcement is, by nature, after the fact. The police do not enforce laws; rather, they arrest people who have allegedly broken the law. If the violence that occurs everywhere, everyday is to be stopped, it will come from society. Somehow society must convince young people who have rejected the parameters of the social contract that every life has value, that conflict can be resolved without violence, and that they will benefit from peace. Sign me up for the contract!

15

Seeing the Glass Half Full, Despite the $4.5 Billion State Budget Shortfall

June 13, 2003

In our typical "out with the old and in with the new" fashion, most of us view the arrival of the New Year as a chance to start over. As we begin again, there's a sense of excitement and expectation. We all have made our New Year's resolutions in good faith in spite of the knowledge that we'll probably disregard most of them before the year ends. This time, however, I am finding it difficult to greet the New Year with my usual anticipation. I find myself asking, "Is the glass half full or half empty?"

Everywhere I turn I am faced with what seem to be insurmountable problems. Our community has one of the highest teen pregnancy rates in the nation, our babies die in infancy three times more often than white babies, cardiovascular disease is a primary cause of death for our mothers and fathers, our women are 100% more likely than the general population to develop diabetes. The likelihood that our young men will die as a result of firearms is 25 times greater than for white youth. Those who survive are overrepresented in the criminal justice system. The plight of our children within both the Minneapolis and St. Paul school systems is worsening.

The State of Minnesota faces a $4.5 billion dollar deficit that could get worse with the next revenue forecast in February. That is a bleak picture, especially for those who are disenfranchised, underemployed and discriminated against. The huge shortfall has cut the heart out of so many ideas for positive change in health, employment, education, and youth development. Will there be enough in the glass to sustain us for another year?

As a community we need to keep this picture in perspective. Although we will be affected personally by our inability to meet expenses or to do all the things we want to do, we have to remember that this is a national condition, not a household or a community or even a state condition. We must avoid being hard on ourselves, because doing so only results in other problems. Instead, we have to bring our collective intellectual, financial, and spiritual resources together in order to obtain the sustenance we will need in 2003.

I believe we must be collectively optimistic and declare the glass

87

half full. We must concentrate on the problems we can solve and the conditions that we can better. For example, community efforts to mediate with the city on the critical issue of police use of force policies have been beleaguered with internal struggle. I know we can solve this conflict, but only if we take seriously the charge to become more unified in 2003 and begin to look at what we are capable of achieving as a community. Only then will we see the potential in all of us as individuals, as leadership groups, and as advocates for the good of every member of our community.

Finally, I wish all of you a happy New Year.

16

Comment on 70% of African American
Children Born to Unwed Parents

October 31, 2003

Many of you know that in my service to this community, I wear multiple hats. One of the hats that I wear is that of President of the Minneapolis Urban League. Thanks for allowing me to wear that hat. Another hat that I wear is that of a husband and a parent, and I am proud and humbled to be able to wear that hat. But I wear another hat, and that is the hat of a preacher. Today I am compelled to write from the perspective of one who wears that preacher's hat.

The topic that I want to talk about is a touchy one for a lot of people, and I'm sure there will be somebody who will accuse me of being judgmental. That's not my intent, but bear with me, because I intend to say what's on my mind.

I was on an airplane a couple of days ago, reading an article that presented some startling figures around African American children born in the United States. Two of the figures particularly stuck with me. And so as a preacher I must ask, why are 70% of all African American children born to unwed parents? And as a preacher I must inquire, why is it that 86% of today's young black women are single when they have their first child? These statistics as presented in the article are deeply troubling to me, and must raise these questions.

As I sat and pondered those figures, I could think of several reasons why so many of our young black women are having babies out of wedlock. One that comes to me right away is the relaxed sexual mores that have permeated our society. For whatever reason, we've decided as a society that having sex whenever and wherever one feels like it is okay, regardless of age, and regardless of whether or not one is in a committed relationship.

A second reason, and one that I think of as the biggest reason for so many black children born out of wedlock, is that it's really not a big deal any more to have a child and not be in a committed relationship. Convergent to that notion, the magazine article goes on to quote the author as saying, "In today's society, Big Mommas don't rant and rave the way they used to when a single daughter or granddaughter turns up pregnant. Fathers and uncles don't go for the shotgun. Some of us remember different times, times when a child born out of wedlock was called "illegitimate," meaning a child with no legitimate status in society. That child and its mother were often shunned, not only by society, but by their own family. The current reality is that with so many children born out of wedlock, society doesn't even refer to any distinction between "legitimate" or "illegitimate."

Another unfortunate reality embedded in this issue of unwed mothers is that people just don't believe that a marriage is going to last, so they ask, "Why bother going through the motions in the first place?" It is a fact that 50% of marriages end up in divorce.

All this leads to a black community in which 70% of the children are born out of wedlock. This causes the preacher in me to be concerned, not only with issues of morality, but with the other implications that this phenomenon carries for the downward spiral of the black family. Let me name a few:

First, single parents disproportionately struggle financially. It doesn't take a rocket scientist to conclude that two incomes are two times better than one. So in the routine process of struggling to feed, clothe, and shelter a family, it stands to reason that the single parent is going to struggle, both financially and mentally, on a disproportionate level.

Second, research would argue that children of single parents have more health, social, and academic issues than those who come from two-parent households, and that forty-seven percent of children in single parent families live in poverty. I can understand why that would be so. The responsibility for meeting financial obligations and protecting the health and welfare of a child can be overwhelming for a two-parent family. Think of the stress that a single parent faces when something goes wrong in that same paradigm.

Then think of the social impact. Let me cite the telling statistic again: Seventy percent of black children born in the United States are born to unwed parents. That means these are children who may never have a relationship, healthy or otherwise, with their biological father. These are children who are growing up with the sense that not having a father is no big deal, that you can't miss what you never had.

But third, and most importantly, we as a community have slacked off of being concerned about unwed motherhood. Instead, we've tended to fall lockstep into the mistaken notion that birth control methods are a solution or that teaching parenting skills and providing prenatal care is all we can do. Well, the preacher in me says that we're missing the point. In order to save the black family from its downward spiral we can't afford to be coaxed into an acceptance of the new social norms swarming around our children, especially when we know full well they bode nothing but ill. Our young black women and men need to be counseled on the full import of being parents. We've got to look to the pulpit for guidance on issues of morality and not to media-driven stereotypes.

I told you I was going to speak what was on my mind, so again, if you find my comments judgmental, forgive me. It is not my intent to pass judgment on my loved ones, but it is my desire to see my people thrive. AMEN!

17

A Think Tank as Repository for the Wisdom of the Elders

November 7, 2003

A few days ago I was thinking (and you know how dangerous it is for me to think), "Where do our black leaders go once they have given selflessly to better our community?" What I mean is, when you stop serving, when you stop advocating, when you stop fighting, or when you get tired and just can't carry the ball anymore------where do you go? What does the community hold in store for our black leaders once their service is done? After being attacked and criticized; after being taken for granted, where do our black leaders go? Where does a pastor who has faithfully served a congregation for a number of years go when he retires?

I started thinking about this, and I thought about the service Gleason Glover gave to the Minneapolis Urban League for over 25 years as its President and CEO. From 1967 to 1991 his vision for the Minneapolis Urban League and for the city of Minneapolis led to many outstanding accomplishments. I also thought about Sharon Sayles Belton, whose ten years on the Minneapolis City Council and two terms as mayor of Minneapolis are unprecedented. I think of Greg Gray, former State Representative, who lost his bid to become the state's first African American Auditor. Where do these people go who have given so much? How do we pay tribute to the Josies, the Matts, the Harrys, the Lizzes, the Mahmouds, and many others who have worked to make this city and state a better place for African Americans and all Minnesotans.

No one can dispute with true conviction the contributions of these and other leaders of our community. And yet, where do they go after their service is done? I suppose it's possible that after giving so much time and energy, some of our former leaders simply suffer from community service burnout. Some might be only too happy to escape the slings and arrows that come from being on the front line. They may even relish the obscurity that comes from stepping down. Unfortunately, I'm inclined to believe that more often than not, those that have given so much to the forward progress of our community suffer from community disuse.

Instead of wasting the wisdom that so many of our black leaders have garnered over years of service, we should establish a think tank. A place where the wisdom of the old and the energy of the young could come together. A place from which we could pull some of the greatest ideas for public advocacy, negotiation and influence. A place where someone like myself could go and sit at the feet of those who have led before me and let their knowledge drip down like honey from a jar.

It's a fact that many who have been on the battlefield so long and have labored so intently have forgotten more about what it takes to move a community forward than young folks like me will ever know. A think tank would provide them the opportunity to teach, and would provide young folk who have picked up the mantle of leadership an opportunity to learn.

A number of years ago, Bill Withers put a couple of dollars in his pocket with a song that goes, "If it feels this good getting used, then just keep on using me until you use me up." That's what should happen to our black leaders. It should feel good getting used. But unfortunately, it doesn't feel that good. As a community, we simply use them up.

18

Taking the Opportunity to Say, "Thanks"

November 26, 2003

By the time you read this, you will have no doubt stuffed yourselves with turkey and dressing, some of momma's candied yams and sweet potato pie, and you've probably imbibed a beverage or two. But in the midst of stuffing yourself, I am convinced that at some point you found time to say "thank you" to somebody. That's what I'd like to share with you--- taking the opportunity to say thanks.

I know most times I write about what's going on in the community--- a particular event or situation; or I write about what we're doing at the Urban League, and the important work others are doing. But today, I really want to take a minute or two to say "thank you" to some people who have deeply influenced my life. Please indulge me, because this is more personal than what I'm used to sharing with you.

First of all, I want to say thank you to my step-dad. Many of you don't know that as a young boy, and one of eight brothers and sisters, my Mom and my biological Dad were divorced. For a number of years my mother struggled as a single parent to raise eight children, ranging in age from 2 to 14. At some point in my early childhood, God allowed a man to come into my life and serve as my step-dad. This man worked two jobs and took on the task of raising eight children who were not his own. He claimed us as his own, and never once complained about the challenge of our upbringing. Thank you, Tom, for giving of yourself without thought of reward.

The second person I want to say thank you to is my oldest brother who, at the time of my parent's divorce was a mere 8th grader. He had to step up and be the man of the house, and step up he did. While my Mom worked two jobs to put bread on the table, my oldest brother made sure our family continued to function. Eventually, he became a 9th grader, then a 10th, 11th, and 12th grader. To be the man of the house he had to make some tough sacrifices. He had to forsake all outside activities--- all of the fun and the foolishness a typical high schooler would get into. In other words, he had to grow up way too soon. When it was time for him to go to college, I'm sure he would have preferred to go away, but he couldn't. He had to attend college right there in our community. Many of you know him now as one of the top NCAA basketball officials in the country, but I know him simply as the person who was a father figure for me in my early years, and who was instrumental in shaping my adult life. So Ed, thank you.

Oftentimes in the life of a community servant, the person behind them goes unnoticed. That is the case with me. I get to lead an institution, I go to the public forums, the press conferences, and the community meetings. But everyday that I am serving in my capacity as a community servant means that I am not at home. There is someone, though, who makes sure that my family functions and thrives while I'm away. That someone is my wife, Beverly. Throughout the 22 years that I have been allowed to do community service, not once has she complained that I have neglected what should be happening on the home front (even though I know I have). So to Beverly, I say thank you.

Finally, let me say thank you to each of you, and each of you consists of so many different families. You are a member of the Urban League family that keeps me on task everyday and gives me a clear vision about the work we need to do for our community. You also consist of my church family, which inspires me to go on everyday in faith and humble servitude. And then I hold dear my community family, which offers freely both criticism and praise, each of which we all need a healthy dose of. Thank you all for keeping me grounded.

So as you digest the turkey of yesterday and sit restively reading "Urban Views," thank you for indulging me as I say "thank you" to the people in my life whom I just don't get around to thanking enough.

19

Five Measures Toward a Happy New
Year for Communities of Color

January 9, 2004

For the next couple of days or weeks, people will greet one another with the traditional phrase, "Happy New Year." We all know every time this greeting is issued, it's intended to recognize the start of a new year for its possibilities--- as an opportunity to make amends for past transgressions or to set new, positive courses of action in motion.

As I began to think about the possibilities for this new year, I asked myself what it would take for Minneapolis--- and in particular, its communities of color--- to have a "Happy New Year." In my mind I can envision at least five resolutions for a happy and productive 2004.

Number one, we need a resolution at the state, city, and county level of government to exercise greater sensitivity towards lower income people. Every one of our elected officials and representatives has to be aware of the impact budget cuts have had on disadvantaged families. Recreational activities have been severely cut, leaving children from hard working, low-income families with nowhere to go and nothing to do. Resources have to be found at the city and county level to enable our schools and our parks to provide after-school and weekend activities that ensure a safe environment for our children. Additionally, I believe more discretionary funds need to be disseminated at the state level to local service providers so some of the worst conditions of hunger and homelessness can be alleviated. Food shelves are finding it harder and harder to maintain enough inventory to meet demand, and the same is true at homeless shelters, where beds are becoming more and more scarce. We as friends or family, as neighbors or as fellow church members can also resolve to find ways to help someone in need in 2004.

Number two, we need a resolution from our city to increase employment opportunities for undereducated people of color. It's an often down-played fact that this softened job market has shifted the balance of employability to such a degree that the educated have now taken those jobs traditionally held by the undereducated, and in turn, the undereducated have had to take jobs traditionally held by the uneducated. These circumstances have caused some of us to develop an unintentional dispassion for the most downtrodden of our community. In 2004, we need to reject the "I got mine" notion. We need to challenge our city leaders to be innovative about creating useful employment opportunities for those of us who are undereducated, because it is this group that stands to experience the most suffering in the current job market. If resources for meeting the economic and emergency service needs of working families continues to dwindle, and the ability of community organizations to meet those needs continues to deteriorate into 2005, then 2004 will not have rung in a good year.

Number three, although we have in place an agreement mediated by the city and the community to institute changes within the police department, we need a resolution for visibly improved community relations. The community must continue its proactive stance with regard to holding local law enforcement accountable for its actions. At the same time we have to be willing to give a new police administration a chance to evaluate and respond to a modified structure. In the next couple of days, Minneapolis will get a new police chief. He will have the task of carrying forward the promises and compromises made by the former chief. As a community, we must be visibly supportive of any positive action that comes out of the police department as a result of mediation. We must laud the department when we find it has increased the number of officers of color. We must offer our congratulations when a strategy of the department leads to increased safety for our neighborhoods without compromising our civil rights. The agreement reached by both sides in mediation has given us a good blueprint for improving police/community relations in 2004. If we have to go into 2005 with no examples of the merits of mediation, it will not have been a good year.

Number four, we need collectively to resolve ourselves to closing the achievement gap between students of color and white students. We've been looking at a downward trend in the achievement of students of color for 8 to 10 years, but in 2004, serious efforts to increase parent involvement in the education of their children need to be implemented. We need to be sure that our schools that are facing sanctions for noncompliance with No Child Left Behind standards aren't unfairly or prematurely closed down. School closings often have an adverse effect on neighborhoods and in most cases need to be avoided. Additionally, state resources need to be more equitably divided between urban schools and suburban schools so that the achievement gap between those students can be narrowed. Overall, in 2004, a new Minneapolis Public Schools superintendent must be prepared to present a plan of action that will excite educators and motivate students around educational achievement. If we face 2005 in the same condition of educational inequity and underachievement, 2004 will not have been a good year for students of color.

Finally, we need to resolve to end the bickering among organizations that either historically or traditionally serve people of color. It would be imperative for social growth in 2004 that community and organizational leadership be of one accord. We need to resolve our differences so that our common constituencies benefit from our unified stance. So if an effort is afoot not to support Turning Point, for example, because of something my good friend Peter Hayden is purported to have done, or the Urban League for something I have been accused of doing, or the NAACP because of infighting among its membership, we as community citizens need to keep our focus on the merits of the organization and how it can serve us, and not on any one individual.

I truly believe that 2004 will more than ever be a year that calls upon all of us to help one another in order for Minneapolis to prosper as a city. In fact, I heard a quote somewhere that strikes me as appropriate going into this new year. It says "Truly, when you helped one of the least of those who are members of my family you did it to me." These are my New Year's resolutions for Minneapolis. Please feel free to share them with me. Happy New Year!

20

Black History Month: Toward Solutions to Lingering Problems on the Foundation of African American History

February 2005

With all of the activities celebrating black history this month, I hope every one of us finds an opportunity to pay homage to the people and the achievements that give us cause to celebrate. Most importantly, I hope we each honor our history by acknowledging a responsibility to continue making progress as a people. After all, every day that goes by is history, and every day we have an opportunity to make our own mark on it.

It makes me wonder: Years from now, what will we be celebrating during Black History Month? Will we still be celebrating the landmark success of Brown vs. The Board of Education and the desegregation of schools in 1954, or will we finally be able to celebrate a public school system in which African American students can achieve academic excellence on a par with all other students? Will we still be celebrating the sit-in demonstrations of the 1960s that led to the integration of lunch counters all across the south, or will we be able to celebrate a Mecca of black economic empowerment and entrepreneurship that spreads across this nation? Will we still be celebrating the passing of the 1964 Civil Rights Act, or will we celebrate new landmarks in the struggle to end institutionalized racism in housing, education, health care, and employment?

In fact, each generation brings with it new challenges. Today's generation certainly has its share: More African American males are in prison than are in college; African Americans represent the highest numbers of those infected with HIV/AIDS; African American students post the lowest rates of achievement in public schools. Our ancestors deserve our best efforts to overcome these challenges. How will Black History Month mark our efforts in celebrations to come?

In case you misunderstand my point about the celebration of Black History Month, let me note that a man named George Santayana once made a profound statement that I agree with wholeheartedly. He said, "If we forget our history we risk losing it." Believe me, I'm not suggesting that we stop paying tribute to the contributions of our ancestors. Their heroic acts should forever be emblazoned in our minds and hearts. I'm just suggesting that we cannot afford to rest on their laurels or fail to build on the solid foundation they laid for achieving true equality.

May the celebration of Black History Month remind us that the struggle for equality is not over. Let our collective spirits be revived and our actions be spurred by the celebration of Black History Month beyond February and throughout the year!

21

Introduction to the Minneapolis Urban League Publication,
The State of African Americans in Minnesota 2004

April 2005

The Minneapolis Urban League has published a book entitled *The State of African Americans in Minnesota*. This book will be released formally to the public at the end of this month. However, because many in the community have been anticipating the release of the Urban League's version of the National Urban League's *State of Black America* for so long, I thought I'd share the introductory chapter with you now. Here it is:

When Dr. Martin Luther King, Jr., spoke of the dream of equality and justice for all, he spoke as one who believed fervently in the ideals expressed in the Constitution of the United States of America, and as one working passionately to change the reality of an American life that came far short of those ideals. In the manner of his hero, Mohandas K. Gandhi, who insistently reminded the British through courageous nonviolent action that their expressed ideals did not match imperialistic reality, Dr. King persistently reminded white America that it was not living up to its own cherished ideals.

This is a message that Minnesotans in 2004 should take to heart. Minnesota is by many measures a progressive state with a high standard of living. Minnesota ranks near the top among all states in per capita income, homeownership, percentage of people with health insurance, number of college graduates, and performance on the ACT college entrance exam. Minnesota has a tradition of providing generous social services to those who need help getting health care, buying food, and finding adequate living quarters.

Minnesotans pride themselves in their concern for the natural environment, air quality, and the relative purity of the state's lakes and rivers. Minnesota is known throughout the nation for good government comparatively untainted by corruption and scandal, and for a political history that has sought to ensure the rights of labor and a good standard of living for working people.

For young African American people who might be considering a move to Minnesota, then, there is much to recommend the state. Particularly to the college-educated seeking employment with progressive companies such as General Mills, 3M, and Medtronic, young African

100

Americans will find Minnesota in many ways a very hospitable place to live. But they need to know also of the numerous challenges faced by African Americans and other people of color in the state. They should understand that, just as the United States is a nation whose ideals have never matched the reality of lives for African Americans, so Minnesota is a state whose progressive reputation falls far short of the reality of life for African Americans and other people of color.

They should know, for example, that

> African American students generally score 20 to 40 percentage points below white students on the Minnesota Basic Skills Tests in math and reading;

> the state government of Minnesota has a poor record of affirmative action and low percentages of African Americans and other people of color employed in the state public sector;

> homeownership among African Americans and other people of color in Minnesota falls far below the national average, while that for whites is substantially above national norms;

> African Americans and other people of color have infant mortality, firearm injury mortality, and teen pregnancy rates far above those prevailing for the white population;

> the percentage of African Americans in the total inmate population of Minnesota is more than 10 times the percentage of African Americans in the general population of the state;

> Minnesota has the highest concentration of inner city poverty of any state in the nation; and

> as a percentage of the general child population, African American children are five times more likely than white children to be living in out-of-home settings.

These conditions and others documented in this book are unacceptable, and particularly daunting, given the increasing diversity of the population of Minnesota. Today there are 171,131 African Americans residing in Minnesota. This represents 3.49% of the state's population of 4,919,479 as revealed in the U.S. Census 2000. By comparison, whites have a population share of 89.45%. The growing numbers of Asian Americans and Hispanics now have population shares of 2.89% and 2.92%

respectively, while American Indians have a population share of 1.12%. Thus, African Americans represent the largest community of color in the state of Minnesota, but both the Asian American and Hispanic populations are gaining. Asian Americans and Hispanics dominate the recently arrived immigrant populations of Minnesota, which as of May 1999 totaled 223,600. Of this number, 55.9% was Hispanic, by far the largest immigrant population. Another 35.78% came from the Asian American community; Hmong Americans alone represented 26.83% of the total recently arrived immigrant population. The next largest recently arrived immigrant population has come from Africa and represented 4.7% of the total recently arrived immigrant population in May 1999. The majority of African refugees have arrived from Somalia, Ethiopia, and Liberia. Over half of all African refugees arriving in Minnesota are from Somalia. Over 72% of Minnesotans whose ancestry is traceable to Somalia, Ethiopia, and Liberia live in Ramsey and Hennepin Counties. Minnesota has the largest Somali population in the United States, a population that as of the 2000 census totaled 11,164 for the whole state and 8,437 in Hennepin and Ramsey Counties.[1]

By far the largest concentrations of African Americans in Minnesota are found in Hennepin and Ramsey Counties. Hennepin County has 99,943 African Americans (58.4% of the total African American population of Minnesota) and Ramsey County has 38,900 (22.73% of the total). The next largest concentrations of African Americans in the counties of Minnesota are found in Dakota, Anoka, Washington, Olmsted, St. Louis, and Steams counties, which have 8,091; 4,756; 3,689; 3,330; 1,704; and 1,110 African Americans respectively. Of all African Americans in Minnesota, 60% live in the Twin Citie. Of these, 68,818 live in Minneapolis and 33,861 live in St. Paul, for a total Twin Cities African American population of 102,679. Within Minneapolis, the urban center of greatest African American settlement in Minnesota, the following communities have the largest concentrations of African American population, with the absolute and percentage figures given as follows: Near North (19,378 [28.16%]), Powderhorn (13,169 [19.13%], Camden (8,970 [13.03%]) and Phillips (5,825 [8.46%]). These four communities alone contain 27.66% of the African American population of Minnesota. Minneapolis as a whole takes a 40.21% share, while St. Paul takes a 19.78% share.[2]

The increasing diversity of Minnesota's population represents a challenge to the state's claim to a high standard of living and to its heritage of progressive standards of governance. The high levels of disparity that one sees between whites on the one hand, and African Americans and other people of color on the other, should provide a wake-up call to anyone who is satisfied with the status quo. Minnesota will not continue to be a leader by so many national measures if it continues to feature the great disparities that exist in education, state government employment, housing, health, criminal justice, conditions of marital and family life, and certain aspects of the social services system. Chapters two through eight of *The State of African Americans in Minnesota* detail the nature and level of these disparities. Chapter nine summarizes the state of African Americans in Minnesota and gives a clear plan of action by which the Minneapolis Urban League intends to work toward erasing the disparities in condition of life for whites and people of color in the state.

In publishing this book, and in setting forth its plan of action, the Minneapolis Urban League expresses both appreciation for the generally high quality of life of the general population of Minnesota and a commitment to make that high standard a reality for African Americans and other people of color. In his essay "Where Do We Go from Here?," Dr. Martin Luther King, Jr. wrote,

> The majority...of white Americans believe that American society is essentially hospitable to fair play and steady growth toward a middle-class Utopia embodying racial harmony. But unfortunately this is a fantasy of self-deception and comfortable vanity. Overwhelmingly America is still struggling with irresolution and contradictions. It has been sincere and even ardent in welcoming some change. But too quickly apathy and disinterest rise to the surface when the next logical steps are to be taken.

In the best tradition established by Dr. Martin Luther King., Jr., the Minneapolis Urban League recognizes the high ideals that in large measure accord with the reality of life for Minnesota's white citizens. It seeks to hold Minnesotans to their own best values and to make these a reality for African Americans and other people of color in the state. The Minneapolis Urban League's plan of action will as necessary shake white Minnesotans into recognizing their "self-deception" and "comfortable vanity," calling upon them to shed the "apathy and disinterest" that too often characterize their attitude toward the conditions of life for African Americans and other people of color in Minnesota. And for this effort, and the achievements that follow in matching ideal to reality, Minnesotans of all races and ethnicities will be the better.

1   *Welfare Reform: Real Possibilities or Empty Promises,*
    Volume Three, *Voices of Change: Families Affected by*
    Welfare Reform, Minnesota Urban Coalition,
    February 2002.

2   *Welfare Reform: Real Possibilities or Empty Promises,*
    Volume Three, *Voices of Change: Families Affected by*
    Welfare Reform, Minnesota Urban Coalition, February 2002.
    Welfare Reform Monitoring Initiative: Fulfilling the Promise,
    A Welfare Policy Brief, Minnesota Urban Coalition, 2003.

Chapter Four

Health and Teen Pregnancy

1

Health Disparities: Causes and Symptoms

February 4, 2002

Amidst all the discussion about how to balance the state budget, one initiative seems to be relatively safe: the effort to eliminate disparities in the health status of populations of color relative to that of the white population. While Minnesota is one of the healthiest states in the union, the health of its populations of color ranks very low.

The discrepancy was first publicly noted in 1997 when the Minnesota Department of Health published *Populations of Color in Minnesota--- Health Status Report.* A year ago, the Minnesota Department of Health began a more detailed study to better understand the health disparities identified in the 1997 report. Many of the distressing facts cited in last week's column appear again in the Health Department's study:

• One out of every ten African American births is a baby born to a teenage mother.
• Over half of all deaths among 15-24 year-olds of color in the metro area are due to homicide.
• The gonorrhea rate among Black teens (15-19) is 70 times higher than the rate for whites.
• Over half of all deaths among people of color occur before age 64.

Some health outcomes can be attributed to social, economic or cultural factors, but there are other findings in the study that cannot be accounted for:

• While poverty appears to be an obvious cause of poor health, the health of populations of color is worse than whites at EVERY INCOME LEVEL.
• Individual behavior regarding diet, exercise, and other health habits accounts for less than 20% of the difference in death rates across races.

105

• Only 7.5% of human genetic diversity occurs between races; 85% occurs WITHIN national populations.

If health disparities cannot be explained by poverty, unhealthy behavior, or genetics, how can it be explained? Certainly, racism and discrimination play significant roles. But what are those roles? Racism often dictates where we live, what our job opportunities are, what type of medical treatment we receive, and how we relate to the larger community. Racism works against the cohesiveness that fosters the belief that the larger community will provide a person with support, safety, and resources to reach that person's potential.

It is not clear what the relationship is, but we do know that adequate housing, safe neighborhoods, good schools, playgrounds and parks, and accessible health care have something to do with it.

Research is quite clear that disparities in health status exist and that they are vast. Much more work needs to be done to determine the cause. What we see now is the manifestation of disparity. We do not know why it exists. This information is so important because our people cannot begin to share in the civic and economic opportunities offered by this state if they are infected by disease, impeded by chronic illness, or vulnerable to their environment.

The trouble is this: We can't wait five more years for additional research. One of the recommendations of this most recent study is that we need to move outside of the traditional realm of public health to address these problems. We know that social and economic factors are closely related to health, but we don't know how. We can't afford to wait until researchers find out.

In 2001, the Minnesota Legislature allocated funds to begin to eliminate the differences in health between populations. The Minnesota Department of Health has made some money available to community organizations, those closest to the problem, to begin the work of preventing even greater disparity. It is a good start, albeit a small one. Yet even those closest to the problem must settle, for now, for treating the symptoms of health disparities and not their cause.

Minnesota: Greatest Increase in African American
Teen Pregnancy among the 50 States

May 20, 2002

I think we are all aware that the number of babies born to African American teenagers has risen dramatically. I for one, though, had not realized until recently that teenage motherhood among African Americans has risen more in Minnesota than anywhere else in the country. In central Minneapolis, there are eight black pregnant teens for every white teenager who is pregnant. This is especially disturbing since the birth rate for other black teens across the country has fallen by 26% since 1991. In fact, according to the National Campaign to Prevent Teen Pregnancy, the national rate is now at the lowest point since 1969, the first year that the rate was calculated. It is clear that African American adolescents in Minneapolis have not "gotten" the messages of pregnancy prevention heard by other black teens across the country. Why?

The factors surrounding teen pregnancy are complex. They include poverty, little hope for the future, the desire to be loved and to love, pressure from an older male, lack of decision-making skills, inability to resist peer pressure, violence and abuse, engaging in other high-risk behaviors, and provocative portrayals of sexuality by the media. Not surprisingly, those same factors can be cited for incidence of STDs, HIV, drug and alcohol abuse and smoking. The interconnectedness of risk behaviors is so pervasive, it is impossible to address only one behavior with success. It is imperative to address them as a whole rather than in isolation.

Minnesota certainly has not ignored the problem. Coalitions, collaborations, task forces, and advisory committees have been formed. They have produced strong programs. The Minneapolis Urban League participates in several of them. But it is not enough.

I propose that Minnesota adopt the model of North Carolina to begin to change these very disturbing statistics. Governor James B. Hunt, Jr., of North Carolina has committed the state to involving churches, businesses, media, parents, agencies, educational institutions, policy makers, and health providers in helping to prevent teenage pregnancy. It is appropriate that teen pregnancy be addressed at the level of the governor's office, in addition to the efforts of a state's Department of Health.

The birth of a baby to a young girl is neither a strictly personal matter nor only a health issue. It has implications for the state. Teenage parents are often unable to complete their education, which later results in unemployment, underemployment, and dependence on public welfare. Teenage mothers often seek prenatal care late, if at all, and frequently suffer higher than average levels of birth complications. Their babies are often born premature and with low birth weights. This can result in years of medical treatment.

I don't know why adolescent pregnancy statistics are so high in Minnesota. But we can't allow it to remain at this level. These are our children. While important programs are underway, we need to do more. When a commitment from every sector of the state is sought by the executive branch to tackle a problem, it gains more attention than it would coming from a state or county agency. The broader the base, the more comprehensive the approach can be. A commitment to changing Minnesota's top ranking in the occurrence of African American adolescent pregnancy would be an important step. This is certainly not a place where Minnesota wants to be number one.

3

May 2003, Teen National Pregnancy
Prevention Month: The Disparities

May 19, 2003

May is National Teen Pregnancy Prevention Month. This is a subject that is important to me because I have a teenage daughter. The good news is that the number of pregnancies among all unmarried teens in the United States has declined steadily since 1991. Both an increase in abstinence and an increase in condom use have been cited as factors that influenced the decline. The bad news is that the number of pregnancies among single African American women in Minneapolis, ages 15-19, has increased during that period.

Between 1993-1997, young African American women had 3,200 babies. During the same period, young white women had 5,000 babies. That fact becomes startling when you realize that there are 8.2 young white women for every young black woman in the Twin Cities metro area. This is a huge health disparity. If the teen pregnancy rate were the same for both black and white teens, there would have been only 600 pregnancies among African American teens instead of 3,200.

The consequences of such a disparity begin the moment the child is born. When the mother is a high school student, the chances for graduation, much less future education, diminish. Families that begin with a teen giving birth are more likely to be on public assistance. In 2001, 53% of all families receiving MFIP in Minnesota began with a teen birth, a 26% increase since 1998. For these young mothers, the barriers to working their way out of poverty are daunting.

The causes of increasing teen pregnancy rates among our young women are complex. Family relationships, peer influence, erratic school attendance, poor school performance, lack of self-esteem, substance abuse, unsupervised time, and poor problem solving skills have all been cited as factors that influence the frequency of sexual activity. Conversely, the presence of strong protective factors emanating from the family, the school, the church, and the community provide a deterrent to sexual activity and unsafe sexual practices.

Every component of a community is needed to build the structure that protects our children from teen pregnancy and a myriad of other risks in their young lives. Having people one can depend on, believing in oneself, knowing one's own value, as well as knowing the facts, are assets that we can all help young people to acquire. Teen Pregnancy Prevention Month, in addition to drawing our attention to a great health disparity, reminds us of the responsibility that our community bears for the future of our young women.

4

The Need to Do More to Prevent Teen Pregnancy

May 7, 2004

May is Teen Pregnancy Month, and programs throughout the State of Minnesota are gearing up to remind communities of the issues, concerns, and problems that arise from high rates of teen pregnancy and premature parenthood. Each year, this focus on Teen Pregnancy gives me a chance to reflect on the efforts that we are making as a community to educate our young men and women about the dangers of having pre-marital and unprotected sex.

I know there are a great many social ills about which the community is concerned, and rightfully so, but being the parent of a 17 year-old daughter, there is no greater social concern for me than teen pregnancy. So clearly, this issue is one that is very personal. To that end, I would like to say **thank**s to teens in Minnesota for the positive direction they are going relative to preventing teen pregnancy. But at the same time let me quickly add that we have not done enough.

Statistics show that since 1992 there has been a decrease of 19% in the rate of sexual intercourse among 12th grade females, and a 27% decrease among 12th grade males.

Perhaps you didn't understand what I just said. Young people are having sex significantly less frequently today than they did ten years ago. That's great, but that's not good enough. It's not good enough because there are several concerns associated with this notion about having sex while still a teen that force us to forge ahead for even better results. One of those concerns has to do with the use of alcohol. In the state of Minnesota, 85% of 9th to 12th graders that have had sex also use alcohol. Folks, that is not right and that hurts. We've got to give our youth the clear, unmistakable message that the cost of illegal alcohol consumption is too high and has no benefits. It only leads to impaired judgment, which leads to poor choices; among those pre-marital sex and unwed parenthood. Linked with other resulting factors, such as fetal alcohol syndrome, depression, domestic violence, and homelessness, it's hard to paint a pretty picture of life for an unwed teen mother.

Another concern is that oftentimes young folks have sex when they don't want to have sex. As a matter of fact, 7 out of every 10 women who have had sex before the age of 14 said that it was involuntary or unwanted. That is not right and it hurts. I understand that peer pressure is a big part of the equation. That's why it's important to have teen role models who can bring the message **peer to peer** that the only safe sex is no sex. I acknowledge that there's some outstanding work being done by peer groups to promote abstinence among teens. We need them to work even harder.

Finally, the notion about having sex and exposing oneself (in the case of a pregnant teen, exposing an unborn fetus, as well) to sexually transmitted diseases is one I'm not sure many of us fully understand. In this state alone there were 11,000 cases of chlamydia or gonorrhea infection among teenaged youth. Hundreds more likely go undetected or unreported.

So what are you saying, Clarence?

I am saying that despite the messages distributed by clinics and health education programs about the importance of practicing safe sex, and despite the warnings about what can happen as a result of having unsafe sex, thousands of cases of STDs among our teens is an indisputable indicator that we have not done enough. I'm saying that teen pregnancy rates have decreased in the last ten years, and we can feel good about that. But there is so much more to do that none of us should pat anybody on the back until teens engaging in sex is at 0, and until the use of alcohol among teens is at 0, and until teens contracting STDs is at 0. I'm saying that achieving these results must not be seen as farfetched or unattainable. Our children's lives and their futures must be that important.

Progress and Continuing Challenges With Regard to Teen Pregnancy

2005

In Minnesota and across the nation, May is the month for giving focus to the issue of teen pregnancy. The Governor has proclaimed the month of May as "Teen Pregnancy Prevention Month." I commend him for having the foresight to give that level of importance to this issue.

I believe that this once-a-year focus on pregnancy prevention is critical to the health, welfare and safety of our children. The reason I believe this month is so important is because it heightens our awareness about the plight of so many of our teens, and it reminds us that teen pregnancy correlates with other social issues that warrant our attention as well.

Consider the young girl who finds herself pregnant, with no access to health care for herself or her unborn child. Consider further a young teen who might be pregnant and suffering from depression because of a negative home environment or personal relationships. There could be a teen whose pregnancy is keeping her from getting an education. Then there could be a child whose low birth weight is causing her or him long-term term health problems that are too expensive to be adequately addressed. Maybe a young child born to a teen mother has nowhere to live because her or his mother is on the run. Somebody may know a teen male who finds out that he's going to become a father and has no clue about how actually to be a father. More and more children born to a teen mother are themselves approaching teen age with no one to guide their decisions about how to be responsible and respectful, and we find the cycle repeated again and again.

All of these conditions are realities for our teens, and throughout the month of May we will get a sense of how adolescent pregnancy and the issues that surround it affects all of our lives.

Now, the report for the state of Minnesota is encouraging: teen pregnancies and birthrates among teen females ages 15-19 are on the decline, as they were the previous year. But even while the news is generally positive and there are certainly some benchmarks to celebrate, I strongly agree with the statement released by the Minnesota Department of Health. They caution that the downside of our limited success in Minnesota and in other states is that the public may tend to believe that the problem has been solved. Nothing could be further from the truth, especially for African Americans. The disparities in the numbers of teen pregnancies, birth rates, and related issues remain steady. African American teen females are still almost five times more likely than their white counterparts to become pregnant. They are still almost ten times more likely to be unable to access healthcare and three times more likely to have a child with a low birth weight.

There is no doubt that people and programs have been doing outstanding work engaging teens in dialogue about sexuality, healthy lifestyle choices, and the realities of teen pregnancy. Peer to peer efforts like The City, Inc.'s "Check Yourself" Crew and the Urban League's HIPPHOPP program that focus on building self-esteem and teach prevention have been especially effective. But as long as there are significant gaps in the progress being made to prevent teen pregnancy, the bottom line is that we cannot become complacent; we cannot afford to let the limited progress that's been made cause us to lose our focus.

I repeat: Having a month to focus on the issue of teen pregnancy is very important to the well-being of our children and our communities. Recently in a news release the Department of Health pointed out that Teen Pregnancy Prevention Month gives us an opportunity to reflect on what must be done--- beyond the month of
May--- by community groups, parents, schools, businesses and faith organizations to reduce adolescent pregnancies. We've made some progress, but I'm confident that if we pull together as a community, form partnerships, and collaborate effectively, there will be even greater progress to report next year and the year after that. It should be our goal, however, to design strategies and seek resources that will ensure that no gap exists in the progress rates for children of color.

Chapter Five

Housing and Concentrated Poverty

1

The Hollman Project and the Issue of Concentrated Poverty

July 26, 2000

It has been eight years since fourteen families living in public housing and the Minneapolis NAACP filed a class action lawsuit against the City of Minneapolis, Minneapolis Public Housing Authority, Minneapolis Community Development Agency, the Department of Housing and Urban Development and, later, the Metropolitan Council. The families claimed that Minneapolis had created racially segregated public housing by confining public housing units in a concentrated area that was the poorest in the city. In 1995, the lawsuit, *Hollman v. Cisneros*, was settled with a consent decree agreed to by the city and its agencies.

The Hollman Decree required that the existing buildings in Sumner Field, and on Glenwood, Olson Highway, and Lyndale be torn down and the residents relocated to areas that did not exhibit "concentrated poverty." This result was considered a victory for those who brought the suit.

Since 1995, we have seen the unfolding of the consequences of the Hollman Decree. Buildings have been demolished, people are living in new surroundings, and plans are underway for redeveloping 73 acres that formerly held some of the worst public housing in the city.

It did not take long for the original intent of the Hollman Decree to start to go astray. In 1998, the plans put forward by the city showed little regard for the former residents of the site or the nature of the Northside community. A group of community organizations got together and presented representatives of the Mayor, the City Council, and Minneapolis Public Housing Authority with a plan to guarantee the participation of community residents in the redevelopment of the Hollman site.

The plan is known as the Wholeman Way. The group was successful in gaining acceptance of eleven out of the nineteen points in their proposal. The proposal covered ways to make the new development affordable to Northside residents, guarantees for business and employment opportunities for community members, and joint decision-making on community issues affecting the development.

An article in the July 19 edition of CITY PAGES called attention to the fact that redevelopment plans now appear to have strayed in another direction. Many of the organizations that have served the Northside community over the years--- organizations like Glenwood-Lyndale Community Center, Phyllis Wheatley Community Center, Sumner Library, Summit Academy OIC--- will be relocated under the redevelopment scheme. Although these organizations have historic foundations in the area, they were never part of the master development plan for the area. The community's agreement with the city (Wholeman Way) tried to correct that by specifically stating in Point Four that space within the project area would be provided for these organizations. Even the state bonding request made by the Minneapolis Empowerment Zone cited, as its first point, "replacement of public housing units in North Minneapolis with well-connected, mixed income neighborhoods with extensive public amenities and a wide range of housing types and community services."

It is this obvious, past omission which has fostered today's growing discussion of the VALUE of continued support of these important organizations now that we have done away with "concentrated poverty." The current discussion of the need for community services rests on two false premises. The first premise is holds that the only people who used the services of these organizations were the residents of the public housing buildings that were destroyed. Sad to say, North Minneapolis has plenty of poverty to go around. Thousands of people who didn't live in those buildings went to those facilities.

The second false premise holds that if one is now earning $8.00 an hour and are trying to support a family of four, that person no longer needs any community services. There are sixty neighborhood or community centers in Minneapolis. There are fourteen community libraries. Not one of them has an inscription over the door saying "for poverty-stricken people only." There is no other neighborhood in the city that would inspire a discussion on whether community services might be threatened by a lack of poor people. Do they ask a person's income at the Nokomis Library or at the Linden Hills Neighborhood Center? Do they check for Medicaid cards at the Lake Harriet Boat Docks?

I am pleased to say that I have not observed any indication that the city intends to walk away from its commitment to provide space for these agencies and the services they provide. Agency directors have been meeting with Jackie Cherryhomes, President of the City Council, and

Chuck Lutz, Director of the city's Special Projects Office. The gist of prevailing attitude at these meetings has been that "the landscape has changed but our need to provide high quality community services has not." I would suggest that the following stance should be taken by all parties involved in the discussion of relocation of services for the people of North Minneapolis: We will use the opportunity offered by the Hollman Decree to create the best neighborhood in the city out of what was once the worst. We will have the best affordable housing, the best community services, and the best opportunities for our residents."

Displacement and Disruption from the Hollman Settlement

February 21, 2001

Several years ago, Reverend Curtis Herron spoke with a great deal of skepticism about our ability to preserve the heart and the spirit of the Hollman Settlement. He was concerned about how quickly and how smoothly low-income, replacement housing would be achieved for displaced residents.

The central allegations in the class action lawsuit, *Hollman vs. Cisneros*, were that both public housing and Section 8 certificate and voucher holders were concentrated in minority low-income neighborhoods. In April of 1995, the Hollman Consent Decree was ratified. The settlement set forth a series of actions to be taken to promote equal housing opportunity, expand and maximize geographic choice in assisted housing, and encourage racial integration.

Now, almost six years later, we are seeing the effects of the settlement. A total of 770 units have been demolished or sold, primarily on the Near Northside. Two hundred units are scheduled to be built on those sites, another ninety-eight throughout Minneapolis. Close to 500 more may be built in the suburbs. Seventy percent of the new units were to be designated for people displaced by the demolition and people already on waiting lists in Minneapolis. But, according to an article in the Star Tribune on February 4, 2001, 54% of the units are occupied by people from suburban lists while only 46% are from Minneapolis lists. This was not the intent of the settlement!

When displaced families were asked if they would be interested in moving to the suburbs, many answered yes. To them, the term suburb is likely to have conjured up visions of Richfield, Brooklyn Center, East Bloomington, or Brooklyn Park. When the options turned out to be Chaska, Eden Prairie, or Woodbury, some very tough choices had to be made. Families now had to ask themselves profound and disturbing questions:

> Is it worth it to travel long distances to be with family and
> friends and to partake of the life we left behind?
> Is it worth it to live in complete isolation in a totally white
> area?
> Is it worth it to give up social networks in the old
> neighborhood that we have spent a lifetime building?

I think the time has come to return the discussion to the heart and the spirit of the Hollman vs. Cisneros issue. Do we solve the problem of housing patterns that create and perpetuate segregation by sending residents of those neighborhoods to newly-created, low-density suburbs on the extremes of the metropolitan area? Isn't there a compromise that could be reached that does not completely disrupt the patterns of daily living: proximity to family, friends, church, doctor, dentist, hairdresser, restaurants, and shopping? Couldn't we find a way to decrease the concentration of minorities without making it difficult, if not impossible, for people who wish to remain in the city?

I think the answer is yes and, for that reason, I support the following actions:

1) Loosen up on the settlement stipulation that prohibits housing from being built in the "impacted areas." This would allow housing for low-income people to be built in the 5th Ward, the 8th Ward, and other areas that are deemed "impacted."

2) Increase pressure on non-impacted neighborhoods, including Kenwood,
Harriet, and Calhoun, to accept their share of meeting the needs for low- income housing.

3) Abandon plans to build 181 units in distant counties like Carver, Washington, and Scott.

Why should the Hollman settlement money be invested in these communities when it will not serve the needs of the people the settlement was intended to help? From today's vantage point, it's clear that the seasoned voice of Rev. Herron was right.

Minneapolis Urban League Role in
Training Workers for Heritage Park

October 28, 2002

It's hard to believe that it's been ten years since we first heard the words, *Hollman vs. Cisneros*. The class action lawsuit, filed in 1992 by the NAACP and Legal Aid Society on behalf of public housing residents, alleged that the City of Minneapolis pursued discriminatory policies over many years by concentrating public housing in poor, minority communities, particularly in Near North Minneapolis. The lawsuit came to an end in 1995 when the parties agreed to a Consent Decree issued by Federal District Court in Minneapolis.

The Consent Decree has resulted in the redevelopment of an 80-acre site in Near North Minneapolis called Heritage Park. This site includes the former Sumner Field, Glenwood, Olson, and Lyndale public housing developments. The passing of a decade seems to be a good time to review the Minneapolis Urban League's role in what is known in the community as the Hollman Project.

After the settlement was reached, the Minneapolis Urban League worked with others in the community to develop the Wholeman Way Plan. The plan had two goals:

• to ensure that an appropriate percentage of the new housing being proposed at the Hollman site (now Heritage Park) be categorized as affordable;
• to ensure employment opportunities for former residents of the Sumner-Olson and Glenwood-Lyndale public housing developments once construction began on the site.

The Hollman Consent Decree contained numerous sections. In response to Section Three, Minneapolis Public Housing Authority issued a Request for Proposals in 1999 to community-based organizations, soliciting ideas for programs to prepare local residents for employment with the Hollman Project.

The Minneapolis Urban League submitted a successful proposal. The Urban League was immediately criticized by some in the community for agreeing to train people to work on this project. That criticism did not resonate with me because helping folks to gear-up to enter the workforce is what the Minneapolis Urban League has been doing for over 75 years. It's part of our mission. In 2001, a total of 1,345 people sought out the Urban League because they needed a job. They arrived in all states of readiness. Some only needed to find out about job openings, some needed a referral, others needed to start at the beginning to prepare for the workplace.

In October of 1999, the Minneapolis Urban League signed a performance-based contract for $270,000 to recruit, train, and graduate 100 Section Three-eligible residents over a one-year period. In the basement of a community church building, we began the first of a series of 4-week workplace-readiness training sessions (known as "soft skills"). Participants who completed the workplace-readiness training moved on to ten more weeks of training, with a subcontractor, to learn specific job skills (known as "hard skills"). A strict requirement of the program was that participants had to attend five consecutive days of training to earn their weekly stipends and move on to the next week. Upon completion of the soft skills course, a formal graduation ceremony was held and attended by participants' families and program staff. Successful participants then enrolled in the 10-week course in hard skills training at Summit Academy OIC or Dunwoody Institute. This is where they learned to use the tools and take the measurements that would be needed on the job.

During the first year of the Section Three Program, the Minneapolis Urban League exceeded all targeted goals. One goal we set was to recruit and assess 150 participants; 173 were actually recruited. Another goal was to graduate 120 participants from soft skills training; 130 were actually graduated. A third goal was to refer 100 graduates for enrollment into hard skills training; 130 were referred. The final goal was to have 70 participants graduate from hard skills training; 91 actually graduated. Based on this success, our contract was renewed for another year, and again we exceeded all targeted goals.

In all, over a two year period, 278 participants were recruited for the program through the use of flyers, public service announcements on local radio stations, and promotion in the Minneapolis Public Housing Authority's monthly newsletter. Out of the 278 recruited, 213 completed the soft skills training, 207 were enrolled in hard skills training, and 144 became eligible to work on the Hollman site.

It is important to note that out of the original grant of $270,000, $135,000 was earmarked for the Urban League to provide a 4-week soft-skills training program, and another $135,000 was earmarked for a sub-contractor to provide a 10-week hard skills training program. Later, it was decided that participants needed a cash incentive to complete both the soft skills and hard skills phases of the Consent Decree Section 3 program.

Thus, $168,000 was added to the original grant and paid out to the people who successfully completed each week of training. The total grant came to $438,000.

Also noteworthy is the fact that 55% of the grant payments received were paid directly to or on behalf of program participants in the form of stipends, equipment costs (work boots and tools), support services (transportation), and drug testing. The remaining 45% represented expenses related to instruction, space, and training materials.

Back in 1999, I was concerned about taking on a performance-based contract for a brand new project. In retrospect, I am glad that we did. A performance-based contract means that we are paid only for our success. Throughout the two-year grant period, we were required to go before an Implementation Committee to report on our progress. In turn, the Implementation Committee would require us to report to an Oversight Committee that was made up of community members. Very detailed outcome data was provided to both committees.

The Minneapolis Urban League received $500 for each Section Three-eligible resident recruited and assessed, $250 for each program participant who completed two weeks of training, and $250 for each participant who completed the full four weeks of training. The same was true for the subcontractors for hard-skills training. Although this is a difficult way to work, both the funder and the community are assured that we didn't get one penny that we didn't earn.

I believe that the 144 community residents who entered and completed the Section Three program, administered by the Minneapolis Urban League, were exposed to a very rewarding experience and gained useful skills and knowledge to prepare them for the workforce. The Hollman Project promised them jobs. Our biggest disappointment is that very few of them were given the opportunity to work on the site. Much of this is due to the time lag in getting the construction underway. The first class graduated and was ready to work on the site in March 2000. Our last class graduated and was ready to go to work in September 2001. The Hollman Project, which is now called the Heritage Park Project, didn't get underway until December of 2001.

Housing: Fundamental Problems (Education and Income) Versus Immediate Needs

December 2, 2002

I came across an article in the St. Paul paper last week that brought a different perspective to the issue of "affordable" housing. Editorial writer D. J. Tice was commenting on a paper published by Ron Feldman, an analyst with the Federal Reserve Bank of Minneapolis. In the paper, Mr. Feldman concludes that, rather than a shortage of housing, "a shortage of income is largely behind the housing affordability problem."

Feldman contends that it is not possible to reduce the cost of building new rental housing to the point where low-income people have enough money to pay the rent. In 2002, the cost of materials and labor coupled with housing codes and building regulations make it impossible to reduce costs. In 1960, 23% of rental units did not have complete plumbing and 10% allowed occupancy beyond one person per room. Although rents were cheaper then, no one recommends returning to the days of substandard housing. But that leaves us with the problem of seemingly irreducible high costs.

The standard ratio used for housing affordability is this: If a person's rent is more than 30% of her or his income, that person is in over her or his head; i.e., the rent is not affordable. When one has very little income, even 30% is probably way too high. People at the bottom end of the income chart use up a greater proportion of their money on food, utilities, medicine, clothes, and other necessities than high-income people do. Percentages probably don't mean anything at that level.

Feldman's answer to the housing problem is not to set a goal of building "affordable" housing. His solution is to build market rate residences for people with higher incomes. This will induce high-income people to leave their old homes and move into newly constructed buildings. The houses/apartments they leave behind can be purchased, at a cost far lower than new construction, for use by low-income people.

This view is an interesting departure from the set of beliefs one usually hears expressed regarding the affordable housing crisis. Whether it was Mr. Feldman's intention or not, the point it brings home to me is that we too readily accept the fact that nearly 200,000 renting households in the Twin Cities make less than half of the median income for the metro area.

I agree that cheaper rent won't move them closer to the median income. What families in the middle of the affordable housing crisis really need is to make more money. Education, job training, safe daycare, reliable transportation, and an employer willing to take a chance on them have a greater pay-off, in the long run, than subsidized rent.

These fundamental shortcomings in our system constitute a greater crisis than the one in affordable housing. Yet, in the near-term, we have people who have nowhere to live. Although the Minneapolis Urban League tries to work on all fronts--- education, employment, health, crime prevention, social services--- we, too, are compelled to try to help with housing. We have plans to work with the Minneapolis Public Housing Authority to build up to 31 rental townhomes for large families with little income. Six are already underway in South Minneapolis.

We realize that our efforts are small, considering the magnitude of the problem. Nevertheless, until the social fabric is strong enough to support all of our poor people in moving up the income ladder, we have an obligation to provide adequate housing.

Sources:

D. J. Tice, "It's Not a Housing Shortage: It's an Income Shortage," *St. Paul Pioneer Press*, November 27, 2002

Ron Feldman, "The Affordable Housing Shortage: Considering the Problem, Causes and Solutions," August 2002.

Governor Tim Pawlenty's Homeownership Initiative

July 2, 2004

On Monday, June 28, Minnesota Governor Tim Pawlenty announced an initiative to close the gap between whites and minorities owning homes. A select group is to develop a plan due to the governor in March of 2005. The goal of the plan is to "increase dramatically" the percentage of people of color owning homes. This is absolutely a needed initiative given the current status of minority home ownership.

Statistics suggest that in Minnesota 78% of all whites who occupied houses owned their homes. This is compared to only 41% for people of color. When one looks more closely at that 41%, the statistics are startling for black folks. In the year 2000, when there were 52,160 African American households, only 28% (approx. 14,604) owned their homes while 71% (approx. 37,033) were renters.

Governor Pawlenty has kicked off this initiative by announcing a $10 million low interest loan to Habitat for Humanity. I 've got three suggestions for those involved in planning and implementing this initiative from the governor.. For one, this initiative should address those banks that red-line in our community and demonstrate a trend of not making loans to people of color. Statistics would show that Franklin Bank, under the direction of Dorothy Bridges, is the only bank in Minneapolis that has stepped out to become a leader for promoting economic opportunity in minority communities. It is imperative that we have more than one bank with that kind of community investment mindset. Secondly, this initiative needs to seek out and create partnerships with minority contractors. The larger contractors are seemingly growing larger with each new development project, while minority contractors, with very few exceptions are struggling. If we are to create more homeowners, we have to be creating more houses, so one partnership should be with minority contractors. Third, there needs to be a major investment in complexes exclusively for our beloved seniors, particularly in North Minneapolis. If there were more complexes to accommodate some of our elders who currently live in houses that are either too large or have become too difficult to maintain, more housing stock would be available for families.

Interestingly, Governor Pawlenty is quoted as saying that this initiative is charged with creating parity between people of color and other Minnesotans. That is precisely the goal of the Minneapolis Urban League in carrying forth our mission, which is to enable African Americans and other minority group members to cultivate and develop their individual and group potential on a par with all other Minnesotans. We're pleased that the governor's plan to increase minority home ownership in Minnesota is parallel to our efforts.

Chapter Six

Leaders and Leadership

1

Jesse Jackson: Reserving Judgment, Appreciating Contributions

January 24, 2001

Over and over again, I have been asked what I think about the public announcement by Jesse Jackson that he is the father of a child born to a member of his staff. I am saddened for Reverend Jackson, his wife, and his children. It hurts. Yet I am clear about what I think: I can't judge anyone.

I find myself struck by the amount of courage it must have taken to continue in the forefront of every issue that concerns African Americans knowing all the while that, sooner or later, his enemies would have a powerful weapon to use against him. The opponents of Jesse Jackson are legion. Their tactics are as varied as their beliefs about politics or religion. They have been after him all of his life. They will never cease trying to neutralize him as a political force.

Yet he went on.

I cannot fathom what it must have been like to summon the courage to stand up, when he himself was so vulnerable, for all people of color, to demand that his voice be heard, to press decision makers in every corner of our country to change their way of thinking, to act on the basic principles of America.

When I reflect on the number of times recently that Jesse Jackson has placed himself in the midst of public controversy, when he might have stayed out of the limelight, I marvel at the strength of purpose that he called upon. He continued to pursue his mission, for the benefit of all African Americans, when he knew he would be defenseless against those who would call him, "hypocrite."

Just in these last two months, Jackson has accused the

Republicans of stealing the election and the state of Florida of disenfranchising black voters. He has condemned John Ashcroft, Bush's nominee for Attorney General, as the enemy of people of color and the poor. He led the charge because that is the vitally important role he plays on the American political scene. He could have kept his mouth shut. He could have ducked the spotlight.

Jesse Jackson has placed himself in a situation that has hurtful repercussions for many people. One could say the same about any of us at some point in our lives.

Life is a struggle that can't be measured on a scoreboard, gaining and losing points as the years go by. Life is a process that, with the help of God, results in an outcome that is, on balance, more positive than negative. The positive cannot discount the negative. It is all of a piece.

God knows that. He is the one who said, "Judge not, that ye be not judged. For with what judgment ye judge, ye shall be judged: and with what measure ye mete, it shall be measured to you again." (Matthew 7:1-2)

On Natalie Johnson Lee and Officer Melissa Schmidt

August 12, 2002

Sometimes we pick a fight that is not our fight and later wonder how we ever got into it. Eventually we realize that in some way, shape, or form, all fights are our fights. As Dr. Martin Luther King, Jr., so ably stated, "We are inextricably bound together--- one cannot fall without the other." Such is the case with Fifth Ward City Council member, Natalie Johnson Lee.

On Tuesday, August 6, Council Member Johnson Lee addressed the following memo to all City of Minneapolis employees:

"It is with great sadness that we grieve with the members of the Minneapolis Police Department, the residents of Horn Towers, the Schmidt Family, the Donald Family, and the entire population of the City of Minneapolis. On this day or mourning, we pause to reflect on the untimely deaths of two fellow citizens--- two fellow human beings.

We salute the work and contributions of Officer Melissa Schmidt. She, like so many others, pursued her special calling to ensure that our streets were safer and our calls for help answered. Officer Schmidt gave meaning to the words, 'community policing.' Her responses to our calls for help transcended racial and economic lines. Her efforts to make our streets safer had no boundaries.

We in the Fifth Ward understand the pain of losing loved ones. We understand untimely deaths. In the wake of this tragedy, let us renew our commitment to community safety--- and strengthen our vow to resolve our conflicts in a nonviolent manner. Let us truly love one another.

On this Sixth Day of August, 2002, National Night Out, - after observing a moment of silence at 7:30 p.m., I encourage our churches, temples, synagogues, and mosques, to ring the bells of freedom in memory of the slain. We pledge to ensure that those who are deceased will have not died in vain. Today, we affirm life and recognize the many lessons in death."

Because of this memo, Council Member Johnson Lee has been accused of being insensitive, a cop-killer-lover, racist, pathetic, unprofessional, and offensive. The police union has called for her resignation. I believe that all of these labels are unwarranted.

I found Council Member Johnson Lee's memo to be compassionate and sympathetic, not only to those who were killed, but to their families who are left to mourn. Further, and equally important, Council Member Johnson Lee calls upon the community to strengthen our resolve to extricate violence from our community.

If you were to speak privately with Council Member Johnson Lee, she would tell you that she and I have sat squarely on opposite sides of some issues. But this is not about what side of an issue you sit on. This is about what's right and what's wrong. What's wrong with this situation is that a member of the Minneapolis City Council is being criticized because she acknowledged the tragic death of two people in the same memo.

My Bible teaches me a unique lesson about life and death. The lesson is that all life, regardless of skin color, age, financial status, or religion is valuable. It is appropriate for Natalie Johnson Lee, and all of Minnesota and the nation, to mourn the death, regardless of the circumstances, of anyone and everyone.

Natalie, hang in there. With head up, shoulders straight, back unbent, head unbowed. Hang in there!

3

Thoughts on the Life and Legacy of Paul Wellstone

November 4, 2002

We take so much for granted. We lead our lives as if nothing will ever change. When tragedy strikes, we are shocked because the unthinkable has happened. The plane crash that killed Senator Paul Wellstone, his family, and five others, was a devastating personal and political event. So much was riding on that plane.

As the days passed following the terrible crash, we started to understand more fully who and what had been lost. Here was a man who had served twelve years in the United States Senate. We thought we knew a lot about him but we didn't know enough.

Hugh Price, President of the National Urban League, captured this feeling in his weekly column, "To Be Equal":

> I had long thought I fully understood how valuable Paul Wellstone was--- valuable to the forces of political progressivism, valuable to people who want to believe that the practice of politics still offers a chance to change things for
> the better for all Americans, valuable to those who like to see a politician who likes ordinary people. Now I'm beginning to think that as much as I appreciated him and respected him, I didn't understand the half of it. Only now, as I read over the comments written to me by our staff who worked with him on legislation, and as I read the comments of media columnists and others who knew him, do I realize that American politics and American society have lost a great deal more than, for the moment, can be put down with precision in words.

We all saw the piece of Paul Wellstone that we needed to see: the piece that agreed with us on a political issue; the part that could help our cause; the part that could right a wrong for one of our community.

What we failed to grasp, until 20,000 people showed up for his memorial service, is that thousands of people saw Paul Wellstone as their champion, as their leader, as the one who would help their cause. One of the speakers at the memorial service was right when he said that Wellstone was the lobbyist for all the people who could never afford to be a special interest group.

In 2001, Senator Wellstone put his thoughts into a book, *Conscience of a Liberal: Reclaiming the Compassionate Agenda*, that gives a sense of the whole man. We all should take the time to read it and understand what motivated him.

One of the lasting memories that I will have of Senator Paul Wellstone is from the opening of the new Glover-Sudduth Center on Plymouth Avenue in October of 2001. He was one of very few public figures who braved an all-day downpour to attend the event. I will never forget him standing next to me and singing, from memory and with gusto, every single word of "Lift Ev'ry Voice and Sing," the black national anthem.

Resignation of Hugh Price: The Legacy of His Service to the National Urban League

November 18, 2002

On November 6, 2002, Hugh Price announced his resignation as President of the National Urban League. His statement included, "There is never a good time to leave the job of a lifetime. But after nearly nine rewarding years and intense years, I think it is time for me to seek a new professional challenge and for the board to enlist fresh leadership for the 21st century."

In a nine-page letter to the 112 CEO's of Urban League affiliates across the country, Mr. Price outlined what his leadership had produced over the past nine years. He brought about a myriad of structural changes that revamped out-dated practices, broadened board membership, strengthened the Movement's research capacity, stabilized funding for the organization, and fortified the relationship with affiliates.

Most importantly, Hugh Price was the driving force behind a clearly- stated strategic direction for the Urban League as a national movement. The agenda calls for:

- Ensuring that our children are well-educated and equipped for economic self-reliance in the 21st Century
- Helping adults attain economic self-sufficiency through good jobs, homeownership, entrepreneurship and wealth accumulation
- Ensuring our civil rights by eradicating barriers to the economic and social mainstream

The Urban League Movement has a dual mission to provide human services AND advocacy for African Americans and other people of color. Other organizations concentrate on service OR advocacy. The Urban League is unique in devoting itself to both endeavors.

There is an internal struggle inherent in having a dual mission. Advocacy and direct services compete for the resources of talent, time, energy, funding, and good will. Some efforts make a difference in the lives of individuals or families; other activities have the potential to reach all African Americans. It is the responsibility of the leadership, both nationally and locally, to find the balance that best fits the current environment. We may see the effects of having this dual mission play out as the National Urban League's search committee moves through the process of identifying a successor to Hugh Price.

As I think about the resignation of Hugh Price and the wonderful legacy he will leave, human nature forces me to think about my own legacy because, for better or for worse, we all produce one. I hope mine will be one of building this community, of moving it forward, of leaving it better off than when I first encountered it twenty years ago.

Natalie Johnson Lee, The Green Party, and the Response to President George W. Bush's State of the Union Address

February 10, 2003

Although 62 million people watched President Bush deliver his State of the Union address on January 28, I suspect far fewer watched the responses that immediately followed the President. One response came from the Green Party and was delivered by Natalie Johnson Lee, a member of the Minneapolis City Council. Being chosen to represent her party in a national venue was a distinct honor for Ms. Johnson Lee. I, for one, wish I had seen more press coverage of her remarks. We might not expect national attention, but I would have expected more local coverage of her presentation in Washington. I want to take this opportunity to publicly congratulate Council Member Johnson Lee on this recognition.

Council Member Johnson Lee pursued the theme "America can wage peace, not war" in her national response to the State of the Union address. She cited the forces for war--- oil, the global weapons trade, unrestricted corporate power, the military establishment, the choice of favored regimes--- and offered the Green Party alternative of a global economic policy whose goal is the elimination of poverty, the creation of sustainable industries, and support for democracy based on the empowerment of working people.

Unlike the Republicans or Democrats, the Green Party is an international movement that is active in ninety countries. Although candidates are elected locally, their affiliation is worldwide. According to the Green Party website (www.greenparty.org), a group of American activists, inspired by the success of the German Green Party, came together in 1984 to form the Green Committees of Correspondence (GCoCs) network. Several national gatherings were held, out of which grew a grassroots process to draft a national Green Program. These activities brought Greens together from across the US, people committed to building a unified vision for a peaceful, just, and environmentally safe society. The first full-fledged Green Congress was held in Eugene, Oregon, in 1989. Since then, activity at the grassroots level has blossomed with local Green Parties organized in 46 out of 50 states. To date, 170 city council members, mayors, county commissioners, school board members, and state representatives have been elected on the Green Party ticket.

For me, Ms. Johnson Lee's accomplishment was not about the Green Party, or the Republican Party, or the Democratic Party. No, for me, this was about a Northsider who done good! So, please, join me in saluting our Fifth Ward City Council member for this wonderful recognition.

6

Thoughts on Leadership

April 14, 2003

One of the topics that is getting a lot of attention these days is, "What does leadership mean in the Black community?" Recently, I have heard comments like, "Who is a leader?," or "She is not my leader," or "He doesn't speak for me." So, I thought I would toss this notion around this week and see where it lands.

As I thought about leadership, I realized that leadership is developed, not discovered. Sometimes people look at a person and say, "There's a natural born leader!" Not so. What they mean, but don't realize, is that the person is charismatic. There is a big difference between charisma and leadership.

Many think that leadership is attaining a position. I disagree. One does not automatically become a leader just because she or he is elected to this, or is head of that, or becomes president of something else. What one has attained is strategic placement. Placement does not necessarily produce leadership.

If it's not charisma, and it's not position, what then is leadership? To me, it is doing the tough work: attending the long, boring meetings; taking the non-glamorous assignments; completing the tedious tasks. To me, leadership means creating a vision of how things can change and developing a plan to make change happen. Then the leader articulates how the plan will work in a way that causes others to follow one's leadership and support one's vision.

But, more than anything, leadership requires humility. I am reminded of a young preacher who was about to deliver his trial sermon. The young man approached the pulpit with his head high, his shoulders back, and a smirk on his face that said, "I got this thing all together."

The new preacher proceeded to deliver the worst sermon ever uttered in that church. The sermon was so bad that it embarrassed him, and it embarrassed those who heard it, as well. He returned to his seat with shoulders slumped and head hanging down. He had been truly humbled. As he sat down, an old, gray-haired woman behind him whispered in his ear, "If you would have went up to that pulpit the way you come back . . . . God could have used you in between."

I recite this story to illustrate that when it comes to leadership, it is better to start out humble than to be humbled by it.

Hugh B. Price's Final "To Be Equal" Column as President of the National Urban League: "Are We Ready for the Development Revolution?"

April 21, 2003

Out of respect for my national president, Mr. Hugh B. Price, who has decided that his work is done as President and CEO of the National Urban League, I thought it appropriate to honor him by making his "To Be Equal" column my column for this week:

"April 11th marks my last day at the helm of the National Urban League. It's been an exhilarating nine-year run. So this is my final "To Be Equal" column.

It seems like light years ago now, but the fact is that barely more than 24 months ago the world euphorically greeted the dawn of the new millennium. The U.S. economy was strong, unemployment was low, and the stock market was soaring. With the Cold War over, former Communist countries were clamoring to join NATO.

Ensuing events, however, dramatically demonstrated that little in life is constant, much less guaranteed.

National economies and Wall Street swing from boom to bust. Conservative U.S. presidents succeed centrist ones. Federal tax cuts can tilt heavily toward the wealthy, while program cuts target working people and the poor, even the middle class. Crippling government deficits can evaporate only to reappear, driving up state and local taxes while destabilizing such vital domestic programs as K-12 education reform, affordable higher education, and accessible healthcare.

We can wring our hands and moan, "Woe is us." Or, we can confront these inevitable vicissitudes by forging a new movement to make certain we reach the economic mainstream—and remain there—whatever ideology prevails inside the Washington Beltway.

The revolution I'm thinking of is what my colleague T. Willard Fair of the Urban League of Greater Miami calls the development revolution.

This follows the two seismic revolutions in the history of African Americans.

First was the Freedom Revolution of the 19th century, during which we cast aside the physical and psychological shackles of slavery that had rendered us someone else's property. The second was the Equality Revolution of the 20th century, whose goal was to secure equal status under law and eliminate government-sanctioned segregation in public schools and higher education, public accommodations and the voting booth.

Racial discrimination is no longer allowed by law; but the work of the Equality Revolution continues in many walks of American life. We can't for a moment relax the pressure on government and the private sector to ensure justice, equality and opportunity for all.

But we must also mount a third great movement—the Development Revolution. Its motivating spirit isn't just to survive as a people. It's to thrive by eradicating the economic gaps that separate far too many Africa Americans from the American mainstream.

As I see it, there are four key components to this 21st century revolution: spiritual development, educational development, economic development and political envelopment.

The foundation for the Development Revolution is our spirit—the deep-rooted values and aspiration in our hearts and heads that shape our dreams and steer us in a positive direction. It's this spirit we must call upon, while respecting individual privacy, to combat the personal conduct among some African Americans that spreads poverty and poison, narcissism and despair, and even death, in our community.

The Development Revolution requires that we instill a collective sense of personal responsibility for the success and the safety of our spouses, our partners, our loved ones and our children, who equal our destiny.

Educational development is vital because in the 21st century world academic failure simply isn't an option. Yet national statistics show that as recently as 2000, nearly two-thirds of black youngsters in the fourth grade can barely read.

Thus, parents and caregivers, pastors and civic leaders must make sure—no excuses!—our children achieve in school so they are well prepared to succeed in life.

Economic development is crucial because economic self-reliance and power are the endgame in a capitalist economy. That means, among other things, buying homes and accumulating nest eggs, and creating and acquiring black-owned businesses that generate livelihoods and wealth, political clout and philanthropy. Not just large firms, but also the smaller shops and franchises that are part of the infrastructure of any economically viable community.

The fourth component of the revolution this time is political development.

No longer should black folk allow one major political party to take us for granted and the other to write us off. At roughly 12 percent of the U.S. population, we exceed the margin in most elections. So we have political clout aplenty, provided we actually vote. In the eyes of today's calculating politicians and their pollsters, we forfeit our right to bellyache if we don't fill out that ballot come election time.

To be sure, the Development Revolution I envision consists of objectives and strategies to fulfill them.

But it's much more than that. Above all else, it's a state of mind.

In the late 1960s, I wrote a column for a weekly newspaper, called *The Crow*, which was published by an organization I headed at the time—the Black Coalition of New Haven in Connecticut. It strikes me as fitting and timely even to this day to close out my final "To Be Equal" column with the question posed in the title for my column for The Crow:

When it comes to waging the Development Revolution, "Are We Ready?"

8

Natalie Johnson Lee and the Cancellation of Family Day

August 7, 2003

Family Day, scheduled to take place on Saturday, August 16, has been canceled. The reason for its cancellation is that the Minneapolis Urban League was unsuccessful in securing a permit to block off Plymouth Avenue from Knox Avenue to Penn. To do so, we needed the support of Natalie Johnson Lee, our 5th Ward city council representative.

The Minneapolis Urban League's Family Day Celebration -- or Extravaganza -- is one of the League's hallmark annual events. Every year we bring together the entire community in the grandest of fashions to say "thank you" to our constituents, stakeholders, contributors, and friends. It is all the more a grand occasion because Family Day encompasses the Plymouth Avenue corridor from Knox Avenue to Penn. The entire five-block area is for one day a year transformed into a festive marketplace where vendors can sell their wares, where community advocates can distribute information promoting family values, healthy lifestyles, and safe neighborhoods, and where empty lots are turned into playgrounds of fun for our children.

Well, this year we again had grand plans. We planned to expand the Family Day Parade, which was initiated as part of the festivities that launched the Grand Opening of our newly constructed Glover-Sudduth Center for Economic Development and Urban Affairs in September of 2000. To make the parade even more spectacular, floats were being designed to show off hometown heroes and sheroes from local high schools. Several area organizations had signed on to march and proudly display their banners. The route was lengthened to give more people an opportunity to catch the parade before it reached the big lot on Penn Avenue for a grand finale performance by all the marching groups.

As I noted, we needed to secure a permit to block off Plymouth Avenue for all of these grand events to happen. We applied for a Block Event permit on May 30, 2003. Our application was hand delivered to the office of Council Member Natalie Johnson Lee, along with the $500.00 application fee. Approximately two weeks later, her office acknowledged our permit request. Johnson Lee stipulated that before signing the permit, she wanted us to meet with tenants of the Plymouth Avenue Shopping Center, who had some concerns about Family Day's impact on their business day. We saw that as a reasonable request, and with the assistance of NRRC, who owns the shopping center, followed through.

On June 16, we met with most of the shopping center tenants to try to resolve their issues. To address their complaints about Family Day, we offered to provide alternative access to the shopping center lot. We offered to buy gift certificates redeemable at each store. And we offered to promote their businesses throughout the day from the main stage. To no avail. Despite our best efforts, we still could not convince our city council representative to support our permit request!

There is something that I want to make absolutely clear about the intent of Family Day. Family Day has become a tradition since its inception in 1989. But it is not just an Urban League tradition, it's a Northside, Southside, Minneapolis, neighborhood, community tradition. For 13 years, families have looked forward to that one day a year when they could be amidst all the fanfare on Plymouth Avenue. It's a social occasion, a networking occasion--- but most importantly, it's a family occasion. The Minneapolis Urban League Guild, our auxiliary arm, has its own booth on Family Day. They make sure that our neighborhood children can get a hotdog, a small treat, and a refreshing drink at a cost any family can afford. The atmosphere created on Family Day is one of neighborliness and mutual acceptance of each and all. We cherish and protect that aspect of Family Day at all costs.

That's our intent. It has never been the intent of the Minneapolis Urban League to disadvantage minority business along Plymouth Avenue. We took seriously the concerns of some of the tenants of the shopping center, and we worked diligently to resolve them. I would point out, though, that Family Day is one time a year when more than 50 small minority vendors and entrepreneurs get the opportunity to share their talents and cultivate new customers from among the thousands of people available on that day to be enticed.

Some folks say the Urban League makes money on Family Day. As a matter of fact, we don't. It costs tens of thousands of dollars to put on this once-a-year event. Each and every member of the Urban League staff is required to work at least four hours that day, which in itself represents 400 staff hours. That's not counting the numerous volunteer hours that the community contributes to provide security, cleanup, and to just be helpful.

Several people have asked me, "What will happen next year? Will there be a Family Day next year?" The answer, quite honestly, is "I don't know." To plan for an event like Family Day we have to know that we have the support of our city council representative. It's just not feasible to spend time with planning and making commitments to suppliers and vendors and not know. It's a drain on limited finances, but more than that, it's a drain on the morale of staff and volunteers, which is something that I just can't tolerate.

143

Despite this current setback, I do have some fond memories of Family Day. I remember five years ago, when I was first named President and CEO of the Minneapolis Urban League. One of the first events I presided over was the Family Day of 1998. It was a wonderfully glorious and proud occasion that I will forever remember. Then I remember Family Day just last year, in 2002. It was around 6:00 in the evening, and about 3,000 people were milling around the streets between Penn and Knox. Music was playing, and folks were eating and having a good time. Major Topps, who conducted the parade earlier in the day, stopped me in the middle of the street and said, "Clarence, this is what community is all about."

Permit or no permit, nobody can take those memories away.

Saluting Al Gallmon upon Resignation
as President of Minneapolis NAACP

October 3, 2003

I'm sure many of you have heard that Rev. Al Gallmon announced his resignation as President of the Minneapolis Branch NAACP. Let it be said by me that he should have no regrets about his contribution to this historical organization. Rev. Gallmon has demonstrated a tireless commitment to this community through voluntary service, and I want to take this opportunity to salute him. He's demonstrated that commitment over and over again as pastor of Fellowship Missionary Baptist Church, as a member of the Minneapolis Public Schools Board of Education, and as President of the NAACP.

All too often, people who volunteer get nothing of substance out of it, but the high likelihood that someone will pass judgment on their efforts. I know, because I am judged every single day. Whenever one stands in leadership it is tremendously difficult, and very few people understand how difficult it can be. It's been my experience that for every person who thinks one is doing a good job, another ten people think otherwise, and for every person who supports a decision one makes, there will be ten others who don't support it. That's why I believe that whenever someone stands up to provide leadership she or he should be applauded for doing so, and I certainly applaud Rev. Gallmon.

With Rev. Gallmon's resignation, a new leadership will emerge at the NAACP. Let me suggest that this is not a time when anyone should be critical. This is not a time when we should look for things that didn't work. What we need to do now is support the NAACP. We must realize how vital the NAACP is to our community. For certain, the work of the Minneapolis Urban League and all those who are interested in equal rights and equal justice is made easier because of the work of the NAACP. As a matter of fact, if there were no NAACP, we'd be trying to figure out how to create one. I am pleased to say that I lead an organization that has always supported the NAACP and will continue to support it and whoever the leadership happens to be.

In my humble opinion, the NAACP, like the Minneapolis Urban League, should not be judged based on any one individual. It should not be supported or not supported because of the leadership that is in place. The history of its purpose is too transcendent, its commitment to the fight for equality too stalwart, and leadership too fluid to be defined by a person or group of people. The NAACP should be supported and lauded based on its solid foundation, rooted in the fight for civil rights and replicated in cities throughout the country. Those who lead such a venerable organization should be supported and lauded for having the desire to carry the fight forward. So again, I salute Rev. Al Gallmon for his desire and for his commitment and for his good service.

Farewell to Bernadette Anderson

October 17, 2003

On Saturday, October 11, several hundred people attended the Homegoing celebration of a friend to many of us, Bernadette Anderson. Through testimonials and song, Bernadette's spirit could be felt within the walls of New Salem Missionary Baptist Church. The poignant stories of her life's journey revived the consciousness of all who stood witness.

Being among those witnesses helped me to remember what it is like to lose a friend. As I sit here and reflect on the program as it unfolded, several things stick in my mind. First of all, I am reminded about the comments several people made about how Bernie "cussed." Let me say that there are two ways to "cuss." One way is when you use your mother's or your sister's or your family's name in disparaging ways. Bernadette never cussed that way, nor would she tolerate you or me cussing that way. But there is another way to "cuss": when a person tells the truth boldly and unabashedly, without any degree of embarrassment. That is how my good friend Bernie 'cussed.

The second thing that struck me during her service was a comment made about Bernadette's legacy. Rev. Jerry McAfee chimed in with reinforcement. Someone asked the question, "Who will continue the legacy of strong advocacy that Bernadette carried for so many years?" The comment challenged everybody in the audience to, in Rev. McAfee's words, "get some heart." That's exactly what it took to be the kind of advocate that Bernadette was. As I look back on her life, I realize it would be disrespectful of me or any one of us who say we're advocates not to go forward with her same courage, strength, commitment, and determination. I promise to do that.

Finally, the third thing that I was reminded of Saturday was the first time I met Bernadette Anderson. I had just settled into my position as Executive Director of the North Community branch of the YMCA on West Broadway, after having spent several years at the Southdale branch. I remember folks telling me that I needed to go across the street to the YWCA and meet Bernadette. Spike Moss told me, "you need to go over and meet Ms. Anderson." Cozelle Breedlove told me, "You need to go over and meet Bernadette.'

Finally, I met Bernadette. My first impression of her was that she was a big woman with a big voice. I don't remember much about our conversation, but there was one thing she told me that day that I'll never forget. As we concluded our meeting and I was preparing to walk out of her office, she said to me, "Boy, don't you let those white folks mess with you." And I said, "Yes ma'am." I will never forget those words, and never again will I let them folks mess with me.

Farewell, my friend.

The Qualifications Necessary in a Chief of Police

November 13, 2003

Police Chief Finney has served notice to the city of St. Paul that he will not seek another term as chief. His announcement gives me a chance to do two things. First, I can publicly state my personal admiration and appreciation for Chief Finney. In his lofty position as chief of police, he has always been the consummate professional, while at the same time maintaining a close relationship with the community. What I really mean is both his professional contacts and people in the community knew him as Chief "Corky" Finney. I admire him for his ability to wear both hats well.

Secondly, Chief Finney's announcement reminds me of the fact that in a few short months, the Minneapolis Police Department will be looking for a new chief. As I thought about that prospect, I thought about the following: 1) What qualities will Minneapolis look for in a new police chief? How should the selection ultimately be made? What kind of allegiances will a new chief form with communities of color, with unions, with the Mayor and Council Members?

Let me share my thoughts on what I see as critical considerations. First, in terms of qualities, a new Minneapolis police chief has to be someone with the ability to provide leadership in a lot of different and distinct areas. By that, I mean there are so many city and community entities that rely on a solid relationship with the chief of police that this person must be able to walk a fine line. His or her skill for balancing the confidence of both the public at large and that of fellow law enforcement agencies has to be proven out by strong leadership. Communities of color must have confidence that their new chief will not be unrelentingly in support of law enforcement at the expense of its concerns, and vice versa. It will be a difficult road to walk, but that's the kind of leadership a new police chief will have to provide.

Another quality essential for a new chief is the confidence to make very difficult and often unpopular decisions. It's no secret that those who make the difficult decisions for the city often feel isolated. Criticism may be so severe as to cause one to question one's own sanity. That's why the new chief must come with the reference of good character, marked by sincere openness and honesty. People must be able to trust in and be compelled to follow the chief when the need for making difficult or unpopular decisions arises. I don't mean to put a damper on the process for selecting the new police chief, but I'm convinced that 2004 will not be a good time for difficult decisions.

The other thing I think about is how the decision should be made. I understand (we all understand) the politics of naming a new police chief. We know that the mayor makes a recommendation that then has to be approved by the city council. It seems to me, however, that there should be another layer to this process. At a minimum there should be some public discussion about the top two or three candidates. In this discussion, the candidates should be given an opportunity to talk openly about how they intend to move our diverse city, with its troubled police/community relations, forward. They should talk openly about their perspective on community policing, about code four, and about racial profiling and the need to recognize its reality in the face of strong denial.

The fact that the next chief of police is going to have to balance so many different allegiances will actually be the litmus test of how effective and influential a new chief will be. The new chief will have to be able to walk in and out of communities of color, go toe to toe in the political arena, and in the end be able to inspire follow-ship from the men and women that make up the police department.

Having said all that, I think you will agree that this is going to be a very difficult task for the city of Minneapolis. Communities of color will have three things to consider in determining the success of the selection of a new chief: 1) What kind of progress is the city making relative to the recruitment of officers of color? 2) What kind of progress is the city making in the promotion of people of color to higher ranks of law enforcement? 3) What is the city actively doing to foster a better relationship between the police department and communities of color?

Despite the difficulties, I am looking forward not only to watching the process unfold, but to pledging Minneapolis Urban League cooperation in forging a partnership for making our community safer and more secure.

Dr. Martin Luther King, Jr.: A Dreamer, But So Much More

January 16, 2004

As I sit in my office today, January 15, I realize that this is the day that one of the greatest leaders in American history was born. And in a few short days we will be celebrating the national holiday recognizing the birth of the Reverend Dr. Martin Luther King, Jr.

Most of us will celebrate Dr. King only because he had a desire—a dream. That's unfortunate, because he was so much more than a dreamer. First of all, Dr. King was highly educated. It's a little known fact that he graduated from college without ever graduating from high school. Dr. King was only 15 when he entered Morehouse College, where he earned a B.A. degree in Sociology. He also earned a Ph.D. in Systemic Theology and authored four books. *Stride Toward Freedom: The Montgomery Story, The Measure of a Man, The Strength to Love,* and *Why We Can't Wait* are publications written by Dr. King that we should all take time to read.

Dr. King was a believer and a dreamer, but being a believer and a dreamer should not detract from the fact that he was an extremely educated intellectual.

Secondly, Dr. King was a tremendously spiritual man. He became a minister at age 18, and delivered his first sermon at Ebenezer Baptist Church in Atlanta, where he served as Associate pastor. At age 19, he was officially ordained a Baptist minister, which is no small fete. Ordination takes you through a process that requires you to demonstrate a thorough knowledge about biblical studies. You have to be able to convince a council of elders that you have achieved a level of biblical understanding that prepares and qualifies you to minister to others. Dr. King entered Crozer Theological Seminary in Chester, Pennsylvania, where he graduated with a B.D. degree in 1951. In 1954, Dr. King became the 20th pastor of Dexter Avenue Church in Montgomery, Alabama, and later served as co-pastor and pastor of Ebenezer Baptist Church.

Dr. Martin Luther King was indeed a dreamer, but being a dreamer should not detract from the fact that he was a tremendously spiritual man.

Dr. King was also a family man. He and his loving wife, Coretta Scott King, experienced the birth of four children. Their first child, Yolanda Denise, was born November 17, 1955. Martin Luther III was born on October 23, 1957. Dexter Scott was born January 30, 1961, and fourth child Bernice Albertine was born March 28, 1963. Dr. King's children thrived under a very nurturing mother and father, and they have grown to reflect the ideals and aspirations that both parents have tried to instill in all Black youth.

Dr. King was truly an insightful dreamer. But being a dreamer should not detract from the fact that he was a great family man.

Finally, Dr. King was passionate about his people and our struggle for freedom and equality. He did more for his people than we could ever do in his memory. He led a successful bus boycott in Montgomery, Alabama, which resulted in giving Black bus riders the right to sit anywhere a seat was free. He exposed racist institutions and took them to court on behalf of black folks, spending many nights in jail as a result. It was in jail that he penned the famous "Letter from a Birmingham Jail" in 1963. Because of these activities, Dr. King's house was bombed and he himself suffered bodily harm and nearly died when he was stabbed in the chest by someone who was incensed by his successes and the notoriety he was gaining in the fight for civil rights. None of the hardships Dr. King encountered deterred him from his dream for our freedom. Dr. King led many sit-ins and demonstrations demanding justice for black folks, and he was successful in convincing a number of eating establishments and other public entities throughout the south to integrate. He led a march on Washington that attracted nearly 1 million followers, and it was at this march that Dr. King delivered his famous "I Have a Dream" speech on the steps of the Lincoln Memorial.

But the fact that he was a dreamer should not detract from the fact that Dr. King fought non-violently and without fear to gain freedom for his people and, in recognition of his efforts, he received the Nobel Peace Prize in 1964.

So, as you celebrate the dreamer, please understand that he was much, much more. Learn about the prophetic wisdom of the man. Read his words and explore his accomplishments. Dr. Martin Luther King, Jr., was unarguably the greatest humanitarian of all time.

The Civil Rights Director Selection Process: A Painful Reminder

April 29, 2004

Back in the latter part of February, I wrote a letter to the mayor expressing the Minneapolis Urban League's concern about the Civil Rights Department and the fact that an interim appointment was made to replace former Director Van Owens Hayes. Please understand, we were not concerned about the person named to fill the position in the interim--- we only felt strongly that a permanent director needed to be appointed as soon as possible. I asked the mayor about the city's plans for the Civil Rights Department, given its current dilemma. The department was facing drastic budget cuts, backlogged cases, and increasing claims, and I wondered about the feasibility of it being able to overcome these problems. I talked about the importance of this department to our constituency, because of its relevance to addressing some of the core objectives of the Minneapolis Urban League's mission. Finally, I offered the assistance of the Minneapolis Urban League in moving a process forward for selecting a permanent director. In response, the mayor appointed a community panel that was charged with helping to shape the criteria for a qualified Civil Rights Department director. This panel would ultimately interview the successful candidates. The Minneapolis Urban League was represented on that panel.

With the process in place and underway, I awaited the Mayor's announcement. Just days ago Mayor Rybak named Jane Khalifa as his choice to be the new director of the Civil Rights Department. His announcement has caused quite a stir in the black community. The stir is centered around both the process and the person.

As I listened to this debate unfold, it took me painfully back six years ago, when I was named President of the Minneapolis Urban League. And it took me painfully back to ten years ago, when I was named President of The City, Inc. In both of those cases people, for various reasons, took exception with both the process and with me, the person. What I felt bad about is that I really could not control the process. Actually, very few people can control their own selection process. I remember feeling terrible inside because some people then began to castigate me as a person. I remember being so inwardly divided in both instances, because I had worked hard--- both educationally and experientially--- to prepare myself for the level of responsibility required for both positions, and I was excited when I was named the successful candidate. But I also remember being so saddened and almost frightful that my wife and daughter would have to read some of the negative comments some people chose to make.

Because of my own painful experience, I have learned to value an honorable process. I know that for African Americans and other people of color to make positive gains in this society, the process for selecting those in leadership positions must be fair, impartial, open, and honest. Given an honorable process, I believe that any African American who is sincere and who has planned appropriately to be successful has the ability to compete on a level with anybody else.

And relative to the "person," I have learned, given the many weaknesses that I have, to just give the "person" the benefit of the doubt, realizing that she or he has a level of responsibility that that individual will either meet or not meet, and that accountability for a quality performance will rest squarely on the chosen person's own shoulders.

I know that in my 11 years of very public leadership, all I have asked for is the benefit of the doubt--- to be allowed to prove whether I could fulfill my given responsibilities or could not.

By the grace of God, in most cases, I have.

14

Paying Spike Moss for His Advocacy

June 4, 2004

For the last couple of weeks, one of the most talked about issues in Minneapolis, and no doubt in our twin city of St. Paul, has been the status of Spike Moss's employment with The City, Inc. On the surface, it would seem like this would be an issue solely between The City, Inc., and Mr. Moss, but quite honestly, this is a much, much broader issue. At its core is this question: How important is advocacy to our community, and if we deem it important, how do we engender support for those who advocate on our community's behalf?

By definition, advocates are the ones out in front on an issue. They are the ones who rally the disenchanted to call to account the powers that be. When the issue is about race, emotions naturally peak, and opinions often collide on both sides. An outspoken advocate like Spike Moss will oftentimes find himself at odds with the majority community and in the distant crosshairs of anyone who finds discomfort with such outspokenness.

But the truth of the matter is this community needs strong advocacy. We need strong advocacy because there are those among us who are less connected and feel less empowered to speak out in the face of unfairness or mistreatment. It's the advocate's job to channel that feeling of powerlessness into action. For someone who has to spend any amount of time advocating in the course of job duties, particularly someone who advocates strongly and forcefully, there are very few organizations or corporations that are able or willing to invest in that person's professional longevity. Advocacy is often viewed as extracurricular or outside the bounds of normal job duties, therefore placing the advocate in the position of committing professional suicide.

Long ago, when I was a young man, advocacy was a valued commodity. Dollars were available to support someone whose role was to maintain a pulse on the community and to stir the pot when the issue warranted it. Nowadays not only is advocacy devalued, but it is looked upon with disfavor--- as something outmoded, having outlived its usefulness. Nowadays funding sources are so restricted that almost every dollar that comes to an institution or organization is tied directly to a specific program that has to produce very tangible results. There are no allowances made in the funding community for the fact that some people will be disenfranchised or even discriminated against in the provision of services. Just consider the disparities for people of color in access to health services, in the allocation of adequate educational resources, in job opportunity growth, or in developing the economy within our neighborhoods.

It brings me back to the real issue for our community as we talk in our intimate circles about Spike Moss's professional fate--- as I know we are doing. The real issue is not about The City, Inc., or about Spike Moss. The pertinent issue, rather, is how as a community we can collectively find the necessary resources to pay for the things that we need. We would be foolhardy to think that the corporate or business community, whether as a result of naivete or by design, will see the wisdom of making sure advocacy is a component of any program for which it provides financial support. The *Star Tribune* called Spike Moss a $1-a-year civil rights leader. Doug Grow wrote that a dollar was all The City, Inc., could afford to pay Mr. Moss. Those statements may sound clever, and they certainly sparked speculation, but they are totally misleading and irrelevant--- missing the point entirely. The point is that we as a community can't afford not to pay Mr. Moss for his advocacy, so it behooves us to figure out how to do just that.

15

Dr. Martin Luther King, Jr.: Advocate
for Education, Nonviolence, and Justice

February 2005

I am not attempting to be funny here (folks know I have no sense of humor), but this time of year always makes me smile. It is the one time a year when it seems like it's okay to be black. It is that time between the celebration of Dr. King's birthday and the conclusion of Black History Month when we will see display after display of people in celebration of "Blackness."

Yesterday I was at a meeting and the notion about what it means to be black in 2005 came up. The discussion surfaced with this question: If Dr. King were alive today, what would he see?

First of all, Dr. King was a strong believer in education, as was his father and mother. His father attended Morehouse School of Religion and earned a degree in theology. King's mother was a teacher. King himself was admitted to Morehouse College at the age of 15, having skipped both the 9th and 12th grades. He went on to earn a Doctor of Philosophy from Boston University. If he could see "Blackness" manifested in Minnesota today, he would see an education system in peril, a system the value of which has seriously diminished in recent years. In Minnesota in 2001, for instance, a study conducted by the MMEP showed that over 50% of African American students and other students of color did not complete high school in four years. Of those who did not finish by 1999, over 34% of American Indians, 31% of Hispanics, and 36% of African/African Americans dropped out of high school. And in the Minneapolis school district, where African Americans constitute the largest community of any race/ethnicity in Minnesota's largest school district, the four-year graduation rate for black students in 2003 was only 39%, compared to 83% for white students.

Secondly, as a man who believed in nonviolence, Dr. King would see "Blackness" manifested in Minnesota communities almost paralyzed by violence. Crime statistics for Minnesota indicate that violent crime increased in 2003, particularly in the city of Minneapolis. The city accounts for over half of the total number of violent crimes committed around the state and contains the highest concentration of people of color. Additionally, the Minnesota Gang Strike Force reports gang activity has been identified in every part of Minnesota for some time, and the trends seem to indicate a continuing growth in criminal gang activity throughout the state.

As a man who hoped for a world that was completely colorblind--a world in which a man was not judged by the color of his skin, but by the content of his character--- Dr. King would see "Blackness" manifested in Minnesotan communities today that are a tapestry of different cultures, but that are as segmented as ever, with each group securing its own little enclave and its own selected leaders.

Finally, one of Dr. King's most poignant statements was his reference in "Letter from a Birmingham Jail" to injustice. King stated simply that "Injustice anywhere is a threat to justice everywhere." Well, if he saw "Blackness" manifested in Minnesota today, he would see injustice in its purest form. He would see that "African Americans are imprisoned at 20 times the rate of Caucasians in Minnesota," that "African Americans are arrested for drug offenses at a rate about 14 times higher than whites in Minnesota," and that "about 20% of African American men in Minnesota are ineligible to vote because they are incarcerated or on parole or probation for a felony conviction."

Yes, for the next month or two, everybody will see that it is okay to be black. But for the 10 months that follow, what will we do to insure that "Blackness" is the commitment to one's culture and not the conditions in which one lives!

16

Sustaining and Honoring Spike Moss

2005

On a Friday evening, when a major snow storm sent many folks scrambling home early from their jobs or from school, a man was honored for his ability to withstand any storm. The honoree was Spike Moss, who was recognized by friends, former foes, and contemporaries. Numerous people rose to offer pungent comments, both seriously and in jest, in recognition of the man as an outstanding advocate for black people, for poor people, for disenfranchised people, and for all people of color.

The honor given to Spike Moss is fitting at this particular time, because standing up in a storm has become a challenge not everybody is willing to meet. All of us can attest to times when we've just had to stop and wonder: What can I do about it? I've done all I can; I can't do no more. I'm sure Spike has had those times, as well. After all, he's human. The reason he deserves recognition and accolades from all of us in this city is that he refuses to give in to wonderment.

Spike will tell you he's been fighting injustice since he was a child. He's seen it, experienced it, and suffered for it over many, many years. Some of us know about Spike at

"The Way," before it became "The City, Inc.," and was moved off of Plymouth Avenue. We know the role he played in bringing calm to a city caught off-guard by the fervor and destruction of the riots that rocked Plymouth Avenue in the 1960s. His influence on processes for bridging a relationship between police and community, and paving the way for urban development in the aftermath of those times is well documented and continues its evolution.

Those were indeed stormy times, and a lot of people who had been on the front line with Spike eventually drifted away, comforted by the goodwill being dispensed by public and private sector institutions who just wanted to avoid confrontation. Spike, one of the most insightful people I've ever met, knew that most of that "goodwill" was meant to pacify, and that in time the struggle for people of color would be against more covert forms of racism and inequality. Spike Moss is able to reveal this covertness in a manner that some call "outspoken," or "confrontational," and so he is tagged as a "controversial civil rights activist," which is descriptive, but which also marginalizes his ability and effectiveness as an advocate for equality.

159

I'm not trying to call out his age, but I know Spike has lived long enough to run into those who think the time for fighting is over. Some are younger folks who think protesting and marching is 'passe.' Others are older folk who are just tired of fighting.

Those of us who know Spike know that he will never get tired of fighting for what's right. But what is it costing him personally? I asked this question back in June, when the talk all over town was the status of Spike Moss' employment at The City, Inc.:

How important is advocacy to our community, and if we deem it important, how do we engender support for those who advocate on our community's behalf?

I said back then that we, as a city and as a community, had to figure out some way to compensate Mr. Moss for service that cannot be measured. I submit again that even while we honor him and praise his commitment to serve, the notion about how we sustain advocacy remains.

Part Two

The Need for Institutional Response

Chapter Seven

Police, Criminal Justice, and Corrections

1

African Americans on the Police Force

October 11, 2000

In September, Minneapolis Police Chief Robert Olson sent me a report on African American police officers promoted by the Minneapolis Police Department. Chief Olson referred back to 1996 when Minneapolis Urban League President Gary Sudduth and other community leaders worked with the Police Department to initiate changes in Department policy to address the issue of equal training and promotion opportunities for officers of color. The group has not met in recent years.

Chief Olson's report describes the work that the Minneapolis Police Department has done in changing the assignment processes, promotional testing policies, and training selection decisions. Some highlights he noted are as follows:

> In 1995, there were no African American police lieutenants; there are four
> today, plus one Acting Lieutenant.
> In 1995, there were 11 African American Sergeants; by 2000, the number had increased to 17.
> The first African American is completing training at the National FBI Academy.
> The overall ratio of promoted African Americans rose from 17% in 1995 to 36% in 2000, exceeding the 32% rate for promoted whites.

This report indicates that progress has been made, and I thank Chief Olson for sharing this information with the Minneapolis Urban League. Most of all, we want to recognize the achievements of the African American officers who have been promoted since 1995: Lt. Valerie Wurster, Lt. Donald Banham, Lt. Donald Harris, Lt. Lee Edwards, Sgt. Medaria Arradondo, Sgt. DuWayne Walker, Sgt. Derrick Barnes, Sgt. Anthony Hines, Sgt. Kelvin Puiphus, Sgt. Douglas Belton, Sgt. Gwendolyn Gunther, Sgt. Michael Davis, Sgt. Arther Knight, and Sgt. Dennis Hamilton.

But the Minneapolis Urban League would not be true to its dual mission of human services and advocacy if we did not point out that the figures cited by Chief Olson represent an effort to correct many decades during which a black officer was unlikely to receive a promotion and many more years when an African American was unlikely to be hired. Even today, African Americans account for only about six percent of the nearly 900 officers of the Minneapolis Police Department. The Urban League is not doing its job if we fail to remain vigilant in our exposure of inequality and vigorous in our condemnation of bigotry in all policies and practices that have an effect upon our community.

According to the 1990 U.S. Census, 22% of the residents of Minneapolis were people of color. African Americans were the largest group, with 13% of the total. We only have to look around us to see the increase since 1990 in the many communities of color here in Minneapolis. As a public institution that serves all residents of the city, the Minneapolis Police Department has a long way to go before it reflects the diversity of the people it serves and protects.

At the same time, our communities of color have a long way to go in building coalitions to bring about change in our major institutions and service systems. We have an obligation to show those in the wider Minneapolis community that their own self-interest lies in embracing all people.

2

Racial Profiling Bills

February 14, 2001

It must be me. How come it's clear to me that racial profiling is a part of daily life and others deny its existence? I must not get it.

There are three bills before the Minnesota Legislature right now regarding racial profiling. All three of the bills call for the collection of data on the alleged practice of stopping drivers based on the color of their skin. Why do we need another study to determine what any black man over sixteen can tell you? It must be me. I must not get it.

All three of these bills are now under consideration. The first bill, sponsored by Representative Gregory Gray, would not only record information about the stop, it would include the badge number of the officer who made the stop. Rep. Rich Stanek's bill would gather information on traffic stops in communities that volunteered to participate but would not identify individual officers. The third bill, sponsored by Rep. Jane Ranum, would conduct a two-year, statewide, mandatory study of traffic stops without including individual officers in the data. Even in the Gray bill, which would collect badge numbers, the information would be used as a training tool rather than grounds for punitive measures.

The executive director of the Minnesota Police and Peace Officers Association, Dennis Flaherty, dismissed the need for any kind of study, especially one that identifies individual officers. On February 13, he told the Star Tribune, "We will vigorously oppose that at all costs . . . There is no need to identify an officer. In fact, we seriously question the need for any data collection . . . the problem is so insignificant in Minnesota that all of the attention is not worth it."

I can only assume that Mr. Flaherty is speaking for the members of his association. Their view, and the view of many legislators, goes like this: People of color seem to think that they are stopped by the police more often than white people. They're probably imagining it, but we'll offer up a study to determine if racial profiling is occurring. If we do find instances of stops based on race, it will probably prove to be an isolated case and we'll give the misguided officer some counseling. If it's not an isolated case, then it can be corrected during officer training. No big deal. What's all the fuss about?

It must be me. I don't think this has anything to do with how police officers are trained. Racial profiling is just what it says. It's racism. It's not about cracked windshields, missing tail lights, obstructed views, or failure to signal a turn. It's about how police officers react when they see a black man behind the wheel. More than that, it's really about how white folks react when they see a black man in their neighborhood, in their store, in their park. This is the most basic manifestation of racism: instinctive response of suspicion and fear.

People spend their whole lives learning that reaction. A few hours of diversity training in the Police Academy won't subdue the antenna that goes up when a black man drives by, nor will it deter an officer from turning a routine stop into a search.

But then again... maybe it's me.

CODEFOR: Minor Offenses and Racial Profiling

March 8, 2001

I was deeply disturbed by a piece that appeared on the Commentary page in the February 28, 2001, edition of the *Star Tribune*. The article was written by Katherine Kersten, a director of the Center of the American Experiment, the national, conservative think tank based in Minneapolis. According to their mission, the Center of the American Experiment "brings conservative and alternative ideas to bear on the most difficult issues facing Minnesota and the nation."

On February 28, Ms. Kersten wrote in praise of CODEFOR, a law enforcement initiative that has been in place in Minneapolis for the past two years. CODEFOR focuses on minor offenses. The theory is that people who commit minor offenses are often wanted for major offenses. Kersten describes the success of this initiative as an "astonishing turnaround." She cites statistic after statistic on arrests made for felonies from motor vehicle theft to murder. In Minneapolis, Kersten discusses traffic stops, pointing out that 34% of those stopped were black. More important, minorities were more than twice as likely as whites to be taken into custody. For her, that proves a point.   She does not see racial profiling in those numbers; she sees good police work.

What caused me the most distress was her inference that blacks, by virtue of their race, are more likely to commit crimes. Her conclusion: "Certain minorities--- particularly low-income blacks--- apparently commit proportionately far more crimes than whites and other racial groups."

What does she mean? Does she mean that I am predisposed to commit a crime and she is not? Does she mean that my beloved fourteen-year-old daughter has a greater propensity for law-breaking than her white classmates? Is she implying that African Americans carry a crime gene that white people do not?

All of us want the bad guys off the streets, but none of us ought to favor a system that assumes a citizen is up to no good because of her or his color. The truth is, police officers can be in only one place at a time. If they spend all their time in areas where most of the people are minorities, most of the people they stop or arrest are going to be minorities.

Surely Kersten must realize that if the police spent as much time in the vicinity of the parking lot at Edina High School, nearby parks, or gathering places for Edina youth, they would find a comparable number of "little offenses" which, if cars and persons were searched, would turn up a comparable number of recreational drugs, drunk driving offenses, petty theft, and other offenses.

Katherine Kerstan's statements in this article support others that she has written for the Star Tribune. On June 25,1997, she brought us "the remarkable fact that between 1940 and 1960, the average black man--- though born in wretched poverty--- increased his earnings by 2.5 times, while black women's earnings rose 2.3 times."

So what? The people to whom she refers were still poor. In reference to changes in school textbooks, she claimed, "authors sought to boost minority students' self-esteem by lowering academic standards." (*Star Tribune*, April 21, 1999)

Katherine Kersten's colleague at the Center of the American Experiment, Mitchell Pearlstein, wrote, " While racism is all around, it is generally not deep, which is to say that it just can't be used as a principal explanation for so much that is working out so poorly for so many people of color in our great cities… While racism is reprehensible and personally painful to be sure, we tend to focus too much on it when trying to understand and fix problems of poverty, bad education, and the like." (*Star Tribune*, December 8, 1996)

If Ms. Kersten and Mr. Pearlstein were the only people who held these beliefs, I would not be so worried. The fact is, I believe Katherine Kersten represents the thinking of a growing number of people in Minnesota and across the county. She has access to the majority press to express her views. Her comments are published in the *Star Tribune* at least twice a month. She is also a commentator on National Public Radio's "All Things Considered." When Kersten suggests that racial profiling does not exist, I believe she speaks for a large number of people. When she denies that some officers see the color before the crime, I am concerned that she is expressing the views of a significant segment of the population.

It seems to me that an organization like the Center of the American Experiment, dedicated to the most difficult issues in Minnesota, would want to examine the reality of racial profiling rather than dismiss the concept. In one of the most prosperous states in the nation, in a city renowned for civic responsibility and economic opportunity, we have the greatest disparity between rich and poor in the United States. I submit that this disparity IS our most difficult issue. It cannot be resolved by ignoring the existence of racism in our midst. Perhaps the think tank could think about that one.

Racial Profiling: Confronting Differences, January 2001 and February 2001

March 15, 2001

On March 14, the *Star Tribune* reported on the difference in traffic stops by Minneapolis police officers in January and February of this year. In January, the police stopped 7,704 drivers and wrote 3,770 tickets. Put another way, 49% of the stops resulted in a ticket.   That means that about 4,000 drivers who were stopped were let go.

In February, police stopped 2,861 drivers and ticketed 2217; this means that 77% of all drivers received tickets. Now, either that is an enormous jump in the Minneapolis Police Department's efficiency rating--- going from one ticket for every two stops in January to one ticket for every 1.3 stops in February--- or something else is happening. Officers would have had to write 5,926 tickets in January to match the efficiency of February.

For me, it raises lots of questions:

> How many of the drivers involved in January's 4,000 unproductive stops were people of color?
> What would be an acceptable ratio of justified to unjustified stops? Is it closer to the 51% in January or the 23% in February?
> Do people commit fewer violations when there is a lot of snow as there was in February?
> Were there fewer stops because, according to Sgt. John Delmonico, president of the Minneapolis Police Officers Federation, police officers "feel their work is being second-guessed"?

The number of traffic stops over two months doesn't provide enough information to evaluate the meaning of the difference. But it seems to me that the answer lies in one of the following, none of the following or all of the following:

1.   Stops were down because officers are genuinely concerned about the possibility of racial profiling.

2.   Stops were down because people are driving more safely.

3.	Stops were down because officers were not focusing on traffic offenses.

4.	Stops were down because officers are concerned about how their actions will reflect on themselves and the department.

Any of those reasons could be valid explanations. If officers are examining their own actions in light of their careers and other facets of their lives, I would consider that enlightened. If traffic stops are down because officers are not performing to the standards of their job description, then that is an internal police matter, a matter on which I'm not qualified to comment.

The issue in the African American community is, as it has always been, with traffic stops that are unwarranted, made in hopes of finding something suspicious, a suspicion that arises because of the color of the driver's skin. No one is going to argue with stops that result from an obvious violation or from behavior that is a potential threat to public safety.

It is the stops that result from a decision made by a police officer based on his or her observation of skin color, rather than observation of a bona fide offense, to which we so strongly object.

Calling on Governor Ventura to Veto Racial Profiling Bill

June 14, 2001

Governor Jesse Ventura should veto the racial profiling bill just passed by the Minnesota Legislature. I repeat: Jesse Ventura should veto the racial profiling bill. Minnesota is better off not collecting information on traffic stops than collecting it in the manner proposed in the bill that the state legislature has passed. We will learn nothing from the bill that will be presented for Governor Ventura's signature. He should not sign it.

If you recall, there was an early flurry of activity around the question of gathering data on routine traffic stops. Based on the experience of eight other states, it was considered important to find out the degree to which traffic stops are made based on the race of the driver. Charlie Weaver, Commissioner of Public Safety, appointed one of those blue ribbon panels to investigate whether we should collect data on traffic stops here in Minnesota. The panel recommended that law enforcement officials who pull drivers over on the road record why the stop was made, the race of the driver, and the result of the stop. Under the present system, information of this kind is recorded only if a ticket is issued. The Commission of Public Safety chose not to follow the recommendations of his blue ribbon panel.

Later, a committee of community representatives was invited to give their views on how traffic stop data should be collected. That group also recommended mandatory collection of data. In addition, the group recommended that police officers be required to give all of the drivers that they stop a small card showing the officer's badge number and a toll free number to call if the driver suspects biased treatment.

Three bills regarding racial profiling were introduced in the Minnesota Legislature in 2001. Each took a different approach to the collection of data. As the session continued, African American community leaders, such as Lester Collins and Bill English, were called in to work with other interested parties to negotiate a compromise bill. This group achieved a delicate balance among competing interests. One example of compromise was that officers would collect data if they were given video cameras mounted in the squad car.

The bill that passed, called the Stanek amendment after the author of one of the original bills, misses the point. It is not useful either in establishing whether racial profiling occurs in Minnesota or in changing the behavior of officers who practice it.

The Stanek amendment eliminates all of the compromises that were worked out earlier. It eliminates the very provisions that would make the bill effective:

> There will be no mandatory data collection.
> There will be no officer information card distributed.
> There will be no incentives for officers to collect information voluntarily.
> Voluntary collection of data that does occur will last for one year, not two.
> The citizen complaint system will remain as it has been for years.

I call on Governor Ventura to veto this bill. Fair, equitable, and community- centered policing is fundamental to a democratic society. The intent of introducing a racial profiling bill was to move the conversation on this issue away from rhetoric and accusations into an informed discussion of the effective deployment of police resources. This bill does not achieve that objective.

6

Police Shooting of Abu Kassim Jeilani

March 18, 2002

Like many of you, I have followed the stories about the shooting of Abu Kassim Jeilani with a deep sense of regret. Mr. Jeilani was shot by six Minneapolis Police Officers on Sunday afternoon, March 10. When I heard the news, my first thought was of all the other stories like this where a black man has been shot multiple times in a rain of police bullets. I thought of Timothy Thomas in Cincinnati and Amadou Diallo in New York.

Now we have Abu Kassim Jeilani of Minneapolis, a refugee from Somalia who arrived in this country in 1997 via the refugee camps in Kenya. It is not surprising that he was diagnosed with a mental illness after witnessing the horrors of the civil war in his homeland. Despite his illness, Mr. Jeilani was part of a family and a member of the growing Somali community in Cedar-Riverside. It is with profound regret that we view the photos of his young wife and baby sons, ages one and three. He must have survived so much and fought so hard to get here, only to be shot in Minneapolis, the place where he believed he would finally be safe.

As I read the accounts of his eleven-minute march down the middle of Franklin Avenue to Chicago, I regret that it all happened so fast. Jeilani's behavior prompted a call to the Crisis Intervention Team trained to deal with the mentally ill. Newspaper reports say a member of the team arrived six minutes later. Five minutes after that, Jeilani was dead. Why did so little time elapse between the arrival of experts on the scene and the fatal shooting? How are these decisions made? It makes me sad to think that maybe, with more time, a different course would have been followed.

Time after time, in tragic stories of the shooting of black men, police officers have perceived the black man as an immediate threat. Without question, in some cases they were. In other cases, these men were black BEFORE they were an immediate threat. That is my deepest regret. After all the talk and all the training and all the promises, black men, because of their color, are still perceived as a cause for alarm.

Police-Community Relations: The Possibilities of Mediation through Patricia Campbell Glenn

September 9, 2002

There has never been a time in American history when the relationship between the police and African Americans can be described as good. One hundred years ago, even fifty years ago, a black man would not have considered making a public statement about police behavior. His primary goal would have been not to be noticed by the police. The use of excessive force may or may not have been greater in the 1950s than it is today. We will never know, because the subject was never discussed.

That is not the case today. It seems that in the last six months, our newscasts and newspapers have been filled with injury and death for black people. I get the feeling it will only get worse.

I admit that there was a time when the death of a black person would not have made it into the news. It was not newsworthy. We are beyond that era. We are seeing for ourselves what is happening. Too often, we are seeing on TV how force is used.

There are some things we should be straight on. The law allows police officers to use force. Police officers are not just guys who ride around in cars with guns. We, the citizens, have conferred upon them the right to enforce laws on our behalf. Their top priority is to protect the public. Their second priority is to ensure the safety of fellow officers. But, there is no law that says an officer must achieve those goals with a gun.

The methods used to meet the two priorities vary widely across this country. A state can set minimum standards for the use of force, but municipalities have considerable leeway in interpreting those standards. The history of Minneapolis shows a pattern of using greater rather than lesser force.

In 1989, Urban League President Gleason Glover said, "The whole issue of police brutality is nothing new to the city of Minneapolis. It almost gives the impression that if you are black and poor, it doesn't really matter if you lose your life." He made that statement at a time when African Americans, Native Americans, Latinos, and Asians were calling for the formation of the Civilian Police Review Authority. Civilian

Review was established in 1990 and authorized to look at allegations of excessive force, language, harassment, discrimination, and other behavior. It never had a role in investigating shootings involving police. Only about 10% of the calls or letters that came in became a formal complaint. Only about 10% of the formal complaints were found to show wrongdoing by the police. That amounts to 1% of the original allegations.

Since the Civilian Police Review Authority was dismantled by Mayor Rybak, this is a moot point. I make it only to illustrate the need for a better way to determine how the police use of force will be exercised in Minneapolis. In the last six months, we have seen incidents that might have been handled another way. The City of Minneapolis has been slow to recognize that there might BE another way.

Before another life-threatening or life-taking event occurs, our city and our communities of color must come together to reach an agreement on how force will be defined and how force will be used in this city in the future. An opportunity exists now through the presence of federal mediator, Patricia Campbell Glenn. Ms. Glenn has been in Minneapolis twice in recent months. She is willing to return. Her work in Cincinnati last spring should convince both sides of her credibility.

Stakeholders and the officials of this city must construct an agreement, through mediation and accepted by all, which makes it clear what will happen, when it will happen, and how it will happen when a situation escalates and force is considered. It is far easier to identify the officials--- we all know the mayor, the police chief, the council members, the union leaders--- than it is to identify the stakeholders. It is important that the communities of color identify the individuals who will represent them in the mediation process.

Mediation can get us past the powerlessness of a Civilian Review Board and the powerfulness of a police union to reach a policy that is accepted and, more importantly, understood by police and citizens alike. I have no delusions that such an agreement will transform perilous police-community relations into perfect police-community relations. I can only hope that it will bring us more peace and safety than we have now.

The Need for Federal Mediation between Community and Police

April 28, 2003

For those of you who were not among the crowd of 1,200 in attendance at the Minneapolis Urban League's Annual Dinner, where Tavis Smiley was the guest speaker, you missed a great event. You also missed the challenge he issued to the audience and to the community, as well. Mr. Smiley challenged us to be courageous. As a matter of fact, he compared the choice to sit in silence to a sin.

In that vein, I ask this question: *Is our community being held hostage to the mediation process with the City of Minneapolis and the Minneapolis Police Department?*

I believe that mediation needs to take place now. Yet good people are arguing over who should be at the table. They're arguing about whether or not there should be a lawsuit to force mediation. The latest rumor is that federal mediation is dead. It's being said that in place of this 'dead' federal mediation, some new entity will arise called 'private mediation.'

As far as I'm concerned, mediation will be dead only when a federally mediated agreement has been reached. It's important that mediation go forward in the manner that it was first outlined. Mediation was presented as a process whereby representatives of the city of Minneapolis and members of the community sit down at the same table until they can hammer out an agreement. The process was to include a representative of the Department of Justice, who has the neutrality and the resources to see mediation through, to serve as the mediating force.

There is instance after instance across the country in which this process has been successful. As a matter of fact, last Monday I received a fax from Grand Rapids, Michigan, with a copy of a mediated agreement between the Grand Rapids Police Department and what is called the Grand Rapids Community Leaders Coalition. Similar agreements were mediated in Cincinnati and other cities across this country.

The same thing can happen in Minneapolis. We just need to be committed to seeing it through. We have to have the will to see it through. Elders have often said, "Where there is a will, there is a way." We need to muster up the "will."

Absolutely problematic are the constant news articles reporting that the problem with mediation is that the community can't get its act together. I am sick of that characterization. It serves no useful purpose to belittle an effort to improve the relationship between police and community. The stakes are too high. The fact of the matter is that there is not, nor will there ever be, agreement on who will represent the community. All of those who are willing to put in the time to abide by the long process of coming to a mediated agreement should be able to sit down and provide that service on behalf of all of us.

We can't wait. Summer is upon us. We're facing a summer of reduced summer school at best. A summer when many more young folks than ever will be out on the street. A summer in which there is an increased opportunity for more interactions between the police and the minority community, not fewer. We cannot afford to sit by and do nothing! Federal mediation must take place now in Minneapolis.

That is my reaction to Brother Smiley's message to the audience at the Hilton on April 17th. It was a powerful and timely message. I'm sure others had their own reactions, but I just want to thank Tavis Smiley for challenging me to be courageous.

On the High Incarceration Rates of African American Males

May 12, 2003

What if I asked you this question: What percentage of Black people will win the lottery? What about this question: What percentage of African Americans will play professional golf? And this one: What percentage of African Americans will own their own business one day?

We don't know the answer to some of those 'what if' questions, but we do know the answer to this one. We know the answer to what percentage of black men will be sent to jail or prison in their lifetime, and the answer is astonishing. Twenty-eight percent of black men will be sent to jail or prison in their lifetime. That's more than one out of every four. At this very moment, 12% of our young men in their 20s and early 30s are in prison. According to a study released in April by the Bureau of Justice Statistics, this is the highest rate ever experienced.

I gotta ask the question, **what the H!!! is going on?** Well, somebody said that 12% is not bad. Let me compare that rate with White America. By comparison, 1.6% of white men in the same age group are incarcerated. While the number of people behind bars is going down across the country, the number of African American young men in prison continues to increase. So here is the question: **What the H!!! is going on?**

The chances of being in jail vary from state to state. That's because of the different ways that states use their prisons to deal with crime. The determination of who is sent to prison and for what offense is not a uniform practice. States make their own rules. For example, Louisiana had an incarceration rate of 799 inmates per 100,000 of its population, the highest in the nation. Maine, which had the lowest rate, had 137 prison inmates per 100,000.

Well, somebody asked, "Where does Minnesota rank?" Minnesota ranks close to Maine in incarceration rates, but the raw numbers are still overwhelming. As of this writing, there are 7,357 adult men and women being held in state prisons in Minnesota. Their average age is 33.8 years. More than 3,300 were new commitments in 2002. Another 1,600 or more returned to prison. Nearly half are held in Hennepin or Ramsey County.

As we look closely at the numbers, two things jump out. First, by and large these young men and women are undereducated. For whatever reason, about 40% have a high school diploma or a GED. And the second item of note is that way too many of them are African Americans. Thirty-four percent, or more than 2500, of those inmates are African American. Somebody said, "That's not bad." But when we look at the number of blacks in the State of Minnesota, the African American population is only 3.5% of the total population of the state, and yet we make up 34% of those in prison. **I am forced to ask for the final time, what the H!!! Is going on?**

City Council Delay on Patricia Glenn and Mediation

September 23, 2003

Two weeks ago, in this column, I pointed out the critical importance of bringing a federal mediator to Minneapolis to negotiate the use of force by police officers before another life-threatening or life-taking event occurs in our community. In fact, Patricia Campbell Glenn, the senior federal mediator with the Justice Department's Community Relations division in Chicago, has been in Minneapolis twice since the August 22 events at 26th and Knox in the Jordan neighborhood. But no negotiation has taken place.

Glenn has thirty years of experience in police-community relations. She's the one who negotiated the agreement last winter in Cincinnati. The Minneapolis City Council can't decide if it will honor her with the task or not. Why are members still negotiating among themselves about who will bring the process forward? What more do they need to know about engaging a neutral party, at no cost, to bring the community together with the police to come to an agreement? Even the head cop in Minneapolis, Chief Robert Olson, has said, "Let's do it." Now, forging such an agreement will be very, very difficult, but deciding to try it is a no-brainer. Is there something that City Council members are not telling us?

Last March, the Minneapolis Urban League, as a representative of the community, sent a letter to Mayor R. T. Rybak urging him to employ mediation. Six months have gone by and the letter has never received a response. What is he afraid of?

On September 13, 2002, despite the fact that Patricia Campbell Glenn was in town and ready to begin work, the members of the Minneapolis City Council took the political way out by sending the question back to the Council's Health and Human Resources Committee and the Public Safety and Regulatory Services Committee for further study. I've got news for them. I have studied the issue and our public safety is in danger right now. What is it that they don't understand?

One of the excuses offered by City Council members is that there is a problem determining who the "community" is. That's easy. It's the people who have been harassed, profiled, and mistreated since they became "free" 135 years ago. All of a sudden, the City Council can't remember that definition.

Time is running while bureaucrats scramble to gain an advantage, or to protect themselves, or both. Minneapolis is considerably less peaceful and less safe today than it was a year ago. No one knows what will happen if there is another police shooting, regardless of the cause. If that occurs, Minneapolis will pay a very high price for the City Council's fiddling around.

Thank You to Mediators of Community-Police Agreement

December 3, 2003

Over the next couple of weeks there will be a lot of fanfare about the mediated agreement between a group of community representatives and the city of Minneapolis. What people will spend a great deal of time arguing about is what's in the written agreement. That is fair, because whenever you put something on paper, you invite people to pick it apart. Besides, we all know that action speaks louder than words.

I want to take this opportunity to say thank you to the group of dedicated community members who labored long and hard on behalf of the community to move mediation forward. They did a great job and we as a community must not let their hard work be wasted.

I can remember in 2002, when many people said, "Mediation is dead." And for all practical purposes, it was. There were several factions out there saying "Let me, let me." There was finger-pointing when the process appeared to leave some out. And the net result was that mediation was at a standstill. I can vividly recall the two events that put mediation back on track. The first event I recall is Ron Edwards making an overture to the city to expand the number of individuals allowed to be on the community team. The second event that I recall having a great impact on moving mediation forward was when Rev. Randy Staten asked, "Why should there be a number at all?" These two observations came together and led to a process that allowed for the participation of anyone who had an interest in mediation and who wanted to put in the time and the effort to make it successful.

Therefore, the first mediation meeting was attended by 37 people who had signed up to represent the community. This group began to meet regularly at the Minneapolis Urban League. Eventually, the initial 37 members got whittled down to a hard core group of 19, and it is to these 19 individuals that I want to pay tribute. It is these 19 people who argued on behalf of the community for long hours. It is this group of 19 that conducted research and came up with quantitative analysis. It is this group of 19 that had to wade through and interpret reams and reams of legal documents. It is this group of 19 dedicated people that came up with a resolution that I strongly believe will move this city and this community forward--- together.

By now you know who those 19 individuals are. They come from various walks of life and brought various viewpoints to the table. And yet they were able to put all of their personal and private agendas aside to focus on a collective agenda that had as a common theme a better community and police relationship. They are the people you should say thank you to when you see them in your neighborhood, or at your church, or where you socialize.

I would be negligent if I did not also mention the other side of the table, led by retiring Minneapolis Police Chief Robert K. Olson. There were several instances throughout this process when Chief Olson could have simply walked away. Let us be fair, when things have not gone the way we thought they should have, we've been quick to criticize the chief's leadership. We should be just as quick to say thank you for not giving up, and for not letting his team give up, on mediation.

Another thank you goes out to Paul Zerby. I remember attending a meeting on the subject of mediation with Paul Zerby and Paul Ostrow in the City Council Chambers, and Paul Zerby said, "Let's just get this thing done." Those were simple words, and in their simplicity, they sum up the work of the entire mediation team. They just "got it done!"

Thank you very much.

The Lack of African Americans in the Pipeline to Become Police Chief

December 12, 2003

One of the most commonly used practices in politics is known as releasing a trial balloon. When using this tactic, powers that be use a major media outlet to release a piece of information to see how the community will react. They use it to test public opinion. The release normally has enough truth in it that it is considered factual, but not so much that it can be attributed to anyone.

In the past two weeks the black community received such a balloon. This balloon was released to test our collective appetite for a new police chief, a potential nominee who is not a person of color. It was released to see how much of an uproar will come from the community if the next Minneapolis police chief is white.

The first time this balloon was released was on December 5, 2003. The *Star Tribune*, in an article about mediation, talked about what it would take to move the mediation agreement forward. It suggested that one way to capitalize on the momentum of this agreement between the community and the police department was to select an internal candidate. And then on Wednesday, December 10, powers that be released another balloon. This balloon informed us that both internal candidates have sufficient city council support to be the next chief. It is a known fact that both internal candidates are white. What is unknown and what folks are trying to anticipate is what will happen, given the tremendous distrust of the department by folks of color, if an internal candidate who is not a person of color is named the chief of police.

What is missing from this discussion, and what I am most upset about, is an important question: Why are there no internal candidates of color? Why are there only white folks next in line to be chief? It has been clear to everyone for at least 18 months that Chief Olson was leaving. During that same time frame, all three deputy chief positions had been vacated. If we are serious about diversity, why wasn't a person of color named to one of the deputy chief positions? If we were absolutely serious about diversity, we would have folks of color in the pipeline ready to step up and provide leadership. We would have a person of color serving as deputy chief!

I am convinced that by not filling any of the vacancies with a person of color we have sealed our fate, desired or otherwise. You may ask what I am saying. I am saying that if the selection is going to come from among internal candidates, and only white individuals have been positioned in the pipeline to become chief, then we will end up with a white chief! If I go into a basketful of apples, and all the apples in the basket are red, then it is a fact that if I select an apple to eat from that basket, I will be eating a red apple! Period! And if all I put in the basket is red apples then you can't tell me that you have the same taste for a green or a yellow apple!! I am not buying it. If I suspected that at some point I might want a green or yellow apple, I would have put some in the basket from the beginning.

And because we didn't promote officers of color to the rank of deputy chief, although we had ample opportunity to do so, we are left with a choice that is not diverse at all. Trial balloon or not… that is not fair!

Findings of Council on Crime and Justice Concerning Racial Profiling

February 27, 2004

In September of 2003, the Council on Crime and Justice released a report that analyzed traffic stops by police in the state of Minnesota. The report showed conclusively that an overwhelmingly significant number of these stops were based on the driver's race, creating a pattern of disparity in the treatment of people of color. The report concluded that "these disparities are particularly large for blacks and Latinos. If officers in the participating jurisdiction had stopped drivers of all racial/ethnic groups at the same rate, approximately 18,800 fewer blacks, 5,800 fewer Latinos, and approximately 22,500 more whites would have been stopped in the sixty-five jurisdictions in 2002. If officers in the study had subjected drivers of all racial/ethnic groups to discretionary searches at the same rate, 2,114 fewer blacks, 428 fewer Latinos, and 2,645 more whites would have been searched.

The public release of the Council on Crime and Justice's report seems to have caused serious repercussions that are being made manifest at the State Capitol. The House introduced a bill during the 83rd Legislative Session that states the following:

Whoever informs, or causes information to be communicated to, a public
official, or an employee thereof, whose responsibilities include investigating
or reporting police misconduct, that a peace officer has committed an act of
police misconduct, knowing that the information is false, is guilty of a crime.

The bill further states that

… if the false information alleges a criminal act, the court shall order [the informer] to make full restitution of all reasonable expenses incurred in the investigation of the false allegation.

The intention of this bill, and what it means to any real effort to address the reality of racial profiling in Minnesota, should be disheartening to every one of us. Roughly, the issue is this: If you file a report with the Minneapolis Police Department claiming police harassment or brutality, then you could very easily be found guilty of making a false report if your claim cannot be substantiated. And if you are found guilty of making a false claim, you would have to pay for all expenses related to the investigation of that claim.

This legislation is horrific to me for this reason: It's indisputable that people of color are victims of racial profiling in Minnesota. But if people believe that a claim against an officer could cause them to be convicted of a crime and that they could be ordered by the court to pay for the investigation into that claim, the net effect is that people will refuse to make a claim against an officer. If people refuse to make claims against police officers, then the condition of racial profiling will remain intact and will run rampant in the state of Minnesota.

I am calling on each and every one of you--- on us--- to contact our state legislators, and even those who are not our legislators, but serve in some capacity in the Minnesota House or Senate. Let us make them understand how horrific we feel this bill is. Even while we consider the intention of the legislature in introducing a bill that appears to be in retaliation to findings of racial profiling in Minnesota, we need to be even more concerned about the ramifications of our inaction. Clearly, this is a time when we need to be proactive. Right now, there's been no Senate action on this horrific bill. Let's not wait for it to be acted on any further. Let's take action now.

A Gang Member or Somebody's Baby:
Toward a New System of Corrections

August 13, 2004

Recent reports in the *Star Tribune* suggest that gang activity on the North Side of Minneapolis has spiked. It's suggested that when you compare the number of homicides in North Minneapolis this year to the same time frame last year, they have doubled. Many reports have come forth about random attacks and shooting deaths with no known motive. Each time we hear about one of these incidents, they get closer and closer to home.

There are several reasons given for this phenomenon. The most prominent reason has already been mentioned: increased gang activity. The reports focus on three different areas as offering potential explanations for the increase in gang activity. First is the suggestion that many so-called gang members who were arrested in the 1990s are just now getting out of jail, coming back to find that the community has changed, and trying to reestablish themselves. Another suggestion is that maybe there are smaller gangs breaking off from larger ones to form "baby" gangs, and that they are in a fight to decide who is going to control what small piece of turf. The third suggestion is that these young men and women are the sons and daughters of former gang members and have not learned the necessary skills to deal with conflict.

Thinking about these attempts to explain the very real conditions of danger and lack of security in our community has caused me to take personal inventory of my feelings. I am challenged to remember that the word "gang" is simply a label with a negative connotation. The fact of the matter is that most of the young women and men who are labeled as "gang members" are somebody's babies. It's not they who are the problem, but rather their behavior that is deplorable. In the early 80s, then Chief of Police Tony Bouza classified these same young people this way: "They are simply a bunch of kids all dressed up with no place to go."

So the issue then becomes how do we, as a community, react to a segment of our population whose behavior does not move our community forward? Historically what we have done is turn to a correctional system that has had limited success at best. The philosophy of that system has been and continues to be, "Lock 'em up and throw away the key." I would argue that it's time that we employ a different idea. I want us to look for a solution that will eliminate the need for any of us--- particularly our young folk---

to turn to violence, to crime, to selling drugs, or to taking the life of another brother or sister. I believe there is a need for a new system of corrections that calls for us to emphasize employment opportunities, educational opportunities, family connections, community connections. A system that causes us to believe deeply and sincerely that we are our brother's keeper.

Clearly, we have bits and pieces of such a system, but I would argue that now more than ever before those bits and pieces need to be knitted together into a community fabric to form a safety net meant to catch any young boy or girl who slips.

I know there are some who will read this and interpret my remarks to suggest that I am for coddling gangs and glossing over inappropriate behavior. Nothing could be farther from the truth. What I am for is creating an environment with so many safety nets that none of our young people will ever again resort to taking a road that leads to the types of negative behavior that shuts them away from society, from the community, and from their families.

Marvin Gaye, in his song, "Save the Children," asked us, "Who really cares, who's willing to try, to save a world that's destined to die?" He said, "When I look at the world, it fills me with sorrow that little children today are really gonna suffer tomorrow."

Let's remember that these young men and women--- some who are given the label "gang member"--- are somebody's babies. We've at least got to be willing to try to save them.

Chapter Eight

Public Policy and Processes

1

Excessive Out-of-Home Placement for African American Children

June 28, 2000

The controversy surrounding Chief Judge Kevin Burke's decision to replace Judge Pamela Alexander on Juvenile Court draws our attention to the very disturbing statistics on the numbers of our children who have been or are now involved in the Juvenile Court system. The most dangerous of these statistics is the number of children who are removed from their homes and placed in an institution or foster care.

There are more black kids in out-of-home placement than any other racial or ethnic group. In Minnesota, where African American juveniles comprise 4 % of the youth population, the number in out-of-home placement is among the highest in the country. In 1997, over 1500 of every 100,000 African American youth were in a residential placement facility. That's eight to ten times what it was for whites. The number of young women coming into the Juvenile Justice system is rising at the most significant rate. According to a 1998 report by the Office of Juvenile Justice and Delinquency Prevention, females accounted for 25% of total juvenile arrests for all crimes. Property crimes showed the most dramatic growth. One reason the rate of out-of -home placement is so high is because the arrest rate is so high. But that's the subject for another discussion.

The point is our children are being taken out of our community in astonishing numbers and placed in foster homes, the County Home School, or Red Wing. Children who reach the point of out-of-home placement have only one choice: They must recognize their ability to take control of their own lives and demonstrate that capacity to the satisfaction of Hennepin County Probation Officers. The alternative is the probability of a life of failure. What everybody wants for these children--- parents, schools, parole officers, courts--- is that they complete their education, not re-offend, and make a successful transition to adulthood. Out-of-home placement is considered the best way to accomplish that.

I agree that these children need to overcome the behaviors that brought them into court in the first place and build on the strengths that they all possess. I believe that beneath the confusion, the anger and the resentment, these young people have the strength to lead different lives. I do NOT believe that their lives will change if the county removes them from their homes and their community.

Out-of-home placement is dangerous for our children. It takes away from them the values and the traditions that can nurture them and give them the strength they need. Out-of-home placement removes our children from the nourishment that has sustained many of us - our spirituality. I don't mean the profession of a particular religion. I mean the acknowledgment of the animating force within each of us that has been given to us by a higher power. The nurturing of that gift results in the recognition of the priceless value of each being and the enormous strength that comes with the knowledge that one is valued by another. Our children need that above all else. They need to remain in their home community. This community can provide programs that are intensive, highly structured, individualized, and behavior changing. We ought to be able to do it better than the county. These are our children. We need to help them change.

We cannot help them to change until we change the way decisions are made, policies are set, and programs implemented in the juvenile justice system. African Americans who know our children must have a place on key committees that set policy for Juvenile Court, probation, and out-of-home placement. More African American must be available as advocates for children and families. African Americans, not outside experts, must create and operate the programs to change our children's behavior. We have the most at stake and we have the most to lose under the current system.

189

Powerlessness before the St. Paul School Board

August 9, 2000

On the evening of August 7, I attended a meeting of the St. Paul School Board. That night, the Board was considering the future of Right Step Academy, a charter school. I went to the meeting to make a public statement in support of granting Right Step Academy a one-year extension before any permanent decision was made. For over two hours, I observed the proceedings going on before me. It would be presumptuous of me to comment on the appropriateness of the decisions made on August 7. However, I feel fully qualified to comment on the procedures that were used and the air of absolute powerlessness that pervaded the audience.

As a charter school, Right Step Academy has entered new territory in American education. Certainly, there have been bumps along the way. I believed that I was attending a meeting to discuss the future. The first act of the St. Paul School Board was to set the agenda. The agenda granted equal time to the St. Paul School District and to Right Step Academy. Each side was allowed to make an initial presentation.

Midway through the agenda, the School Board called a recess. When the members returned, they voted to change the agenda. Suddenly, more speakers from the St. Paul School District were invited to the podium. It appeared that they were allowed unlimited time to deliver their comments. In actuality, it took about forty more minutes!

Following this lengthy diatribe, Right Step was given five minutes to present again--- five minutes to rebut what the school district had been given forty minutes to state. That's powerlessness!

Then each side was given the opportunity for a ten-minute summation. The St. Paul School District went well beyond the ten-minute limit. Right Start Academy was held to a strict deadline. At the ten-minute mark, they were told, "Time's up." The founder of Right Start wasn't even given a chance to speak. That's powerlessness!

The most disturbing aspect of the evening was that representatives of Right Step Academy could not change the situation that was unfolding before them. In my opinion, representatives of Right Step were treated as if they were children who had misbehaved in class and must be made an example of to all the other children in the classroom. But they are not children. They are adults who went there to present their side of the story, but they were powerless to do so. When one has power, one controls resources. In the case of the St. Paul School Board meeting, the resources, at that moment, were time and the agenda. But resources come in many forms--- natural resources, financial resources, human resources, spiritual resources. Any of them can produce power. For example, if one lives in the desert and controls the water, one is the most powerful person around.

One of the greatest forms of power is political power. A resource that we have, as a community, is the vote. Every time we vote, we make a choice. Each time we don't vote, we make a choice. Too many people regard voting as a personal matter. They focus too one-sidedly on the question, "What will this candidate, or this party, do for me?" In reality, voting is a source of power. In the African American community, we have enough votes to change the outcome of elections. In St. Paul or Minneapolis, in a primary election or a school board election or a city council election, the African American community could use the vote as a resource to exert some control over the outcome. We seldom look at power that way.

If half of the members of the St. Paul School Board were African American, would the outcome for Right Start Academy have been the same? I don't know. As I said at the beginning, I'm not in a position to judge the wisdom of the decisions that were made. What I can and do judge is the humiliation that was visited upon the representatives of Right Step Academy and their inability to stop it. By controlling the resources, the School Board rendered them powerless. As African Americans, we are acutely aware of powerlessness. We live with it every day. We are not as aware of the potential for power that we have but do not use.

NAACP Litigation Spawns "The Choice is Yours" Program

January 3, 2001

Next Tuesday, January 16, 2001, marks the deadline for Minneapolis families to exercise an unprecedented option to send their children to school in the western suburbs--- AT NO COST *and* WITH FREE TRANSPORTATION PROVIDED.

Five hundred students from low-income families will be given priority in their choice of eight suburban school districts for the 2001-2002 school year. An additional provision provides priority spaces at designated magnet schools in the city. This is an historic opportunity for children from low-performing city schools to take advantage of the possibilities that exist in some of the metro area's highest performing schools.

The choice being offered is the result of more than five years of litigation between the Minneapolis Branch of the NAACP and the State of Minnesota. The settlement of that lawsuit commits suburban school districts to providing a total of 500 open enrollment slots per year for the next four years.

But you have to exercise your preference nine months BEFORE the school year starts. The deadline was established by the Open Enrollment statute and cannot be changed. If you fail to enroll by January 16, your application will remain in the pool but will not have priority.

Eligibility for the program, "The Choice is Yours," is based on income and follows the guidelines for free or reduced price school lunch. For example, a family of four is eligible with an income of $31,500 or less. The application process consists of a number of regulations and exceptions. Don't let that deter you. You can get more information at the Minneapolis School District's website: www.mpls.k12.mn.us. Look for NAACP Settlement. The important point is to apply by the deadline.

I have no doubt that some city parents will be apprehensive about making a choice that sends a child miles away to an environment that promises to welcome all new students but may not be able to fulfill that commitment. Nor do I doubt that some suburban parents will resent classroom space being devoted to "outsiders." Their children will reflect the prejudice and resentment of the parents.

I fully expect that the students who make this move will experience racism, loneliness, and fear. The irony is that those students will experience racism, loneliness, and fear whether they enroll in a suburban school or not. That is the price of not being white in America.

Taking advantage of an alternative that is untested and unproven is risky. It takes courage to make a decision that places one's child in a situation that one might not have been comfortable in oneself. I contend that it is worth the risk.

The Minneapolis Urban League has offered assistance to the NAACP in its efforts to give all low-income families a chance to take part in the program. This has been a crusade on the part of the NAACP since the mid-nineties.

After a long, hard-fought battle on the part of the NAACP lawyers, two thousand children over the next four years can benefit from the course offerings and extracurricular activities available in suburban schools that are not offered in city schools. Families that are ready to take the risk can reap great rewards.

The choice is yours.

Families can obtain applications at State of Minnesota Hotline, 1-877-766-5485.

The Lingering Issue of Excessive Out-of-Home Placements

March 22, 2001

Minnesota has more African American children living away from their families than any other state in the union. "Out-of-home placement," as it is called in the child welfare system, occurs three to five times more often among African American children in Minnesota than anywhere else.

Out-of-home placement comes at the end of the child welfare road. A child should arrive there only after passing the mileposts of family support, early intervention, family preservation services, in-home services and parental rehabilitation services. Being ranked number one in out-of-home placements means that African American children get to the end of the child welfare road faster than anyone else. They are on a fast-track, so to speak.

On another front, Minnesota has had a Minority Child Heritage Protection Act on the books for nearly twenty years. When it was enacted, it was the first time an order of preference was established for out-of-home placement of minority children. Relatives were given priority, followed by adults who shared the same racial or ethnic heritage as the child. There is much concern over the erosion of those provisions throughout the 1990s. But that is not the issue that concerns me here.

The question is this: Why are there so many African American children in the system? Most people have accepted the time-honored view that there is a direct relationship between poverty and child maltreatment. The traditional wisdom is that since African American households have disproportionately lower incomes than Caucasian households, the effects of poverty drive up the incidence of child maltreatment. There are many important studies that support the correlation between income and maltreatment. But not all of them do.

According to accepted beliefs, one would expect that factors that are believed to influence child maltreatment--- family structure, number of children, income, or illicit drug
use--- would occur more frequently among African Americans than among the general population. This would serve to explain why African Americans occupy such a large number of cases in the child welfare system by comparison with those of other races/ethnicities.

In fact, they do not. The incidence of these life factors are about the same for everybody.

If children are not found in the welfare system in proportion to their presence in the total population, then one has to wonder if the system treats people differently or is less successful in its interactions with some people than with others.

Consider this scenario: A two-year-old boy, wearing a diaper, flannel pajamas, a sweat shirt, and one boot, is found unconscious in the back yard. It is estimated that the child has been outdoors in below zero temperatures for almost four hours. A parent, who has five other children in the household, reports that the child had been out with him until 2:30 am. When they returned to the house, the parent played a "Winnie the Pooh" video for the child. The parent sat down to watch with the boy but promptly fell asleep. He awoke at 6:40 a. m. to find the door open and his son missing. When the paramedics arrive, the child's temperature is 65 degrees. He is rushed to the hospital, where he remains in critical condition for weeks.

What would you predict would be the consequences of this episode for the parent? Where would it fall on the continuum of child neglect, endangerment or abuse? If the child were Paulie Jones, living in public housing in North Minneapolis, the chances that little Paulie would now be in out-of-home placement might be high. As it happens, the real-life child who survived this trauma is Paulie Hynek, who lives on a farm near Eau Claire, Wisconsin. There has been an overwhelming outpouring of support for his parents from all across the state.

We know that African American children and families are more likely than white families to have the child welfare system step in when child maltreatment arises.

The nature of this intervention is more likely to last longer, involve separation of family members, and may mean the separation is permanent. Aside from the possible implications of racism in these facts, there is an additional danger. Valid cases of abuse and neglect in African American families may go unreported because of mistrust of the system and resentment of the intrusiveness of child protection services.

Sources:
Thomas D. Merton,"The Increasing Colorization of America's Child Welfare System: The Overrepresentation of African American Children " *Policy and Practice Journal*, December, 1999.

"Child Welfare Reform," National Center for Children in Poverty.

Accomplishments of Kenneth White at the
Minneapolis Department of Civil Rights

April 13, 2001

There is new leadership at the Minneapolis Department of Civil Rights. Amidst the political and media misunderstandings and misinterpretations that surrounded the change in leadership, the accomplishments of Kenneth White have been overlooked. Although I have great respect for Vanne Owens-Hayes, I will miss Kenneth White's presence at the helm of the Minneapolis Department of Civil Rights.

Many people may not realize how much has changed at the Department since Kenneth White took over in May of 1994. A significant accomplishment has been the development of the Small and Underutilized Business Program (SUBP). The program has certified over 700 minority and women businesses to work on state projects. Among those businesses are several Native American owned businesses. In the past, Native American business owners have been reluctant to pursue a contract with the city.

Hand in hand with the development of the Small and Underutilized Business Program has been the nurturing of a working relationship with all Minneapolis city departments to make use of the businesses that have been certified. During the last fiscal year, the City of Minneapolis spent $16.8 million with SUBP companies; over $6 million of that went to minority-owned businesses. Contrast that with $480,000 spent by the city with minority businesses in 1998.

The current Convention Center Expansion is a good example of how beneficial the leadership of Kenneth White has been for businesses in our community. The Small and Underutilized Business Program goal for the Convention Center was 25%. By late 2000, the project was at 37%, almost one and one-half times the original goal. Minority contractors have been awarded $17 million in contracts for the expansion.

Another important responsibility of the Minneapolis Department of Civil Rights is to investigate complaints of discrimination. It is disheartening to learn that the nature of discrimination complaints has not changed much over the past thirty years. Last year, 58% of the complaints filed with the department were in the area of employment and 73% were based on race.

Kenneth White, as Director of the Minneapolis Department of Civil Rights, played a leadership role in the EEOC v. Holiday Inn Express complaint that gained national attention over the issue of undocumented workers having the ability to file a charge of discrimination against their employer. What has changed is the amount of time it takes to investigate a complaint. In 1995, more than a quarter of the complaints took about 21months to process. Today, that time period is closer to seven months.

Monitoring City of Minneapolis contracts, with an eye toward identifying job opportunities for minorities and women, has been a long-term commitment of the Minneapolis Department of Civil Rights. In the year 2000, the equivalent of 940 full-time jobs were created for minorities through their vigilance.

When Mayor Sharon Sayles Belton approached Kenneth White, informing him of her desire for new leadership, to his credit and as a result of his commitment to the accomplishments of the Minneapolis Department of Civil Rights, he did not resist the exercise of her prerogative. I am pleased with the way that the mayor, in turn, handled the situation. Although mainstream media continually tried to drag Mr. White through the mud, Mayor Sayles-Belton, Council President Jackie Cherryhomes, and Council Member Brian Herron refused to participate. The changeover was handled smoothly and professionally.

It is important for all of us in the community to pay attention to what happens at or to the Minneapolis Department of Civil Rights. These days, there is talk of getting rid of the department altogether. This is a conversation that has come up periodically over the last twenty years. The argument is made that Minnesota has a State Department of Human Rights that reports to the governor and can act on any complaint made in any part of the state. Therefore, we don't need additional, local departments of civil rights.

During the Civil Rights Movement, local civil rights commissions proliferated across the state and across the country. Many of these groups did not have any enforcement power, as the Minneapolis office does; since the groups were closer to the local situation, though, they were valued as beneficial to the community. Local groups could be more responsive because they knew the environment and the players. Monitoring of city contracts would be a good example of why a community might want its own commission or department.

Minneapolis has gone a step beyond that. The Minneapolis Department of Civil Rights reports to the mayor, as we have seen. It can enforce city ordinances and exact penalties for violation of those ordinances. Because the MDCR is closer to the problem, it can act more quickly and more efficiently, and it may require a different remedy from that of the state. That's important for all of us to think about.

The Minneapolis Department of Civil Rights promotes the elimination of discrimination through investigation, dispute resolution, education and community involvement. The Department is more likely to be familiar with a problem in Minneapolis. It can act faster if a complaint is validated. It is in our interest, since most civil right complaints involve race, to be vigilant ourselves in monitoring the fate of the entire Minneapolis Department of Civil Rights.

6

U. S. Census, Redistricting, and the Implications for African Americans in Minnesota

October 15, 2001

The U. S. Census and the political reapportionment and redistricting that result from the Census are subjects that excite few people. Discussion of these topics is often needlessly complicated. People tune out before they have a chance to understand how it works.

The fact is that in this country population is power. When population shifts, opportunities arise for more money and more clout. Public policy can change to reflect the interests of a changed population. The people who understand how it works and use the changes to their advantage increase their power.

Reapportionment is what happens to the United States Congress after a census is taken. According to the Constitution, there will always be 435 members of the U. S. House of Representatives. The population count, taken every ten years by the U. S. Census, determines how many of the 435 representatives are assigned to each state. In the 1940s and 1950s, Minnesota had nine representatives in the U. S. House. There have been only eight since 1960. The number will remain at eight for the next ten years. As for Senators, that number is always two per state regardless of population size.

Redistricting is what happens INSIDE each state after the census is taken. The Minnesota State Legislature will redraw the boundaries for the 201 districts of Minnesota legislators as well as for the eight U.S. House members. Who lives inside those boundary lines determines the direction the district is likely to take. If more people of color are concentrated in one district, does that mean more power and more resources? Or does it mean less power and few resources devoted to that district?

District lines will be realigned down to the smallest units of government. Boundaries for election precincts are the last to be set. When those lines are determined, voters in each precinct can vote only for the candidates who are eligible to run in their precinct. Boundary questions don't come into play in a presidential election, but what about city and county elections? Will new boundaries make it easier or harder to elect a person of color? How will district changes influence issues that pit urban

199

interests against rural interests? We all need to pay attention to this. Redistricting is a topic that separates those who know how to use the system from those who do not. Not knowing how the system works, not knowing how to make it work to our own advantage, has had tragic consequences in the past for African Americans and other people of color.

Please make the effort to learn about redistricting:

Redistricting Hearing
Tuesday, October 16, from 7:00 to 9:00 p. m.
Glover-Sudduth Center
2100 Plymouth Avenue North

Sponsored by Minneapolis Urban League, League of Women Voters, Council of Black Minnesotans, and the Minnesota Senate Redistricting Working Group

Poor People Hit Hard by $1.95 Billion State Budget Deficit

December 10, 2001

Last week, Governor Jesse Ventura released the state budget forecast. With a projected $1.95 billion dollar deficit, it signals a recession deeper than the one in 1990-1991. Pam Wheelock, Minnesota Commissioner of Finance, stated that, "This is not a temporary problem. will be with us for awhile." In Minnesota, we are faced with a structural deficit, one that cannot be remedied with a quick, one-time fix. We are probably looking at deficit problems through 2005.

In 1998, Governor Ventura rode into office on the biggest budget surplus in our history. He has taken credit for the surplus, subsequent tax rebates and, finally, tax cuts. Now many people say that the governor needs to take blame for the downturn in the economy. Senator Roger Moe, Minnesota Senate Majority Leader, said that Governor Ventura, "ought to suffer the consequences of his cost-cutting victories." Moe went on to say that he "looks to the Governor for a road map."

The fact is, the consequences will **not** rest on the shoulders of Governor Ventura; they will fall, rather, on the backs of poor people. I say this for two reasons. First, poor people are the first to feel the effects of a recession. They are the first to be told to tighten their belts.

Minnesota has already lost 23,000 jobs. That number will reach 34,000 in the next year or so. Those who have been laid-off are out looking for other work. If they can't regain their previous job level, they will take the next best thing. The trickle-down effect of overqualified people taking jobs they would not have considered a year ago will continue until there is no room left for the person struggling to get off welfare, the person trying to move up from a minimum wage job or the inexperienced person trying to enter the job market.

The second reason that this recession will fall on the backs of poor people is that all new or renewing state grants have been temporarily frozen. The freeze includes grants to cities, counties, businesses and others. It also includes more than $200 million in grants to nonprofits, most of them in the health and human services area. The temporary freeze will be considered on a case-by-case basis. Some programs have had to curtail services already because they cannot finance the uncertainty. Since poor people feel the effects of a recession first, the numbers of people needing assistance is likely to increase at a time when the level of assistance may decrease. One suggestion to resolve the budget crisis has been to institute a flat ten percent reduction across all line items in the state budget. The ten percent reduction would include the grants that the state agencies disburse to nonprofit social service and health organizations.

The consequences of having ten percent less to work with can have a vastly different impact. To illustrate the point, let us imagine the person who makes $150,000 a year. A ten percent pay cut means that he or she would have to get along on $135,000 a year. The consequences might be no new car, no winter vacation, no home remodeling project, or fewer investments for retirement. For the person making $15,000 a year, a ten percent cut may mean not being able to pay the rent, make the car payment, keep up with daycare, or make the co-pay at the clinic. Does that sound fair?

We need to find a better way. It's too late to expend our energy on the horrible outside events and faulty internal decisions that got us here. After all, we've all already cashed our rebate checks. We must tell our elected officials that there is no one answer to this. Every avenue that will bring in more revenue must be explored, including higher taxes on cigarettes and alcohol, entertainment, and luxury items.

There is no quick fix here. A structural change is needed to protect the state's revenue systems from such steep and rapid downturns. Eventually, we will all feel the consequences of a $1.95 million state budget deficit. The most needy among us are already feeling it.

R. T. Rybak and the Elimination of the Minneapolis Civil Rights Department

February 18, 2002

On February 11, 2002, Mayor R. T. Rybak decided to eliminate the Minneapolis Civilian Police Review Authority, the mechanism for investigating complaints of misconduct against Minneapolis police officers.

While the mayor's proposal to stop investigating citizen complaints against the police is part of a larger strategy to cut the city budget, it is nonetheless a curious move. Does he intend to do nothing about the incidences of excessive force, harassment, discrimination, inappropriate language or conduct, or failure to respond in a timely manner that occur regularly in Minneapolis?

The logic of the decision seems to be: the Civilian Review Authority is ineffective, so let's close it down. That's like saying the mayor is not doing his job, so let's do away with the position of mayor and let the City Council run the city.

If Mayor Rybak examined the work of the Civilian Review Authority and found it lacking, he should be looking for ways to make sure that people who have suffered at the hands of the police are heard and their complaints are resolved. To stop listening to victims and witnesses is to give the Minneapolis Police Department free rein throughout the city.

Over 4,700 people have contacted the Civilian Review Authority since 1996 by telephone, by e-mail, by filing an in-person complaint, or by inquiring as to whether there are grounds to file a complaint. It is true that many of the complaints are groundless, but just as many bear investigation.

If the police know that there is no longer a process for making an allegation against their behavior, they have license to do as they please. Do we want to live in a city where the police cannot be held accountable? Does Mayor Rybak want to live in a city where the police cannot be held accountable?

Seventy percent of the complaints to the Minneapolis Civilian Police Review Authority come from people of color who live in the poorest parts of the city. That fact alone should trigger an inquiry into police behavior. Rather than eliminate any possibility of an examination of these complaints, a responsible mayor would want to know why the Review Authority has not represented the interests of the citizens of his city.

Martin Luther King Avenue: Cedar or University?

March 11, 2002

The Mayor of St. Paul, Randy Kelly, wants to name a street after Dr. Martin Luther King, Jr. I applaud his intentions. Neither St. Paul nor Minneapolis has a street that bears that name officially.

The street that mayor Kelly has chosen is Cedar Street, one of the oldest streets in the city dating back to 1849. Cedar Street traverses the heart of downtown St. Paul from the Mississippi River, past the Minnesota State Capitol to Como Avenue. The name change would not be the usual honorary subtitle to a real street name. This would be an official change. Mayor Kelly described his idea in an article in the major St. Paul newspaper: "My thinking is that rather than locating some street in some neighborhood, we could find a street that had some prominence. This way, it would give some dignity to Martin Luther King, Jr., and all the work he did." ("Mayor: Rename Cedar St. for MLK," Pioneer Press, February 7, 2002)

Although I believe that the mayor wants to do the right thing, I don't think he has thought his decision through. Picking one of the oldest streets in St. Paul doesn't speak to the work or the heritage of Dr. Martin Luther King, Jr. Cedar Street is the home of the white establishment: the *Pioneer Press*, the old St. Paul Athletic Club (now the University Club), Wells Fargo, World Trade Center, Chamber of Commerce, and Minnesota Public Radio are all located on Cedar Street. I agree with the folks who have offered up University Avenue in St. Paul as the most fitting tribute to Dr. King. University Avenue is neither beautiful nor historic. There are still blocks that are sorely depressed and unsightly. But there is no denying the hustle and bustle going on there. There are more entrepreneurs of color per square foot on University Avenue in St. Paul than anywhere in the Twin Cities, with the possible exception of Lake Street or Broadway.

University Avenue is the street Dr. King would have chosen, I'm sure. It is a street full of potential for the future, not an avenue of the past. It is home to every culture, every racial and ethnic group living in the Twin Cities. The street is full of people of color engaged in free enterprise, an essential tool for building a future.

Changing a street name is not as easy as it sounds, however. Every piece of paper that bears the former name, be it Cedar Street or

University Avenue, will have to be changed: stationary, invoices, promotional materials, web sites, business cards, phone books, voter records, driver's licenses, and on and on. Could Mayor Kelly's choice of Cedar Street have been influenced by those considerations? Cedar Street is only about a mile long and has mainly large institutions or businesses that could handle the impact of a name change.

University Avenue, on the other hand, is over six miles long in St. Paul. The burden of changing the name of University Avenue would fall on the hundreds of very small businesses that line the street. On University, what used to be known as mom-and-pop businesses are now more likely to be uncle-cousin-grandmother-brother-niece businesses. To ask them to bear that cost of a name change would not only be unfair; it would be contrary to the spirit of having a Martin Luther King Street.

University Avenue is clearly the best location for a street named after Dr. King. Mayor Kelly will have to find the resources for those who live and/or work on University Avenue to make the needed changes. After that, Mayor Kelly can meet with Mayor Rybak to discuss continuing the name change on the Minneapolis end of University Avenue.

Implications of Recent Supreme Court Ruling on Vouchers

July 8, 2002

On June 28, the United States Supreme Court decided that the use of school vouchers is constitutional. It is important to note that the Supreme Court said that vouchers do not violate the separation of church and state. The Supreme Court did NOT say that vouchers will create better education for our children.

Now families will be able to use public funds to pay private-school tuition. The Supreme Court is not required to be concerned with the consequences of its decision. Nevertheless, finding the use of school vouchers constitutional could bring about long-term, debilitating change in education that should be of concern to all the rest of us.

I expect the debate to begin immediately in Minnesota as a campaign issue and as a bill before the 2003 Minnesota Legislature. It is estimated that 167,000 families in the state now claim the education tax deduction for private education, and 50,000 other families use the tax credit program ("State Voucher Debate is Revived," *St. Paul Pioneer Press*, June 28, 2002). This is a state where vouchers might pass.

The argument has been made that nonpublic schools give children a better education at less cost. If you compare only the published cost of tuition at a private or parochial school with the average cost per student in the public school system, you might be inclined to agree. Keep in mind, however, that public schools have costs not incurred by other schools and public schools pay some of the costs to run nonpublic schools. Textbooks, health and counseling services, and bus service for private and parochial schools are all part of the public schools' expenses. Public schools may be required to have a social worker, English-language teacher, special education teacher, psychologist, gifted and talented teacher, and/or an occupational therapist that non-public schools can opt not to employ.

By limiting their resources, nonpublic schools can limit who will be educated.

If only the "fittest" students can move from public to nonpublic schools, children with the greatest needs will remain. If three or four students per classroom opt to transfer to a different school, that classroom retains all of the overhead costs of a full complement of students, but the school receives less money to operate the classroom. In the early days, when few families know how to use the voucher system, and the voucher amounts are small, the change will not be great. When and if usage grows, great harm could be done to our public schools.

I have to agree with the president of the National Education Association. In his keynote speech at the National Education Association's annual conference last week, NEA President Bob Chase said, "Because the Court can say that vouchers are constitutional--- just as the Court for 60 years said that segregated schools were constitutional--- that does not make it right. And it certainly does not make it wise public policy." ("Teachers Criticize Voucher Ruling," *Star Tribune*, July 2, 2002)

Dramatic Rise in African American Male Prisoners

October 14, 2002

Late this summer, an article appeared in the *New York Times* that stunned me. A recent study by the Justice Policy Institute reported that there are five black men in prison today for every black man who was incarcerated in 1980. In 1980, about 143,000 black men were in jail or prison compared to nearly 792,000 in 2000.

These numbers, while confirming what we all know to be true, are far larger than I had imagined. The United States entered the 21st Century with over two million of its citizens, of all races, behind bars. Since human nature is not likely to change in the space of twenty years, these huge jumps must be attributed to changes in public policy. One explanation is certainly the prison building boom that has occurred since 1980. We have four times as many inmates today because we have four times the space we had twenty years ago.

Another explanation is the disposition of drug offenses. The Justice Policy Institute has done another study that addresses the imprisonment of drug offenders. The number of people imprisoned for drug offenses first surpassed the number of incarcerations for violent crime in 1989 and continues to this day. There are now about the same number of people behind bars for drug offenses as were incarcerated for ALL crimes in 1980. Changes in public policy regarding punishment for drug offenses have had a great impact on young black men. Even though surveys consistently show similar drug usage rates for young blacks and whites, far more blacks end up in jail.

We have to look at the cost of these policies to the African American community. For example, twenty years ago, there were three times as many black men enrolled in college than confined in prison. Today the ratio is almost one to one. While we must be mindful that it is primarily young men who attend college and the prison population includes all ages, these devastating figures bring us face to face with the loss of potential and the loss of opportunity for our community.

When $9 billion is being spent to hold drug offenders alone, we know that's $9 billion NOT being spent on educating young black men. That is a public policy decision that was made twenty years ago that is now devastating our community. Here in Minneapolis, less than half of African

American kids pass any part of the Minnesota Basic Standards Test that is required for high school graduation. More than one out of three African American students drop out before graduation. Our public education system is not prepared to deal with this, but our prison system is.

Sources :

Fox Butterfield, "Study Finds Big Increase in Black Men as Inmates Since1980," *New York Times*, August 28, 2002.

"Poor Prescription: The Costs of Imprisoning Drug Offenders in the United States," Justice Policy Institute, a project of the nonprofit Center on Juvenile and Criminal Justice.

12

Why the Rush to Invade Iraq?

February 3, 2003

On Wednesday, Secretary of State Colin Powell will present evidence to the United Nations Security Council that Iraq has indeed hidden weapons of mass destruction from U. N. inspectors and has prevented inspectors from learning about Iraq's weapons program from the scientists who develop them. His job will be to identify a threat that is so grave, so immediate, and so certain that a military response cannot be delayed.

Whatever Secretary Powell says, it may not be enough to push world opinion to agree with President Bush on the urgency to invade Iraq. Colin Powell has to show a very real discrepancy between what Iraq claims to have--- nothing--- and what is really there. Even if he is able to make a strong case, there is no assurance that the countries of the United Nations will be convinced to start a war. It has been proven, time and time again, that facts are not the same as opinion or perception.

This constitutes the real danger for us as Americans. President Bush is backing himself into a corner by proclaiming that he has enough evidence to invade Iraq and will begin a war alone if other countries do not believe him. There is no doubt that the United States of America could move in, take over Iraq, and remove Saddam Hussein.

That would be the beginning, not the end, of military engagement. How will America maintain Iraq, rebuild the country, and prevent another Saddam Hussein from rising up? If America is the sole aggressor in such a war, it may be impossible to ever bring a world coalition together to keep peace in the Arab world.

As Hugh Price, President of the National Urban League, has pointed out, "Attacking terrorism alone and engineering temporary ceasefires doesn't ensure peace. Not only must the cycle of violence be broken; the dynamic that rationalizes resorting to violence must be destroyed so that violence as a tool of politics becomes unequivocally unacceptable."

The acquisition of nuclear, chemical, and biological weapons by would-be aggressor nations is a global problem. The use of terrorism by these nations and by non-affiliated operations like Al-Qaida is a global problem. The United States cannot solve it alone. The whole process of the proliferation of weapons of mass destruction must be dealt with at the level of the United Nations Security Council. The fight against terrorism can only succeed if there is a large anti-terrorist coalition that covers the globe. In the 1991 Gulf War, 28 countries--- European, Arab, North American--- joined together, under a U. N. resolution, to eject Iraq from Kuwait and defend other countries in the region. Although the U.S., under the first President Bush, supplied the bulk of the personnel, technology, and resources, there was never any doubt that this was a global effort.

The current President Bush has not made his case here or abroad. We have not heard the kind of debate that should precede an undertaking with such grave consequences. The President doesn't need a debate. Congress gave him the authority last fall to use force to disarm Iraq. He doesn't need a second vote. But, as the leader of this country, he has a responsibility to make us understand why war is inevitable. Why now? Why not next year if all other alternatives fail?

If Bush is right, and Saddam Hussein has the destructive power that Bush claims, he may use it on his neighbors and his own people when an invasion begins. It is already an accepted fact that there will be a retaliatory terrorist attack on the U.S. when Iraq is invaded. Those are the risks that the world faces. No one can justify accepting such risks without global understanding and active global support.

Need to Increase Income Tax to Cover the Educational, Economic, And Health Needs of the Poor

March 10, 2003

Does reducing government hurt poor folks?   I am puzzled, given a historic shortage of money to run the State of Minnesota, that there has been no constructive, public discussion of this topic. Instead of a thorough debate about the purpose of government in this state, the question has become: What government services should be cut and by how much? Instead of a dialogue about what we should rely on government to do, we are cataloging what government will NOT do.

Nationally, President Bush has proposed a tax cut despite a rapidly rising national deficit. Statewide, our governor has pledged that taxes will not be increased--- period--- despite the fact that President Bush has made it clear that there will be no help for states coming from Washington. Locally, as counties and municipalities lose state aid, their power to impose new taxes may be limited.

The option of finding more revenue seems to be off the table. Have we considered all of the ramifications of this position? Do we really know how what this means for poor people? People who are poor come in all varieties, colors, and sizes. And far too many of them are children. For poor folks, life is a continual struggle to get enough to eat, to live in a place long enough to call it home, to find a job that can provide a modicum of security. They are in constant combat with poor health, depression, or anxiety. Poor folks don't know how to make the system work in their favor. They are at its mercy. Most poor people are WORKING people. They are contributing members of society. But they do not have enough to make it on their own. Do we really want to make their lives harder?

This is a fundamental question. It is not just a matter of balancing the books. When there is a shortage of money, is it better to maintain a basic quality of life for everyone or reduce services and let people fend for themselves? In my limited view, it seems it would be better to raise income taxes to a level that keeps poor people afloat.

The alternative is to deny some people opportunities that are taken for granted by the rest of us; there is, for example, the matter of finding and retaining a job. If you have never held a job, you probably don't know how to fill out an application form, don't know how to act in a job interview, don't know what will be expected of you in the workplace. You may never have the chance to find out if government programs are reduced. Although K-12 education has been spared the biggest cuts in the governor's proposed budget, the programs that are in jeopardy are the ones used most often by the poor. Then there is health care. If one cannot afford to buy private health insurance, that individual is scrutinized for eligibility for coverage for what the government determines the person needs. Poor folks take what they are given.

Most of us can find a way to cover an emergency repair at home, especially in the winter. Poor folks used to be able to get a loan in a situation like that. This is no longer true under the new budget.

Is this really the way we want people to live? From where I stand, it looks like Minnesota, known across the nation as a place that takes care of all of its people, has no choice but to increase the income tax rather than diminish its regard for people most in need.

14

Budget Cutting: "Nonessential Services" and the Threat to Diversity

March 17, 2003

Hard times bring hard choices. We've seen the governor's proposal about how to solve the problem of a $4.5 billion deficit. We are now seeing the county's response. The City of Minneapolis is trying to sort things out. The recommendations from all levels of government focus on cutting nonessential services. Each one has made a judgment about the definition of "nonessential" services. Libraries, parks, nutrition programs for children, the arts, early childhood education, have taken a hit at every level. I worry about who makes these judgments and how the decisions are made. Hard times change more than service delivery. The word "essential" can take on many meanings.

For more than a decade, we have seen growing evidence of a commitment to diversity in the Twin Cities. Minneapolis had a black mayor, the Vikings had a black head coach, the University of Minnesota had a black athletic director. On the surface anyway, it looked as though there was some movement.

We even began to see some change in the make-up of the police and fire departments in Minneapolis. The police had an African American deputy chief, there were ten black sergeants, and there were a few more African Americans on the beat. I don't think any of us were satisfied with the rate of progress, but it was something.

I'm concerned about what will happen to our limited progress when the final budget ax comes down. We know some people are going to lose their jobs in every department in the city, the county, and the state. How will those decisions be made? I have read that the Mayor and City Council are looking at cutting over fifty firefighters and nearly 100 police officers.

With regard to treatment of employees of color, a standard practice in many industries is "last hired, first fired." A corollary is often "last promoted, first demoted." Hiring more officers and firefighters of color is a relatively recent phenomenon. Many of the men and women whom we looked at as symbols of progress haven't been in their jobs very long.

Do we now stand to lose the fragile commitment to diversity that was beginning to take hold? Will there be no deputy chiefs of color? Will there be no captains of color among firefighters? Will African American police officers suffer a devastating loss of sergeants? How about all those rookies and cops with little seniority?

I am troubled by these questions: Are we about to lose all the ground that has been gained in the last ten years? Will the "hard choice" that is made mean that officers of color, along with the commitment to diversity, are out the door?

15

Redistricting: Exercising Political Power

March 25, 2002

Last week, the Minnesota Legislature announced its redistricting plan. Every ten years, after the results of the census are in, the legislature redraws the boundaries for all 200-plus districts in the state, as well as for the eight people that Minnesota sends to the U. S. House of Representatives. The purpose is to try to balance the number of people represented by each elected official.

In theory, every person in the state legislature or the U.S. Congress speaks with an equal voice among his or her peers. In theory, the people who live in a district have the power to determine the direction that district will take. Public policy can change to reflect the interests of a changed population.

How did folks of color fare in the redistricting plan? It's hard to tell. This could play out in a lot of different ways. Take Rep. Gregory Gray's district 58B, for example. District 58B got bigger in the new plan. It now includes downtown Minneapolis. As a result, several scenarios could occur. Will the political emphasis now shift to the bigger business interests and more affluent residents of downtown? Will there be a better balance between the interests of high and low-income residents based on population numbers? Will 58B now have additional clout at the state legislature because it represents the power of downtown?

According to the 2000 census, there are now nine Minnesota districts where thirty percent or more of the voting age population is made up of minorities. The Special Redistricting Panel has termed these locations "Minority Opportunity Districts." At present, that is all that they are. Redistricting is a subject that separates those who know how to use the system from those who do not. For the first time in Minnesota, we have the opportunity to make the system work to our advantage. Do we know how to do that?

There are four districts in Minneapolis and St. Paul (58B, 61A, 61B, 65A) that could elect a minority candidate simply because over 50% of the potential voters are minorities. Two other districts (58A, 66A) have over 40%. It's possible for a close race to occur there. In each district, African Americans are the largest minority. Do we know how to make those elections a reality?

Redistricting is a very important topic that deserves careful discussion in the African American community. With four state legislative districts that, according to the numbers, should be sure bets for minority candidates in the next election, this is a subject that demands attention at Lucille's Forum, the Urban League's Minnesota Pipeline, and other venues. It is a matter of power. If we don't exercise it, someone else will. The first thing we can do is convey to our community the potential for power that they possess if only they will show up at the polls on election day.

16

African Americans as a Neglected Political Constituency

March 31, 2003

Years ago, African Americans couldn't vote. After a long and bitter struggle, we won the right to vote and to elect people to represent our interests. Yet, we have never held those that we helped to elect accountable for representing the interests of African Americans. As a result, we are rarely, if ever, asked by an elected official to state a position or give an opinion.

Take the war on Iraq, for example. While polls show that 70% of all Americans support the war, 60% of African Americans believe that it is wrong for American troops to be there. Television coverage of the war goes on 24/7 with discussion of every conceivable aspect of the conflict. No one knows how long the troops will be there or at what price in terms of dollars or human lives. And yet I have never seen a conversation about how African Americans and other people of color view this war. Nor am I aware that any of those we elected to represent us in Washington have exchanged views with members of our community.

Closer to home, in the State of Minnesota, low income African Americans will be among the first to feel the impact of budget reductions in health care, work programs, education for young children, and crime prevention. I can assure you that neither the governor nor his administration have asked low-income African Americans how they would advise balancing the budget. While the Minnesota House and Senate have heard testimony about the impact of budget cuts on the social service structure, there have been no legislative hearings that addressed how things will change for communities of color when the full impact is felt in 2004. I think I know what low-income people would say: "Please, raise my taxes! I don't have much money anyway, so if you raise my taxes by 5%, you're not really taking anything away from me. But if you cut the services that sustain my life, it will be a great loss."

Then there is the City of Minneapolis. The City Council faces severe budget problems. Under the governor's plan, Minneapolis lost $25 million out of its general fund of $260 million. No one is asking the people who are most dependent on city services what they think is the best way to deal with that loss. Our opinion is not wanted and our voices are not heard.

And for another example, there's a plan on the table to reduce the Minneapolis Civil Rights Department budget by 19%. Did the people we voted for ask the people whose civil rights are the first to be threatened what they would recommend? As things get tighter in affordable housing, access to health care, and employment, I have not seen a poll that shows how we perceive the decline in civil rights protection. People who depend on the government for this support are not on the call list.

17

Lack of Summer Jobs for Teens

June 2, 2003

This is going to be a tough summer for high school students. Many students look forward to a summer job to help pay for car insurance and clothes or to save up for college expenses. Some young people need the money to survive. All of them benefit from having structure and responsibility during those long, lazy summer days.

Unfortunately, the summer of 2003 will present too many long, lazy, aimless days for too many kids. Summer school has been curtailed, summer activities in the parks have been cut, few organizations have funds left for summer programs, and few employers are hiring extra help for the summer. I know first hand. Ashley, my 16 year-old daughter, has applied at several places, all unsuccessfully. The lack of summer jobs presents a problem, not just of lost opportunity and work experience for our youth, but of potential danger for many young people who do not or do not know how to make constructive use of their time.

As we have watched the stock market plummet, companies downsize, new investment postponed, government deficits sky-rocket, and workers lose jobs, we have been most concerned about adults responsible for families. Now the results of an economic slide have come face-to-face with our children.

Despite Ronald Reagan's efforts to convince us of the merits of the "Trickle Down Theory" in a formerly strong economy, we are now seeing the results of a bad economy trickle down through society. Summer jobs have made it possible for cities and counties to spruce up parks, for small retailers to stay open longer hours or give regular employees time off, or for youth to explore careers through summer internships. Although there are advantages to this type of employment, summer jobs are at the bottom of the list when it comes to self-sufficiency.

And yet today we are seeing teens lined up behind people who have been laid off, people in welfare-to-work programs, and college students for short-term, part-time, low-paying jobs without benefits that high school students have traditionally held. Parks, beaches, malls, movie theaters, amusement parks, and fast food chains can now choose from over-qualified adults if they have job openings.

In this economy, it's not possible to create additional summer jobs to give young people purpose and direction during the summer months. According to a *Star Tribune* article last week, unemployment for teens 16 to 19 is at 18%, an eight-year high, and the rate is expected to get worse this summer. Traditional programs for disadvantaged youth have been hit hard. Tree Trust, for example, funded by both state and federal sources, has only half as many jobs to offer as last summer.

I don't know what the answer is, but I do know that each of us has to face the problem of too much time and not enough constructive activity in each of our homes this summer. We would do well to give it careful attention.

Source: Paul Levy, "One More Teen Worry: Too Few Jobs," *Star Tribune*, May 25, 2003.

18

The Likelihood That No Persons of Color Will Be Heading Minneapolis Public Schools, Civil Rights Department, or Police Department

December 26, 2003

Minnesota is a great state. We're the state that produced Hubert H. Humphrey, a champion for equal rights. We're a state that prides itself on diversity. But right here in Minneapolis, the largest city in the state, there's every possibility that we could end up with an administration totally without a person of color in its ranks. Think about that for a moment. There are three appointed positions that will be filled in the very near future. These are critical positions, for which the individual appointed will be responsible for making decisions of great consequence to this city.

First, there is the superintendent of Minneapolis Public Schools. Now keep in mind this is a school system where students of color make up more than 60 percent of the student population. In fact, in 2001 the Minnesota Minority Education Partnership's report on the State of Students of Color indicated that increases in K-12 enrollments among students of color will cause Minnesota's future workforce to rely more than ever on the academic achievement and college graduation of students of color. Who then will we find that will be sensitive to and knowledgeable about the unique issues facing a growing population of students of color? Who will have the experience and toughness required to gain political and community support for innovative solutions for closing the achievement gap that exists between white students and students of color? It's at least conceivable that in the city of Minneapolis, that individual may not be a person of color.

The second position that could be filled by someone other than an African American or person of color is that of Minneapolis Civil Rights Department Director. It's a known fact that current director Vanne Owens Hayes has been told that she won't be reappointed by Mayor Rybak. The Mayor now has to look for someone else to provide leadership on civil rights issues. Mind you, this is the city department that investigates complaints of discrimination in Minneapolis, a city which incarcerates African American men at a rate 27 times that of white men. Racial profiling in Minneapolis is now an undeniable reality, thanks to a comprehensive study and published report by the Council on Crime and Justice.

The Civil Rights department must be led by someone who will not deny the undeniable. In order to protect the civil rights of our citizens, that person must be willing to confront city leadership with what is often the "ugly truth" about our city as it relates to discrimination that clearly continues to exist in the workforce, in education, in housing, and in law enforcement. With cases backlogged, and complaints on the rise, with budget problems plaguing the department, the pressure is on the Mayor to make some drastic changes. It's possible, even probable, that the next director for our city's Civil Rights Department will not be a person of color.

Lastly, the city is in the final process of selecting a new Minneapolis Chief of Police. We were down to two finalists before the mayor announced his choice just days ago. Charles Moose, whose educational credentials and vast experience in the field of law enforcement are impeccable, was not surprisingly one of the finalists. And I believe he would have surfaced as a finalist, regardless of the national attention he received for his role in the D.C. Sniper investigation. The other finalist, and the mayor's choice for police chief, is Dayton, Ohio, Police Chief Bill McManus. From all indications, McManus has done an outstanding job in Dayton. I've personally heard from a colleague of mine at the Urban League in Dayton that we'd be getting someone with a reputation for establishing and practicing sound police policy. Quite frankly they're both outstanding candidates; they are well-qualified and deserving of the opportunity to serve Minneapolis, whatever the council decides.

But what does it mean for the city of Minneapolis that it had to look outside of itself for a candidate of color? We've long since addressed the issue with the city and with the police department concerning the need to recruit officers of color, and we've also raised the issue of their upward mobility within the police hierarchy. It's time that we begin to see the fruits of our collective efforts emerge at the highest level.

Having said all that I have said, I don't mean to imply that the appointment of a person of color to any one of the positions that I've outlined should be automatic. It has never been the Urban League's position - locally or nationally - to support an individual simply on the basis of skin color. It is, however, our position and our mission "to enable African Americans and other people of color to develop and realize their full potential on a par with all other Minnesotans." I hope that my comments will be regarded in that context.

19

Empowerment Zone: Truly Benefiting African Americans?

March 18, 2004

A few years ago, the City of Minneapolis applied for and was granted Empowerment Zone designation by the U.S. Department of Housing and Urban Development. Along with this designation came significant dollars to improve the life and lot of Minneapolis residents by revitalizing communities. To justify the need for such a designation, the City of Minneapolis included in their proposal the following language:

Economic disparity by race is perhaps the most significant problem facing Minneapolis today. In Minneapolis, people of color are disproportionately represented among the economically disadvantaged. People of color living in Minneapolis are impoverished at rates higher than any other city in the country, and Minneapolis has one of the highest economic disparity ratios in the country, especially between white children and children of color. Consider the following statistics:

- *The Twin Cities has the highest rate of poverty for people of color in the 25 most populous metropolitan areas.*
- *Minneapolis has the highest rate of African American unemployment of any metropolitan area at 27.5 percent but one of the smallest African American populations in the country.*
- *The unemployment rate for workers of color is higher than for whites, even though workers of color participate in the work force at a lower rate than whites*
- *Poverty rates among people of color are six times greater than that for the white population in the region.*
- *The African American child poverty rate is 49.5 percent in Minneapolis. The white child poverty rate is 9.7 percent. Minnesota ranks fourth in the country for disparities in child poverty rates based on rac.e*
- *The statewide high school dropout rate for Minnesota is 19.2 percent. In Minneapolis, however, the rate is 89.6 percent of Native American students and 65.6 percent of African American students.*

Clearly, this city's designation was born of the misery of African Americans in Minneapolis. Now, because of the designation, dollars did flow. On Monday, March 15, there was a forum held at the Minneapolis Urban League to talk about how African Americans have benefited from the city's EZ designation. Some troubling facts emerged. First, there has been $24 million committed to the City of Minneapolis. The City of Minneapolis has spent or pledged $18 million. The remaining $6 million has to be spent by 2009. The question that I have is, if $18 million have been spent to revitalize urban communities in Minneapolis, then how have African Americans benefited from this multi-million dollar investment?

Kim Havey, Executive Director of the Empowerment Zone, stated that the poverty rate among African Americans in Minnesota has dropped by 60% as a by-product of having Empowerment Zone dollars working on its behalf. Mr. Havey also stated that, of the $18 million spent, $13.8 million, or 77%, has been spent to support African Americans. Further, he alleges that $4.14 million dollars, or 23%, went directly to organizations headed by African Americans.

I am troubled by these statements. I'm troubled that the figure of $13.8 million that Mr. Havey claims was spent to support African Americans includes $4.7 million given to Heritage Park, because "there will be African Americans living there." If there are more instances like this one factored into the $13.8 million figure, it must be concluded that the benefit to African Americans that Mr. Havey speaks about is hugely a "benefit by association."

The Empowerment Zone produced a document that lists every organization that has received Empowerment Zone dollars. I took the liberty to go through this document, trying to identify the $4.14 million that went directly to organizations headed by African Americans. Going through the list, I was able to find 11 organizations that were headed by African Americans that received dollars. According to Mr. Havey's own information, the following organizations received $1.1 million, not $4.14 million: Siyeza ($184,000), Summit OIC ($134,000), Harvest Prep ($25,000), Hollywood Dance Studio ($31,000), Mad Dads ($75,000), North High School ($125,000), Pilot City ($90,000), Sabathani ($98,000), The City, Inc. ($138,000), Turning Point ($139,000), Minneapolis Urban League ($103,000).

Now, clearly I could have missed someone that Mr. Havey included. My point, brothers and sisters, is that these dollars came to the City of Minneapolis to improve the lives of African Americans and other low income minority groups. Efforts towards improving those lives should not be based merely on association, they should be direct. More minority directed jobs, increased minority training, minority start-up businesses, are examples of direct efforts.

226

Certainly, $18 million could and *should* improve the "life stake" of a whole lot of folks of color. That's why I am calling for a thorough accounting of how these dollars have *directly* benefited the African American community and other communities of color!

20

Keeping the Empowerment Zone Moving Forward

July 16, 2004

Several months ago, a group of community citizens led by Al Flowers, Zach Metoyer, Ronald Edwards and Booker Hodges brought to the community's attention the status of the Empowerment Zone. In particular, they provided a clearer picture of how the Empowerment Zone was affecting the city of Minneapolis according to its prescribed intent.

Many of us are very much aware of the fact that Minneapolis received Empowerment Zone designation from the U.S. Housing and Urban Development Office. We know that dollars have been allocated to this city to direct resources at reducing poverty and promoting economic development, but no one had taken the time to look closely to see if African Americans and other low-income communities were directly benefiting from this investment of revenues. Now that the issue of EZ resource distribution has been broached with the city in such a clear-cut and comprehensive manner, progress, although slow, has been put in motion to ensure that there is clarity on that process. This is an attempt to report on the progress a small group of concerned community citizens has been able to make towards opening up the eyes of city officials and members of the community in general. But first, I just want to say thank you to those folks for bringing this issue forward.

The group, which formed an alliance a little less than a year ago to study in depth the Empowerment Zone's effectiveness, began holding regular meetings with community residents just to discuss what it should expect of the city's Empowerment Zone designation. I was pleased to have been invited to join in the facilitation of those meetings. As an alliance, we have been able to secure periodic meetings at the Mayor's office to formally present our findings from a community viewpoint. On July 7, the alliance met formally with Mayor Rybak, key members of his staff, and representatives from the Empowerment Zone Board to present a 13-point plan that we feel best represents the expectations of the community as the Empowerment Zone process plays itself out. At that meeting, time allowed us to discuss only the first five points of the plan. We will present the remaining points at future meetings until all of our recommendations have been discussed.

The five points that were discussed in the Mayor's Office on July 7 included the following recommendations: 1) that two thirds of all current and future EZ/EC funds directly benefit EZ residents; 2) that the African American community receive no less than 30% of any and all funds the Minneapolis Empowerment Zone receives utilizing Empowerment Zone status; 3) that there be equal opportunity of access to all EZ/EC expenditures exceeding $50,000; 4) that a portion of real property owned by the city of Minneapolis be made available for the economic and livability needs of the African American community; and 5) that the city of Minneapolis account for and return all funds received as repayment of EZ loans or unused EZ funds. These recommendations were received exceptionally well by both the Mayor and those members of the EZ Board who were present.

Outcomes established at our meeting for follow-up benchmarking and strategic goal setting included: 1) decreasing African American unemployment in the Empowerment Zone; 2) increasing African American home ownership in the Empowerment Zone; 3) increasing African American business ownership in the Empowerment Zone; 4) reducing health disparities experienced by African Americans/African immigrants; and 5) increasing the achievement of African American students and closing the achievement gap between students of color and white students. At the conclusion of our presentation, it was agreed by all parties that a group would be formed from the Alliance and from the Mayor's staff to work towards moving these objectives forward.

An added bonus of our meeting was that we also had an opportunity to talk about issues involving youth and the fact that conditions likely to shape the scene for this summer would produce a dangerous environment stemming from too much idle time. It was agreed, therefore, that something needed to be put in place immediately to address the dire need of young folks who are struggling to get 'no-hoops' jobs. The Alliance will pilot a program for the city for the rest of the summer to link youth with area businesses for readily available work opportunities. This, along with several city and community efforts to promote a safe summer, is progress.

Our next meeting at the Mayor's Office, although not yet scheduled, promises to lay out a systematic process for moving the remaining recommendations outlined in the Alliance's 13-point plan forward. Let me say on behalf of the Alliance that Erik Takeshita, representing the mayor's office, has maintained a cooperative relationship with the group and has sought to move our issues forward in a very positive manner. We greatly appreciate this relationship.

I began my remarks by stating that the progress of the city's Empowerment Zone in making its process for addressing poverty in city neighborhoods clearer is moving ahead--- slowly. Let me close with those same words, adding only that it's encouraging that progress is coming about and that this community can rest assured that the Alliance will stay the course.

Six Major Political Concerns for the 2004 Presidential Election

September 10, 2004

In my 25 years as a resident of the state of Minnesota, I have never seen this state being courted in a manner so aggressive and so consequential to the national political scene. In the last four months it seems as though every time I turn around President Bush, Laura Bush, Vice President Cheney, Senator John Kerry, or Senator John Edwards is visiting Minnesota, offering that political figure's ideas for moving this nation forward.

I have three thoughts on this phenomenon. First of all, is there really that big a difference between what one candidate is going to do and what the other proposes to do? As a young boy, my father always told me that politics didn't matter because all it was about was two rich white men trying to outdo each other. Rarely do I disagree with my dad, but in this case I strongly disagree.

Despite the fact that the two major candidates for president are indeed both rich and white, politics do matter for Black America. They matter because in the almost 40 years since we fought for and gained the right to vote according to clearly worded statutory law, our lives have changed significantly. Our treatment at the hands of a previously segregated society improved drastically. But those gains are eroding and today we are missing in too large a number at the polls on election day. Today we're once again being disenfranchised by an election process that tries to discourage or negate our vote, as was the case in Florida four years ago. And there's no getting around the fact that we remain underrepresented in other areas of political influence. How many people of color do you see on local commissions and task forces that make major decisions for Minnesota? Like it or not, politics--- and our involvement or lack of involvement in the political process--- is the key to any gains we will make as people of color, as well as for every setback we will endure.

My second thought on all this political attention being paid to Minnesota lies in these questions: Who pays the tab? Who pays for the security considerations that are involved when these high-level politicians come to our state? Are those dollars that could be used to support our educational system, broaden access to health care, or improve public safety and the environment? With states already facing grim challenges to their budgets, I don't think it's out of line to be thinking about these things.

Thirdly, I've always found that what the candidates say when she or he gets here is a lot different from what I think they need to be saying. Aside from attempting a discussion on local issues, I think they should be having an honest dialogue with us as American citizens about the critical issues facing the United States. But in every visit we've had so far, the politician hasn't done that. Bear with me as I take the liberty of telling you what issues I think the candidates should be raising, the same issues that we in turn should be talking about.

1. We should be talking candidly about the rising national debt and what role my generation and my child's generation will have to play in repaying that debt.

2. We should be talking coherently about whether or not we made the right decision about going into Iraq with force, what the true costs of war with Iraq are and will be for America, and what we can or cannot afford due to the high cost of war!

3. We should be talking about how to stimulate the economy in a way that allows low- income people and disenfranchised people of color to end up with more money in their pockets. This means creating more stable jobs, safer and more affordable places to live, and better access to healthcare and affordable prescription drugs.

4. We should be talking frankly about the educational and economic gaps that exist between people of color and whites, and what constructively we need to be doing to close those gaps.

5. We should be talking about how we, as Americans, can reestablish ourselves as a highly respected nation amongst other nations in terms of how we handle our wealth, power, and global stature.

6. Finally, we should be talking about how we can better demonstrate goodwill, kinship, and fellowship with the people of all nations suffering from widespread disease, agricultural devastation, and political unrest or upheaval. I'm talking about simply being better neighbors.

As we face the pomp and circumstance of yet another round of political posturing, I think it is important for us as black Minnesotans to put all of these things in their proper context. Are we hearing about the things that are important to us as a people, or is the agenda for America being decided for us? Are we being challenged to be active participants in the political process, or are we just being asked to be rubber stamps?

The only way we can be sure is to GET OUT AND VOTE!

22

Impact of City Charter Amendment on the
Minneapolis Civil Rights Department

September 24, 2004

As many of you may be aware, a city charter is the constitution governing the municipal government. The charter defines the powers the citizens agree to give their city government and how the government is to be structured. The charter defines which officials are elected; their term lengths, duties, powers and responsibilities; and establishes the lines of authority for the departments. The Minnesota State Legislature may pass special laws which supersede, contradict, or preempt the city charter.

The Charter Commission for the City of Minneapolis was first established in 1898, but the Commission was unable to get voter approval for a new city charter until 1920. At that time, the Charter Commission simply compiled all state laws to serve as the charter. The Commission as it exists today has the responsibility for reviewing and formulating Charter proposals. To accomplish this, members of the Commission solicit ideas from citizens, city staff, and elected officials.

Why in September of 2004 am I citing this? I do so because on September 29 a tremendously important charter amendment is being proposed by the 15-member Minneapolis Charter Commission. The Commission is poised to move the compliance, penal, and sanction authority that now rests within the Civil Rights Department to city ordinance.

As a matter of fact, the Charter Commission is proposing that specific language be deleted from the current charter that gives jurisdiction to the Minneapolis Civil Rights Commission for ensuring that all city departments, boards, commissions, agencies, and branches of the City of Minneapolis are in compliance with charter provisions and codes. The commission is recommending that the City Charter be amended to place that jurisdiction in a city ordinance rather than the charter. What does that mean? It means that the City Council would then have the authority for ensuring compliance and imposing penalty and sanction that has long been the purview of the Civil Rights Department.

I am tremendously concerned about this prospect because, in my mind, the ability for the Civil Rights Department to hold all other departments of the City of Minneapolis's governmental structure accountable in terms of their compliance would be weakened. As a community, I believe there are three things on which we should press for clarification with regard to this proposed amendment.

First, this question needs to be asked: What has happened in this September 2004 that would cause the Charter Commission to bring this change forward for consideration? Second, we need to understand better the ramifications of the proposed language changes (deletions). Third, the Commission should be more respectful of due process. I believe that the Commission's procedures in handling this issue have not followed the requirements of due process. I would argue that this issue should not even be considered for one year in order to give the Charter Commission ample time to assemble a study group consisting of members of the community who are the most likely to be affected by the commission's proposed amendment. I believe that those likely to be affected are low-income people and people of color.

We need to all be aware that the Charter Commission is moving this amendment forward on a fast track. A public hearing is scheduled for Wednesday, September 29, at 7:00 p.m., in the City Council Chamber, Room 317 City Hall. This is an opportunity for citizens to come down and ask for clarification about the proposed amendment, and to give testimony about whether or not they support this proposed change to the City Charter. I believe that this is something in which this community needs to get involved, and I urge you to attend this hearing.

23

Lack of Leadership on Affirmative Action
From Minnesota State Government

2005

In enforcing the laws that promise equal opportunity for all Americans, we look to the state to take the lead in ensuring that Affirmative Action happens in state and local jurisdictions. But evidence furnished in *The State of African Americans in Minnesota 2004*, published by the Minneapolis Urban League, would seem to call into question the state's ability to be effective in its enforcement obligations.

Chapter 3 of the book on affirmative action examines the effectiveness of the state of Minnesota in enforcing laws passed by congress to ensure equal opportunity, particularly in the area of employment. It begins with this paragraph:

"In 1972, the United States Congress passed two laws that were intended to open up job opportunities for women and people of color, who had historically faced severe discrimination in gaining access to jobs and education. The two laws, the **Equal Employment Opportunity (EEOC) Act** and the **Equal Opportunity Act**, were referred to as the "affirmative action" bills. In time, the scope of affirmative action came to include the provisions of the **American Disabilities Act (ADA)**, which promoted equitable consideration for jobs in behalf of people with physical or mental disabilities."

The book examines statistical data that reveals startling realities about the state's own record on affirmative action. The following items represent just a sampling of that data:

• According to a late 1990s study of affirmative action compliance by agencies of the Minnesota state government, <u>60% or fewer agencies</u> were <u>in compliance</u> with <u>eight of twenty requirements</u>.

• Less than 50% of the state agencies responding to the survey indicated that they analyzed availability, utilization, and underutilization of their workforces.

• Half of these Minnesota state agencies were using 1980 census data well into the 1990s, rather than 1990 census data, to assess the ethnic and gender composition of their workforces.

• Agencies are free to be so lax in fulfilling the requirements for an affirmative action plan because they rarely receive any retribution or consequences for being out of compliance.

• The percentage of <u>affirmative action hires</u> among total hires by the agencies of the Minnesota state government dropped from <u>30.3%</u> in <u>1985</u> to <u>21.3%</u> in <u>1996</u>.

• The number of women hired by agencies of the State of Minnesota for managerial/professional positions increased 77% faster during 1985-1996 than did the number of people of color in these higher paid positions.

• By 1998 in Minnesota, employees of color represented 11.6% of personnel employed among 190 private companies studied; this compared to a rate prevailing for the state government in 1998 of 5.6%.

• As of January 2004, the percentage of persons of color on the payroll of the state government of Minnesota was about 7%, far behind the comparable figure of 21% for the City of Minneapolis.

This less than favorable performance for the state of Minnesota is a red flag, signaling not only a lack of conformity on the part of state government, but perhaps an indifference to the landmark decisions that were instituted to establish a level playing field for all of the state's citizens. It's up to each of us to make sure that key decision-makers and the state agencies they represent are held accountable for these major short-comings.

Watch for further excerpts from the Minneapolis Urban League's *State of African Americans in Minnesota 2004* in future submissions to "Urban Views."

24

Impact of Public Transit Cuts on Poor People and People of Color

2005

On September 10, the Metro Transit Company instituted changes in its bus service throughout the metropolitan area, and several routes that didn't meet prescribed "performance standards" were either cut or significantly reduced. The recommendation for these changes came from the Metropolitan Council, reasoning that it has the obligation to policy makers and the public "*to review our polices and practices every so often to make sure we are getting the most for our investment.*" There are two reasons why this is disturbing. First, the changes, as they were recommended and implemented, have the biggest impact on communities of color. How can that be? How can the design for public transportation be such that the people who will suffer the biggest hardship from a cut in service are mostly people who don't have and can't afford cars?

Secondly, fare hikes over the past two years have already created some degree of hardship for people who work at low-paying jobs and don't qualify for any kind of transportation subsidy from the city or state. It would seem to me that tying the transportation needs of people who are struggling to maintain a livable wage to the performance standards of a state-sponsored public service is not serving the best interests of the public. I believe there is a solution that does not hit any one community with such disparate impact, and I question whether the Metropolitan Transit Company or the Metropolitan Commission have done all they could to find that solution.

Prior to the Metro Transit route changes that took effect on September 10, the Minneapolis Urban League expressed its concerns about transportation issues and the impact that would be felt by communities of color if routes were cut or changed significantly. We invited Metropolitan Council and Transit officials to explain their rationale and answer questions from the community in a series of Pipeline Forums. Out of those forums a collaborative was formed with other concerned community groups, such as the Council on Black Minnesotans, MICAH/OPAAC, and the Access Transit Coalition. This group analyzed the impact these changes would have on disadvantaged communities and presented its findings to Metro Transit. This collective effort has resulted in some restoration of service along Plymouth Avenue in North Minneapolis. We are pleased that Metro Transit has been receptive to taking this initial step, but make no mistake, we believe there is much more work that needs to be done.

The Urban League and our collaborative partners will continue to monitor key issues like public transportation, and to represent the best interests of our constituents. Our goal is to advocate, but also to empower. That's why it is critical that each of us recognize our individual roles as key stakeholders in matters that will affect our place in society. I strongly urge each person who has been affected by state budget cuts and by the trickle-down effect on city services to participate in public hearings: Give your testimony, and ensure that your voice is heard by the elected or appointed officials who make decisions about your future.

Let me close with this quote from Frederick Douglass, who said: "Power concedes nothing without a demand; it never has, and it never will."

25

Closing UM General College: Impact on Students of Color

2005

The University of Minnesota recently announced its intention to take bold action in an effort to become known as one of the top three research institutions in the world. The university has submitted a strategic plan to the Board of Regents that calls for a major restructuring of some of the University s oldest colleges, one of them being the General College. According to the plan, the General College will be merged into the College of Education and Human Development, with the eventual result being totally elimination in two years. According to University officials, the college has to eliminate programs like the General College in order to ensure a higher echelon of student admissions.

The Minneapolis Urban League is greatly concerned about this direction.

Many of you are probably familiar with the General College. For 75 years, it has prepared a particular student population for transfer into the university s many degree programs.   A significant portion of that population has traditionally been comprised of students of color.

This is not the first time that the University of Minnesota has attempted to rid itself of the General College. In fact, it has happened multiple times. But this time, in the strategic plan offered by University officials, the relevant word referring to the fate of the General College is not "*elimination*"; it is, rather, the word, "*merge*."

So why does the University of Minnesota want to be considered one of the world's most elite research institutions? What will it gain by that distinction? Here are a few answers: 1) The University will be able to recruit and retain the best teachers in the country; 2) the institution will be able to garner more research dollars; 3) it will be able to attract the best and the brightest students across the country. Needless to say, test scores will go up and probably graduation rates, as well. It should be noted that a report prepared by the University's own researchers indicates that the institution is already retaining and graduating students at higher rates, and in 2003-04 the university conferred 12,356 degrees, the highest ever. The report also indicates that the university ranks fifth among all universities and third among public universities in additional revenue received from the commercialization of university technology and research. The University is nonetheless concerned that its current admission criteria may be keeping it from becoming one of the top 3 research institutes in the world.

The flip side of the question. "What does the University gain by becoming a top research institution?," is this question: "What will the community in and around the University of Minnesota gain by its becoming one of the top three research institutions in the world?" The answer: nothing much that can be viewed as tangible. When one considers that there will be less access to the University of Minnesota, I see no gain for the community. Clearly, unless a student is one of the brightest, she or he will not be selected for admission to the U, but if one's parents live in the state of Minnesota, one will still be required to pay, regardless of how bright that prospective student is. When a university supported by public dollars obviously feels it has the historical weight and the current authority to tell the state of Minnesota that it doesn't want your kids anymore, I see no gain for the community. Further, numerous reports suggest that of the jobs available in the future, 70-85% will require someone with a post-secondary education. If the University of Minnesota is not going to educate the vast population of state residents who need to be trained for the job market of the future, where will this group get trained to occupy jobs in this state? This is particularly problematic for students of color. Currently students of color represent 17% of the student of population at the University of Minnesota, many of whom enter the University through the General College. With the General College's eventual demise, the question becomes: How, then, will these students enter the University?

These are the things about which we have to be concerned as a community as the University focuses on reshaping itself. It is obvious one cannot appeal to the logic of University officials on this matter: They view changes in the demographic, economic, political, and cultural makeup of the state as a challenge to their ability to gain a competitive advantage in the global higher education market. They translate the paramount of goal getting ahead of these economic, social, and global challenges into eliminating the General College and phasing out programs and efforts that prepare students who show great potential, thereby decreasing their opportunities to eventually become part of the overall university community.

The problem in my mind is that in trying to gain status as one of the most elite institutions in the world by picking its students and faculty only from the "cream of the crop," the University of Minnesota is missing the possibility that the "cream of the crop" might be growing in its own back yard.

Chapter Nine

Current Issues and Commentary

1

The Impact of Social Security on Children

November 1, 2000

As I mentioned last week, I have been working my way, chapter by chapter, through **The State of Black America 2000**, the National Urban League's annual assessment of the most important current issues for African Americans. One article that intrigued me is entitled, "The Impact of Social Security on Child Poverty" by Valerie A. Rawlston. Like the rest of you, I have been bombarded by the Presidential candidates' pronouncements on Social Security: preserving it, changing it, preserving it while changing it. Not once have I seen or heard the words "child poverty" mentioned in the same sentence with social security.

Old Age, Survivors and Disability Insurance Program is the technical name for what we call Social Security. The benefits of Social Security are not just for the worker but for the worker's dependents and spouse. This distinction becomes important when we look at the rates of disease and mortality for our community. The greatest differences in life expectancy between whites and African Americans who are working occurs among people in their 20s and 30s. Very often these workers leave behind families with young children. In fact, one-third of African Americans receiving Social Security today are children.

Presidential debates, campaign slogans, and 30-second ads have focused on the returns for retirees. That's not hard to understand since children do not vote. Nevertheless, we need to be careful when we base a discussion of Social Security on the rate of return. Such a discussion fails to consider how children would be affected. They are the survivors that are also included in the provision of Social Security.

The author, Ms. Rawlston, set out to discover what impact Social Security benefits were having on children in poverty. She found that for families in the lowest income group, families whose income averaged $13,117, Social Security payments represented more than fifty percent of their annual income.

As we listen to discussions about how to strengthen Social Security--- and they will go on long after Tuesday's elections--- it is important to remember that fact and insist that our politicians broaden the scope beyond retirees who vote. Social Security is more than a retirement program; it has important benefits for children. Policy-makers must be careful not to cut a lifeline that keeps over one million children from sinking into abject poverty. We must be careful to watch the progress of the debate on Social Security because so many of the children clinging to that lifeline are our own.

And one final plea -- PLEASE VOTE ON TUESDAY!

Final Four, Exploitation, Youth, and Community Development

March 29, 2001

We are in the final moments of The Final Four. The hype, the hysteria, and the media coverage have been building across the country along with the pools in every office in America.

When you look at the tournament brackets, it's pretty clear how it works. Each step toward the finish means millions of dollars for colleges, universities, and the NCAA.

Nobody seems to know exactly how much money schools or the NCAA make on the tournament, but we do know that the television contract alone is upwards of $560 million. That's just for starters.

Then there is the city, at every level of the tournament, that benefits from the arrival of fans ready to spend. On the Final Four weekend, the money increases exponentially. Base price for a ticket ordered in advance, if you can get one, is $240. Scalpers drive the price of good tickets up to $8,500 or more. In Minneapolis this weekend, everybody gains: the Minneapolis Convention Center, hotels, restaurants, taxicabs, bars, Mall of America, corporations that use tickets as a sales tool or a P.R. event.

Everybody gains, that is, except the communities that raised the players. In every city where the NCAA tournament is played, there is an inner-city neighborhood that has produced and NCAA star --- maybe more than one. Year after year, African American youth, from some of the most depressed neighborhoods in the country, dominate the NCAA tournament. These young men are exploited by their schools, the NCAA, and the cities where the games are played. They rarely realize any benefit from the Final Four beyond a moment of glory on the court. The brass ring dangled before fourteen-year-olds seldom pays off in an NBA contract or a position as a coach, trainer, scout, or administrator for their alma mater or the NCAA.

NCAA tournament players have come out of inner city schools and neighborhoods that hold basketball programs together with love, determination and little else. These players grew up in dilapidated gyms in under-funded community centers. Why is there no benefit to the communities that the players left behind? No benefit to their high school coaches, their schools, the community centers, the after-school programs that provided the countless hours of practice that nurtured talent into precision and skill?

Why should only one sector of our city reap the rewards of a Final Four? Why don't the restaurants, newspapers, or shops in our community get a piece of the action? Neither *Insight News* nor the *Spokesman-Recorder* has sold any advertising space to the NCAA. Neither "Sallie's" restaurant nor "Lucille's" expects increased business. Why?

Why doesn't an overblown event showcasing inner city youth give any thought to today's inner city youth who could never get into a game? Why doesn't a system that exploits black youth make any restitution to the local institutions that offered up their children?

Why is no thought given to the establishment of scholarships, basketball clinics, mentoring programs, or coaching clinics by a city that is raking in hundreds of millions from a Final Four or by the NCAA that rakes in hundreds of millions every year?

Cincinnati Riots: Larger Implications

April 19, 2001

As I watched the images of rioting in Cincinnati, I could not help but think how little has changed since the death of Rev. Martin Luther King, Jr., in 1968.

Following the fatal shooting of Timothy Thomas, who was unarmed, by a police officer on April 7, Cincinnati was the scene of three nights of arson, store looting, beatings and clashes with police.

Thomas, wanted on fourteen warrants for misdemeanors and traffic violations, was shot while running from police. He was the fourth black man killed in a confrontation with police in the past five months, the fifteenth since 1995.

The images, so like thirty years ago, were disheartening. Many would argue that there has been enormous progress since 1968. Some of the worst neighborhoods in cities across the country have been rebuilt. Communities have more of a say in their future. Employment, housing, and education programs exist today that were unheard of thirty years ago.

Nevertheless, what happened in Cincinnati could happen anywhere. Granted, Cincinnati's problems are egregious. They have ignored charges of police brutality since the findings of the Kerner Commission. The power structure has been in place for generations. Cincinnati has a police succession policy that makes change impossible.

Yet, as you look across the country, the differences between the black community and the police are so fundamental and the gap in perception is so wide, every city is a potential Cincinnati.

The underlying fear and distrust, on both sides, has lain dormant for years in some communities, the fires well banked. In others, the embers smolder just beyond reach. In every case, given the right conditions, the flames could burst forth again.

The fact remains that African Americans, especially young men, view the police as a determined threat to their safety and freedom. Consider that perception in contrast to the rest of America that views its police force as its protector and looks to its officers for assistance. Too many police officers view young black men as real or potential criminals, thinking, "If he didn't do this one, he's guilty of something else."

At the risk of being accused of contributing to the hate, fear, or mistrust, I assert here my belief that there is a disconnect among the different segments of our own community, whether it be in Cincinnati or Minneapolis or other cities across the country.

The Rev. Damon Lynch, a Cincinnati clergyman, said the city's youth do not know how to channel their anger. "They just feel like nobody's listening. Their anger is not just at officers, but their own black leadership. The feeling is we're not listening, and we have to turn that around." (*Star Tribune*, April 16, 2001)

It's not surprising that our young people can't understand why the older generation allows this to go on. They wonder where the leadership is.

Leaders did come to Cincinnati. NAACP President Kweisi Mfume and Rev. Al Sharpton arrived pleading for calm and an end to the violence while, at the same time, calling on the Bush Administration to address the problem.

Black leadership, in fact, is ever-present. Day in and day out, someone, some agency, or some organization stands in the breach doing battle for and advocating on behalf of people of color and those who are poor and vulnerable. Oftentimes, it goes unnoticed and unappreciated, but it happens.

The imposition of a curfew by Cincinnati Mayor Charles Luken brought an eerie silence to the Easter weekend and increased both the solemnity and the tension at the young man's funeral on Saturday. Though there is now order on the streets, the images of the past week cannot be denied.

The question is: Why are things still the same? The anger, the desperation, and the hopelessness that were the tinder in 1968 remain today. No city in this country is immune. No city has truly resolved the issues of 1968--- including ours.

247

Ku Klux Klan at the Minnesota State Capitol: Current Significance

July 21, 2001

The Ku Klux Klan is coming to town. Leaders are of the organization's expedition to St. Paul are planning a rally at the Minnesota State Capitol on August 25 from 1:00 to 3:00 p. m. Michael McQueeney, a Grand Dragon of the National Knights of the Ku Klux Klan from Wisconsin, plans to have a group of fifty on the Capitol steps for the event.

White supremacists have held rallies at the Minnesota State Capitol before. Somehow, I find this event more troublesome than the others. It's troublesome because it presents a dilemma. Are there limits to free speech? The Minneapolis Urban League, and all other civil rights organizations, depend upon the principle of free speech. Free speech is what allows us, without fear of official retribution, to make the tough statements, to point out the things no one wants to see, and to say the things no one wants to hear. We treasure that right and we need that protection.

Why, then, am I so uneasy about allowing the Ku Klux Klan to exercise the same right? Part of the answer is easy. The sight of the letters KKK sends shivers down the spine of every African American, Jew, or gay person who sees them. The rest of the answer is more difficult.

You won't see any white capes and hoods at this rally. Nowadays, KKK members only wear those for the annual, ceremonial cross-burning at the White Christian Heritage Festival in October. The last fifteen years have brought giant steps in sophistication for the Ku Klux Klan. The Klan has shifted strategy from personalized terror to public relations. The organization has embarked on an aggressive use of television, radio, and print advertising that is well-planned, well-financed, and does not always bear the Ku Klux Klan name. The Klan has the money and the volunteers to give substantial support in political campaigns. The organization is no longer a rural, Southern, secret society even if correspondence still comes in a plain brown wrapper. The KKK has learned how to reach people who don't even know they are receiving the Klan's message.

A trip to the Klan's website (www.kukluxklan.org) provides an illustration. The website is extensive, professional, and slick. The vision, goals, legislative agenda, and interpretation of news events are represented clearly and openly. There is something for everyone--- even an on-line gift shop.

I went to the website link entitled "Just for Kids." The slogans that scrolled across the screen looked, at first glance, like they belonged to the Urban League: Stay in School, Obey the Ten Commandments, Love Your Heritage. It was unnerving. The page for children has 24 sections to answer questions that children might have about the KKK. One section, entitled "But I Know Some Really Nice Black People," was so insidious that my blood froze. This is how Klan publicists create members from among the youth. It all sounds so harmless. It all sounds so reasonable. Hatred is cultivated as a virtue: "We don't hate Negroes, we love OUR people."

The August 25th rally forces me to both ask and answer the question: Is the Ku Klux Klan far less dangerous openly holding a rally at the Capitol than when its members work behind the scenes?

National Baptist Convention in Minneapolis

August 16, 2001

Two weeks from today, the 121st annual session of the National Baptist Convention, USA, Inc., will begin in Minneapolis. Headquartered in Nashville, Tennessee, the National Baptist Convention is one of the largest and oldest African American organizations in the world. Its annual meeting is the largest African American convention held in this country. Attendance for the five-day Convention is expected to be between 30,000 and 35,000.

The annual session will be the kick-off for a major new faith-based initiative, Rally for Health and Wellness. This new initiative will address the major health disparities that exist in the African American Community throughout the nation. Beginning last June, Rallies for Sobriety have taken place across the country. Teams of volunteers have gone door-to-door distributing literature on health care and chemical dependency treatment and offering to bring those in need in for immediate assistance. The Rally for Sobriety will continue during Convention week here in Minneapolis.

The fact that the 2001 National Baptist Convention will be held at the Minneapolis Convention Center on September 3 –7 is remarkable in and of itself. You wouldn't expect an event of this magnitude to happen in a state that is almost 96% white. For five days or more, the African American population in Minneapolis will increase by 50%. Attendees are expected to generate over $35 million dollars for city businesses while they are here. This will have a noticeable effect upon the city.

It is a great tribute to the Minnesota State Baptist Convention, led by Reverend Ian Bethel, that the local organization has attracted the second largest convention ever in this state. After more than four years, the tireless efforts of the State Convention's all-volunteer, Local Host Committee, in collaboration with the Greater Minneapolis Convention and Visitors Association, have paid off in a landmark occasion in Minnesota history.

African Americans have played a part in the history of Minnesota since before 1800. African Americans published their own newspapers starting in the 1870's and the press became a strong, unifying force for the people scattered throughout the area. By 1880, Minnesota had more than

1500 African American citizens. Although most members of the black community worked as servants and laborers; there were black doctors, dentists, lawyers, and entrepreneurs in the Twin Cities. Before the end of the century, one black resident had been elected to the state legislature and another was an assistant in the governor's office.

Black residents started churches in both Minneapolis and St. Paul in the 1860s. Pilgrim Baptist Church, founded in the late 1800s, is still thriving. Today, the Minnesota State Baptist Convention includes thirty-three churches across the state with a total membership of about 5,000. These churches have endured over the years because of the same faith, fortitude, and courage that caused them to attract the biggest African American Baptist event in the U.S. to their doors. We wish them every blessing in their labors.

Events open to the public:

> Welcome Celebration on September 3 from noon until 5 p. m.at Boom Island. This free event features plenty of gospel entertainment, food, merchandise and a health fair.

> Gospel Musical on September 3 at 7 p. m. at Target Center with a 300- voice mass choir, a 150-voice youth choir, and "special guests." Call 612-588-0106 for tickets.

> President's Educational Banquet on September 4 featuring U.S. Surgeon General David Satcher. Call 612-588-0106 for tickets.

> Rally for Sobriety March and Health Fair on September 7. Rally assembles at 1:30 at New Salem Baptist Church and proceeds on Irving to Phyllis Wheatley Community Center for health screenings followed by a worship service.

Donald Watkins under Racist Scrutiny as Buyer for the Twins

February 11, 2002

I have been reading the stories about Donald Watkins, potential buyer of the Minnesota Twins. Every media outlet seems bent on proving that Watkins is not a qualified buyer. No one questioned Glen Taylor's offer to buy the expansion team that became the Timberwolves. Red McCombs became a hero when he decided to buy the Vikings. When Donald Watkins comes along, he is suspected of misrepresenting his ability to become an owner.

Major League Baseball has a clearly defined, detailed, complex process for the disclosure of a potential owner's net worth. Donald Watkins is engaged in that process right now. Major League Baseball has every right to conduct its review with due diligence. For other buyers, due diligence is not conducted in the press. For Donald Watkins, it is.

I suspect that the reason for the intense media scrutiny is that no one believes that a black man, who is not a professional athlete or a rap star, could have the money to buy a sports franchise. That is a racist premise. Watkins appears to have numerous business interests and investments in a number of companies. If he were Irwin Jacobs, those holdings would be considered savvy business practice. When Watkins's business holdings are discussed, there is the implication that they involve shady business practices. The media, and the interests that they reflect, display a distinct lack of comfort with a buyer that they did not pick, who is not "one of us," not a member of the club.

Watkins is most certainly not a member of the club. He grew up with the Civil Rights Movement. As a teenager, he saw blacks vote for the first time in his home state of Alabama. He attended the University of Alabama Law School on an NAACP desegregation scholarship. Watkins' law practice for twenty-five years centered around discrimination cases. In 1976, he won a full pardon for the last surviving "Scottsboro boy" in Alabama. Death threats followed the disposition of that case.

No, definitely not a member of the club. I think that is what fuels the concerted effort in examining Watkins' background. He is not what the sports establishment expected to see holding out an offer for the Twins-- new stadium and all.

I don't know anything about Donald Watkins's net worth. What I do know is this: If Carl Pohlad were the potential buyer, rather than the anxious seller, no one would be interviewing his boyhood friends, college classmates, or business associates. No one would be examining his involvement in the political process.

For Donald Watkins, the media investigation has now gone beyond the question, "How can a black lawyer/businessman have the money to buy the Twins?" to "Is this the kind (read color) of person that we want for the owner of *our* Twins?" That's racism.

April 30th Gathering of Eight Gubernatorial Candidates

May 6, 2002

It seems as though we just had an election. Nevertheless, a new political season is about to open. Candidates have declared their intentions and are actively wooing party endorsement and nomination. In a few weeks, the betrothal will be announced by each party. By the time the orange blossoms bloom, we will know who the Republicans, DFL, Green, and other parties have chosen, for better or for worse.

In this time of courtship, it is interesting to hear the whole field of candidates, listening for the man or woman who speaks to us and might speak for us. We had a chance to do just that on April 30 when eight Minnesota gubernatorial candidates joined in a forum at the Glover-Sudduth Center. Sponsors of the gathering were the Minneapolis Urban League, the Minneapolis NAACP, the Minnesota Black Political Action Committee, the Coalition of Black Churches/African American Leadership Summit and the SubZero Collective.

The candidates represented the spectrum of political thought. From the Green Party, there was Ken Pentel and Nick Raleigh. Brian Sullivan sent Jerry Blakey to represent the Republicans. DFLers included Judy Dutcher, Roger Moe, Ole Savior, and Becky Lourey. Leslie Davis was there from Protect the Earth.

Of course, the "elephant in the living room" at this political wedding shower was Governor Jesse Ventura, who won't announce his candidacy for the Independence Party until July or later--- if at all. A true independent, however, was in the mix on April 30. Booker Hodges is running without party affiliation.

Matthea Little Smith of the Minnesota Black Political Action Committee played a key role in organizing the forum, and she and Dan Williams performed ably as facilitators. All of the candidates welcomed the opportunity to come into our community. Observers could tell that each candidate had given serious thought to the prepared questions. Forum organizers wanted to get at the issue of how a candidate would interact with the African American community and other people of color if elected.

One of the highlights of the evening occurred when Ken Pentel, Green Party candidate, responded to the question, "How do you plan to incorporate the HIP HOP generation into your political future?" After a moment's consideration, he broke into a political rap that was greeted with enthusiasm by the audience.

Other questions about police/community relations, affordable housing, economic development, and health disparities revealed that the candidates still have more to learn about communities of color. After we find out which candidate has walked down the aisle with which political party, it will become our responsibility to provide

It seems as though we just had an election. Nevertheless, a new political season is about to open. Candidates have declared their intentions and are actively wooing party endorsement and nomination. In a few weeks, the betrothal will be announced by each party. By the time the orange blossoms bloom, we will know who the Republicans, DFL, Green, and other parties have chosen for better or for worse.

In this time of courtship, it is interesting to hear the whole field of candidates, listening for the man or woman who speaks to us and might speak for us. We had a chance to do just that on April 30 when eight Minnesota gubernatorial candidates joined in a forum at the Glover-Sudduth Center. Sponsors of the gathering were the Minneapolis Urban League, the Minneapolis NAACP, the Minnesota Black Political Action Committee, the Coalition of Black Churches/African American Leadership Summit and the SubZero Collective.

The candidates represented the spectrum of political thought. From the Green Party, there was Ken Pentel and Nick Raleigh. Brian Sullivan sent Jerry Blakey to represent the Republicans. DFLers included Judy Dutcher, Roger Moe, Ole Savior, and Becky Lourey. Leslie Davis was there from Protect the Earth.

Of course, the "elephant in the living room" at this political wedding shower was Governor Jesse Ventura, who won't announce his candidacy for the Independence Party until July or later . . . if at all. A true independent, however, was in the mix on April 30. Booker Hodges is running without party affiliation.

Matthea Little Smith, Minnesota Black Political Action Committee, played a key role in organizing the forum and she and Dan Williams performed ably as facilitators. All of the candidates welcomed the opportunity to come into our community. You could tell that each candidate had given serious thought to the prepared questions. Forum organizers wanted to get at the issue of how a candidate would interact with the African American community and other people of color if elected.

One of the highlights of the evening occurred when Ken Pentel, Green Party candidate, responded to the question,"How do you plan to incorporate the HIP HOP generation into your political future?" After a moment's consideration, he broke into a political rap that was greeted with enthusiasm by the audience.

Other questions about police/community relations, affordable housing, economic development, and health disparities revealed that the candidates still have more to learn about communities of color. After we find out which candidate has walked down the aisle with which political party, it will become our responsibility to provide these candidates with the information that they need to better understand our community and the most pressing issues for African Americans and other people of color.

8

Thoughts on Jesse Ventura's Ability to Get People to the Polls

June 24, 2002

Last Tuesday, when Jesse Ventura announced he would not run for a second term as governor of the state of Minnesota, he changed the political dynamics in Minnesota for the second time in four years. Minnesota has gone from the biggest upset in its political history to the possibility of its most conventional election. Ventura's departure leaves Minnesota Senate majority leader, Democrat Roger Moe and Minnesota House majority leader, Republican Tim Pawlenty, both career politicians, as the leading contenders for a traditional gubernatorial race.

The election of Jesse Ventura in 1998 was both implausible and improbable. He appealed directly to individual voters without a party apparatus to stand in the way. Although 37% of the electorate voted for him in 1998, he made no attempt to bind them to the Independence Party. There does not seem to be a groundswell among Ventura voters to find his successor. While there is some talk of Tim Penny running on the Independence ticket to succeed Ventura, there does not appear to be a legacy of Ventura supporters eager to rally under the party banner. He is a party of one.

Still, Jesse Ventura may have unwittingly created possibilities for candidates who run outside the Democrat and Republican bureaucracies. Since 1998, the Green Party has achieved major party status. Candidates like Booker T. Hodges are recognized as independents. Although the door opened wide for Jesse Ventura, it may have left a small opening for other candidates to pass through.

As I look back on the past three and a half years of Ventura's term and the astonishing four months of his campaign, I am struck by two things. First, I am not aware of any evidence that demonstrates that our community has benefited from Ventura's tenure. I don't believe I can point to anything besides our Jesse checks and say, "We have Jesse Ventura to thank for that." Second, I have to admire the way he got people to the polls. More first time voters showed up at their local precinct in 1998 than ever before. We should be studying how he did that. No one will deny that it was the big persona that got people thinking about the election. But what else was going on? Two years later, in the presidential election, I wonder if those same people participated again.

As we head into the 2002 election season, the Minneapolis Urban League is making plans for voter education and registration drives. We want African Americans to be as well informed on the issues and the candidates' positions as any other Minnesota resident. But information doesn't always result in a trip to the polls on election day. Somehow, we need to transform the passive presentation of facts into the active execution of our right and obligation to vote.

Cooling Things Down in the Jordan Neighborhood

September 2, 2002

For the past ten days or so, there has been a great deal of media focus on the Jordan neighborhood in North Minneapolis. On August 22, while in the process of executing a search warrant for drugs at a house near 26th and Knox, Minneapolis police officers shot a dog released from its leash by a resident of the house. A police bullet ricocheted off the sidewalk and struck an eleven year-old boy standing outside the house. The incident caused an angry crowd to gather and ultimately led to the destruction of property and injury to several people. Racial tension in the area was reaching the breaking point.

A series of leadership meetings, community meetings, street patrols, and prayer vigils occurred over the following weekend. While the situation was very tense, the violence did not escalate. In the second week after the drug raid, racial volatility in North Minneapolis remains a fact that must be dealt with over the long-term.

There are three points that we mustn't lose sight of in the discussion, planning, and negotiation that will take place in the coming weeks. First, firing a gun with kids around is wrong. The police should not have fired when children were so close by. Other options would have been to throw a net over the dog, kick the dog away, or beat it with a nightstick, even hit him upside the head with the gun instead of firing.

Second, selling and using drugs is wrong any way you cut it. People can make tons of excuses as to why it happens. They can twist the facts. But when all is said and done, we're left with the fact that selling and using drugs in our community is wrong.

Third, we cannot reduce racial tension without turning our attention to economics. People need jobs and they need them now. People need the kind of job that allows them to live decently. They need the kind of job that makes it possible to afford a place to live, have nice clothes, have a car that runs, and partake in the American Dream that we have all been sold. Too many are left out of that dream. As long as we have people on the outside, existing without hope, we will have the potential for violence.

In closing, I just want to say, "hats off," to a lot of brothers and sisters who put their own safety at risk to promote peace and calm. Many of these people will never be seen on TV or mentioned in the paper. But they were there. I know that they were out there, because I was out there with them. To Brother Tyrone Terrill and the Men of March, Brother V. J. Smith and the MAD DADS, sisters and brothers from New Salem Baptist Church, and others, I say. "You were there." I want to acknowledge that and give you my respect for your efforts.

Trent Lott: Not Fit to Be Senate Majority Leader

December 23, 2002

I believe that Trent Lott should step down as Republican majority leader of the

U. S. Senate, not because of what he said at Strom Thurmond's 100th birthday party, but because of what those words revealed about Mr. Lott. On December 5, Trent Lott said that if the rest of America had voted for Strom Thurmond when he ran for president in 1948, "we wouldn't have had all these problems over all these years."

Sen. Strom Thurmond ran as a Dixiecrat in 1948. The Dixiecrat platform was devoted to the preservation of a segregated South. It said, "We stand for the segregation of the races and the racial integrity of each race." That's exactly what the Ku Klux Klan website says today.

Trent Lott, born in 1941, grew up in Mississippi in the pre-integration days before Brown vs. Board of Education, voting acts, and civil rights. He was in college when integration came to Mississippi schools and vigorously opposed the admission of African Americans to his fraternity. Everything in his background would support segregationist views.

In the 1970s, with the force of the U.S. government behind new laws and policies, integration moved painfully into the mainstream of American life. In our community, we have always said that we cannot stop people from being racist. The most we can hope for is that people will stop behaving like racists.

Trent Lott has revealed that he has changed his behavior to accommodate integration as the law of the land. He has never changed his belief that segregation is a better arrangement. He is not alone. Many people, not affiliated with the KKK, would like to return to the 1940s.

Trent Lott is neither a mystery nor a pariah in the eyes of his fellow Republican Senators. He has worked in government since 1968, being elected to the U. S. House of Representatives in 1972 and the Senate in 1988. In 1980, he was the first Southerner to be chosen as Republican Whip in the House of Representatives, the second ranking leadership position in the party. He was reelected three times. In 1995, he became Senate Majority Whip, the first person to hold that position in both houses of Congress. He serves on important Senate committees and has been secretary of the Senate Republican Conference. In other words, Trent Lott is a known quantity in the Republican Party. The Republican Party has honored him and elevated him within their ranks.

It stands to reason that the Republican Party is likewise acquainted with Trent Lott's long history of racism. His positions are a matter of public record: his opposition to the Voting Rights Act extension, the Martin Luther King federal holiday, the confirmation of a highly qualified African American judge. His association with the Council of Conservative Citizens and Bob Jones University are well-documented. Even since December 5, Trent Lott has exhibited little understanding of the concepts of affirmative action or even inclusiveness. It is disingenuous of the other Republican Senators to claim Trent Lott's past has come as a surprise.

The mistake that Trent Lott made on December 5 was to reveal his beliefs, beliefs that are unacceptable in the person who leads the United States Senate. He didn't mean to reveal himself, of course. When he says he didn't mean it, he is really saying that he didn't mean for us to see the reality behind actions.

There are a lot of voters in Mississippi who believe as Trent Lott does. They may not feel that he was out of line at all. They have voted for him in the past, and I think that they should have the opportunity to vote for him in the future. As a Senator from Mississippi, Trent Lott has a right to express his views.

But being Senate Majority Leader is altogether different from being a senator from Mississippi. As a political leader of a major party in 2003, it is not enough to BEHAVE as if one believes that all men are created equal. Such a leader must, in fact, BELIEVE in that principle without hesitation. Upholding the principle of equality is the promise of America. Keeping the promise is the burden of our national leaders.

11

"Call... Don't Shoot"

September 19, 2003

I'm troubled by the violence in Minneapolis. There are far too many news stories lately of shootings and killings right here in our community where the wanton nature of the crimes has claimed innocent children as victims. I believe that the level of gun violence alone has reached a point that it's no longer an aberration to hear that the neighbor down the street got shot. Worse, the sounds of a violent act occurring can be heard right outside one's window. If one doesn't witness the actual crime, she or he witnesses the dismal aftermath that follows once the police arrive. Shootings have become so commonplace in our neighborhoods that many of us have sadly become desensitized to it. There is no worse condition for a community.

How many people know that earlier this month a 16 year-old boy was found shot to death in an alley in Minneapolis? Or that a 29 year-old father of four children was just recently sentenced to more than 35 years in prison for shooting and killing one man and robbing another?

I don't profess to stand in moral judgment of anyone, but it troubles my mind and spirit that violent crime has risen to the level it has in Minneapolis, and that our own people are so disproportionately the perpetrators and the victims. Think of the grief and suffering these violent crimes have caused. Families on both sides are devastated and need help. Children lose a parent who they have a right to believe will be around to guide them into adulthood. And there's no safe haven for our children when they cannot even feel safe in their own homes.

Some 15-16 years ago, a combination grassroots and community organizational effort called "Stop The Violence" attempted to address the drastic rise in black on black crime in Minneapolis. Its formation evoked a widespread sense of community purpose to confront gang violence that was literally destroying our neighborhoods at the time. The group gained momentum for awhile, because it worked to improve tens police-community relations at the same time that it focused on ways that the community could take responsibility for decreasing the violence. But at the first sign of conflict within--- as soon as parties faced the first roadblock to consensus, the Stop the Violence movement was quelled.

263

It has been on my mind for awhile that, like those who started the "Stop the Violence" movement, more of us have to find ways to intervene in response to the violence that devastates our families, plagues our communities and destroys our neighborhoods. I applaud 3rd Ward Council Member Don Samuels, who holds protest Vigils for Peace at the site of tragedy in the Jordan neighborhood, for his efforts, and I'd like to do something too. So today, I'm asking you to support another movement that calls on all of us to do what we can to stop the violence and increase the peace in Minneapolis. Not possessing many intellectual skills, and being somewhat unsophisticated, I am calling this movement "Call... Don't Shoot."

Please understand that I'm not so naive as to think that someone in the throes of a crime is going to stop, pick up a phone, and call before she or he shoots. No, what I have in mind is more preventative, and more realistic. Let's face it, the people committing the gun violence and street crime right here in our communities are our sons, brothers, cousins, nephews, boyfriends, or at least an acquaintance. We've probably seen the signs and know what that person is capable of, where that individual is headed. We've got to step in and offer ourselves as counsel. Let that person know that you're available to talk to them whenever they're troubled or find themselves caught up in a situation that is bound to escalate into violence. Listen, but be honest about the consequences that he or she faces as a result of committing a violent crime. Make them understand that shooting someone or taking someone's life is always a lose-lose situation.

I was truly touched by a story I read in the paper recently about a 23 year-old African American man suspected of killing a store clerk. This young father of three was just 45 minutes away from going on trial for murder. He decided, after talking it over with relatives, not to put his family or the victim's family through the hardship of a trial, and to take full responsibility for the crime he committed. He received a 30-year life sentence. Having his family at his side, willing to listen but also offering honest advice, brought this young man to his decision. Although nobody comes out the winner, I believe he made the right decision. I'm convinced that having family or someone to call or to talk to might cause someone with a notion to pull a trigger to step back from that bad situation, look at it for what it really is, and walk away.

If there is someone reading this who is troubled and can't find your way out of a cycle of violence, call someone close to you. Don't shoot out of a need to belong or to maintain an image among peers. If you don't have anyone to talk to, I offer my counsel. Call me. I'm at the Minneapolis Urban League and my phone number is (612) 302-3101. But please, call... don't shoot!

Appeal for Financial Aid to Pilot City

March 5, 2004

Rarely do I use this column to sing the praises of other community service agencies, but I know this is something I need to do at this time. I attended a meeting last Friday at Pilot City Neighborhood Services where several people in the community gathered to hear testimony about the tremendously effective work going on at Pilot City.

For 37 years Pilot City has been around to help the most needy residents of our urban neighborhoods. They've grown in size and in focus. They've undergone a name change, become a merge partner, and have even taken on boarders. But nothing has changed about Pilot City's mission to alleviate the miseries of poverty. In 2003, Pilot City distributed $900,000 in groceries through its food shelf. The organization placed 119 area residents in jobs and another 107 in job training programs. Pilot City empowered 900 senior citizens to be able to live independently. Four hundred eleven residents received financial counseling, while 911 households received counseling to meet their housing needs. Pilot City advocated for 2,308 households in 2003, responding to crisis and emergency needs such as housing deposits, utility bills, furniture and appliances, and other human service needs.

Over the years, the number of people seeking the free services offered by Pilot City has increased markedly, but the amount of funding it receives from the county has significantly decreased. That means that individuals and families facing hardship may suffer even further if the level of service delivery provided by Pilot City Neighborhood Services is diminished.

Pilot City is asking for community support. The venerable institution needs moral support for the work that it does, but equally important, it needs our monetary support. The work that I described above and the outcomes that Pilot City has managed to achieve over the years have resulted in a wealth of positive outcomes for neighborhood residents. I'd particularly like to point out that Pilot City is distinctly responsive to the unique needs of a growing and diverse Minneapolis community, and that its efforts are helping to foster cultural unity among several ethnic groups. But don't just take my word for it. The organization's leaders and dedicated staff invite you--- and I encourage you--- to go and take a look at what's going on at 1315 Penn Avenue North, or to give them a call at (612) 348-4700.

Realizing how difficult it is for all of us in this current economic climate, coming out of our pockets almost seems like an unreasonable thing to ask. However, imagine what a little bit from each one of us could do--- $10.00 from you, combined with my $20.00, added to something from your neighbor. What I'm saying is that if we are willing, we have the ability to ensure the future viability of Pilot City Neighborhood Services. The organization is a trusted community partner that has served the urban neighborhoods of Minneapolis well for decades. I truly believe it is appropriate for us to do that.

North and Henry High School Basketball Teams: State High School League Acts to Ensure Only One Can be Champion

March 11, 2004

At this time last year, North High School Boys and Girls, and Henry High School Boys, were starting a journey that would lead all three teams to state basketball championships. In between the final whistle of last year and tip off of this year, in my opinion, something lamentable has happened. The Minnesota State High School League has ensured that this will never happen again.

First, the State High School League changed their boundaries and placed North and Henry in the same region, which means only one of these two teams can be a regional champion, and consequently, only one will be vying for a state title. Let me offer just a tad bit of history on team placement. North High's basketball team, which is a 3A school, has opted to play 4A basketball competitively. The team had a four-year agreement with the State High School League to do that. But as the League went through this redistricting structure, it allowed other schools to opt up or down. The League refused, however, to allow North High to opt out of its agreement.

The second thing is that Henry High School, which historically plays 3A basketball, had 40 more students this year than it had last year. This increase means Henry had to go 4A, so we're seeing the same picture, which is essentially this: North has an agreement to play 4A that the League is not letting the school out of, and Henry has 40 more students over last year, so they are required to play 4A. With this scenario, the High School League is saying in essence, "Let's put these two powerhouse teams, primarily made up of students of color, in the same region and ensure that only one of them will even get a shot at winning a state title."

Let me preface my next comments with an acknowledgment that inner city youth can and do excel in any manner of school sports competition, whether individual or team, whether in golf, swimming, hockey, or any other sport. But history tells us that it is the sport of basketball where people are going to find inner city teams that are likely to reach championship level. The point is, in these times--- times when inner city schools are being trashed by low student performance on standardized tests, decreased enrollment (meaning possible school closures), and under-funding, these kids need something to celebrate. One of the causes for celebration could be around the crowning of multiple inner city state basketball champions.

In my mind the State High School League, with its new structure, has unfortunately taken steps to ensure that never again will more than one North Side inner city school take the title of state champion.

While I'm on this basketball bandwagon, let me also point out the lack of acknowledgment Larry McKenzie has received as a coach. No other coach in the history of Minnesota high school basketball has won four consecutive state championships. Larry McKenzie stands alone in that arena. And his Henry Patriots are one of only two teams in state history to win four state basketball championships. Henry has a chance to be the only state high school to win five consecutive championships. But that road has been made much more difficult as a result of the actions taken by the Minnesota State High School League.

Implications for More Competitive Cable and Satellite Television

2005

There is an issue looming over the state of Minnesota that has serious implications for residents of the city of Minneapolis. That issue involves the cable and satellite industry, and it concerns local laws that regulate the industry's ability to provide certain consumer services. Matters like this are usually negotiated out of the public arena by industry powerbrokers who basically take their case directly to state and local officials. But I believe residents need to take a close look at what these communication entities want our state and our city to consider.

What I've learned is that the state legislature is considering a proposal to grant an additional cable service franchise that would open cable service up to more competition. The question for residents is this: Will the competition be an advantage or a disadvantage? My chief concern is that it could lead to redlining, since a new franchise would be able to locate in particular areas and provide services that meet specific needs. My question is this, then: What areas and whose needs are we talking about? Will a new franchise only build in those neighborhoods where decision makers feel the enterprise will get the best return and not where the service might be needed? Or will the franchise's management apply a "one size fits all" approach, opening up the potential for discrimination due to Minneapolis' diverse population?

There is a lot at stake in the delivery of cable services, and it is up to the city to protect the public's interest. City officials must insist on a level playing field in granting competitive cable franchises. I believe there are questions that the community needs to have answered by our state representatives and by our local officials as this proposal moves along. Because of the rapid growth of this industry, and because the issues are so complex, the state needs to establish a comprehensive policy for ensuring that consumers are protected, and the city must follow suit.

The Minneapolis Urban League has contacted Senator Steve Kelley, one of the authors of a bill (SF688) amending previous law governing the granting of new franchises. We are asking for the rationale for his support. We've also contacted the Minnesota Telecom Alliance, a group that actively represents and advocates on behalf of the state's telecom industry to get an understanding of that organization's support. Once we've had a chance to get their responses, we will issue our own position statement.

Chapter Ten

Hiring Practices

1

The Haskins and Boston Situations: A Double Standard at the University of Minnesota

May 16, 2001

When I was a little boy, I took a test. The test showed that I wasn't the smartest kid in the world but that I had the ability to figure things out.

Today, I'm beginning to think that the test was wrong.

For the last ten to fifteen years, I have been trying to figure out what's going on at the University of Minnesota. I can't figure out why black folks are treated with such disrespect there. I can't understand why there are two sets of rules--- one set for how black folks are treated and another set for how everybody else is treated.

Others tell me that this double standard has existed for a long time. The first time I saw it play out was when the men's basketball team went to Madison, Wisconsin, for a game. The end result of that basketball trip was that two basketball players were publicly hung by the University of Minnesota. The players were accused of raping a white female from Wisconsin.

Although the law provides for due process, the University of Minnesota does not. The legal process gathered evidence, conducted a trial, allowed both sides to tell its story, and then reached a decision. In contrast, the U. of M. immediately removed the students. The University said, "You're guilty. You're outta here. Enough said."

Then there was the issue with Clem Haskins and Dr. McKinley Boston. In that case the University of Minnesota said, "Haskins, you did something wrong. Dr. Boston, it happened on your watch. You're both outta here." The decision was the same regarding several white employees--- all dismissed.

But a few weeks ago, the U. of M. leadership quietly approached one of the white employees with the message, "We changed our mind. You can stay. " A similar approach was not made to Dr. McKinley Boston.

Now we have this latest mess. Several months ago, Sid Hartman wrote an article in the Star Tribune stating that the University of Minnesota was dissatisfied with women's basketball coach, Cheryl Littlejohn, and would try to buy out her contract. When the U. of M. couldn't come up with the money to buy out the contract, Sid Hartman predicted, "Look for her to be fired." A few days ago, Cheryl Littlejohn was fired for breaking NCAA rules. Coach Littlejohn reported to a white supervisor.

Let's be clear about this:

Dr. Boston was fired because something happened on his watch. Whatever Coach Littlejohn did or did not do happened on her white supervisor's watch. Was the white supervisor fired? Absolutely not. In fact, she was praised by University officials for her undercover work on the case.

This double standard is a blatant slap in the face for every black person in Minnesota. One thing I can figure out, one question that is clear to me is: How much longer are we going to keep taking this? The University of Minnesota gets hundreds of millions of tax dollars every year.

We, as Minnesota taxpayers, contribute to that allocation. And, yet, black folks can't even come close to being treated fairly at the University of Minnesota.

Look closely at the number of tenured African American faculty, talk to them about some of their horror stories. Look at the student population. How many are African American? Of the African American students who start out at the University of Minnesota, how many graduate? Of those who graduate, how many go on to graduate school at the U. of M.?

On another front, take a look at the amount of business the University of Minnesota does. How much of that business is done with minority-owned businesses?

I believe that, at some point, I should be able to figure all of this out. I sure can't figure out what's going on at the University of Minnesota relative to black folks. On second thought, maybe I have.

271

2

Lack of Non-Player Job Opportunities
for African Americans in Sports

January 27, 2007

On January 18, I went to Williams Arena to watch the Gophers play Michigan State. Before the game, as I flipped through the 96-page, glossy program of photos and stories, I saw only three black faces besides the ten Gopher players. It struck me that, if I am a black man, I can play sports for the University of Minnesota but I probably can't get a job there.

On page 95, I saw the photos of all of the Golden Gopher Head Coaches: twenty-four white men and women. On page 25, featuring 20 members of the Athletics Administration, there is one black face: Sam Owens, Director of Spirit Squads. On page 63, I saw the 15 members of the coed cheerleading team, the 13 members of the all-girl cheerleading team, and the 17 members of the dance team. Not one African American.

When it comes to basketball, there are nineteen players, both eligible and ineligible. Eleven of those players, or 58%, are African American. It takes 32 staff, in addition to the players, to put on a Gopher basketball season. Thirty of the staff are white. From what I could see, basketball has one Assistant Coach, Vic Couch, and one Director of Basketball Operations, John-Blair Bickerstaff, who are African American. Not one of the trainers, medical staff, P. R. people, or recruiters is African American. Not one of the student managers or student office personnel is African American.

Millions of young black kids across the country are playing basketball. Some will play at the college level. Fewer will play at Division I schools. Only a tiny fraction will be considered for the NBA. That leaves hundreds, or maybe thousands, of young people who love sports, who have grown up in the sports system, who can't get a job in collegiate sports.

Young black players are heavily recruited from the age of sixteen. They receive a barrage of scouting visits, phone calls, and promises of glory. When their student days are over, the attention and the promises cease. Collegiate sports no longer have a place for them.

The lack of African American coaches is the most glaring example. But there are many jobs in collegiate sports that are not so

272

visible. There are jobs in marketing, media relations, business management, equipment management, arena management, academic counseling. There are jobs keeping the players in shape, rehabilitating their bodies after injuries, calling the games, applying technology, and recruiting new athletes. But African Americans don't have those jobs. Their sole purpose seems to be to produce wins as students and then get out.

It seems to me that college athletic departments want our children to play but they don't want them to work.

Super Bowl XXXVIII and the Long, Hard Road Traveled by African American Head Coaches and Quarterbacks

January 29, 2004

Today, as opposed to talking about community politics that affect the Black community (and there's a lot to talk about), I want to make an announcement about an event that has an importance of its own. I only get to make this announcement once a year, so please bear with me as I gather my thoughts.

As the community waits with baited breath for me to make this announcement, I want you to note that I am imparting this information to you on Thursday, January 29. Everybody knows the Superbowl will be held this Sunday, and yes, my announcement is about who is going to win. What I want you to understand is that I made my prediction well in advance of Sunday's kick off. You can call me at my office on Monday to let me know what a remarkable prediction it was.

Now, before I announce my pick, let me point out that neither of the two teams in the Superbowl are my favorite teams. For some reason, I gravitate to those teams that give black coaches or black quarterbacks an opportunity to prove their worth. That's probably due to the fact that I am a product of an era when blacks weren't given the opportunity to coach or to quarterback a National Football League team. So many times, black quarterbacks who came out of college with phenomenal ratings were turned into wide receivers or defensive backs. Then came guys like James "Shack" Harris, Doug Williams, and Warren Moon, guys who could flat-out play the game, but who had to be so much better to strip away the long-held belief that blacks couldn't quarterback.

I was also the product of an era when black coaches weren't invited to join the fraternal order of NFL coaches, an exclusive organization reserved for whites. In fact, that probably still is the case. Attorney Johnnie Cochran released a report two years ago called "Black Coaches in the National Football League: Superior Performance, Inferior Opportunities. The report pointed out that since 1986, there have only been five black head coaches. As of today, only three remain, one of which is former Vikings coach Denny Green, who's back in business after being picked up to coach the Arizona Cardinals. Two of the three, Tony Dungy and Herman Edwards, made history when the Indianapolis Colts and the New York Jets met in this year's playoffs. The bottom line is this:

Until black folks can acquire a team franchise here and there out of the 32 available, the makeup of NFL coaches will remain disproportionate to the racial composition witnessed in the league's player rosters (almost 70% Black) and will continue to be more a matter of one man's (or woman's) whim than of another man's ability.

But back to my prediction about Superbowl XXXVIII. I am picking the Carolina Panthers to win. Let me tell you why. To make this selection, I had to do two things: first, I had to factor in all the tangibles, determining which of the two teams has the best passing game, defense, success in the t-zone--- something any computer can do. But secondly, and most importantly, I had to factor in the intangibles. These are the ingredients that most of you don't understand. These are the things that cause us to hesitate and to vacillate from one team to the other. But my philosophy is simple in this regard: If you think long, you think wrong. **The only intangible factor important in a situation wherein two of the best teams are vying for the Superbowl title is the color of their helmets.** The Carolina Panthers wear a silver helmet, but it's not just the silver helmet that puts the team in front of New England; the determining factor is actually that Carolina has blue trim going down the center in twin lines and thereby holds a decided edge. Any knowledgeable sports person realizes that the combination of the silver with the blue trim is an intangible that just cannot be denied!

GO PANTHERS!!!

Samuel Alito as the Choice for Supreme Court Justice:
When All Else Fails, Hire a White Man

2005

At a time when this country is becoming more and more diverse, when growing populations of color are lending numerous threads to the social, economic, and political fabric of our cities and states, and when women continually demonstrate their ability to lead at all levels of business, corporate, and governmental affairs, sadly we fail to take advantage of our diversity. Worse, there is an underlying sentiment that prevails across this country holding that "when all else fails, just find a white man."

The recent appointment of a white male to the U.S. Supreme Court reinforces that sentiment The appointment underscores the fact that there is a purposeful lack of commitment to diversity in this country. Here was a perfect opportunity to improve on the diversity of the Supreme Court. Here was a chance to show that, if need be, extra effort would be exerted in identifying a person of color or a woman to occupy a place on the highest court of the land--- a position of such import that whoever is chosen will serve for a lifetime. Instead, we resorted to prevailing sentiment.

My comments should not be taken as a slight against Samuel Alito; they are no reflection on the man's fitness to be on the Supreme Court. I don't know him, nor do I know his background; the confirmation process will determine his readiness to be a Supreme Court Justice. It simply disturbs me that his appointment is just another example of our lack of true commitment to diversity. What bothers me is that--- particularly in the case of people of color, and oftentimes women--- we give one shot to trying to ensure inclusion, and if for some reason it doesn't work out, we find a white man.

In the Minneapolis, Minnesota, for example, there was a period of time when we had a black female as mayor. Now, both candidates for Mayor of Minneapolis are white males. At one time the University of Minnesota had both an African American male and an African American female as head coaches of their basketball programs. Since then, the head coaches have all been white.

Over and over again, the hopes of people of color to pursue the heights of their abilities in jobs matching their talents are reduced because of a lack of commitment to diversity. Over and over, the opportunity to dispel the mindset that leadership in this country falls within a domain reserved for white America is lost because we only pay lip service to our cultural wealth. The weakest excuse for this country's inability to break the mold is, "We can't find one." Unfortunately, the appointment of another white male to the Supreme Court is a prime example of our shortcomings.

We've often heard the mantra that we are "One America." If this is truly the case, then I believe we must look long and hard at how we can change the "one shot" standard that seems so often to apply to people of color and women.

Part Three

Uniting People and Institutions

Chapter Eleven

Minneapolis Urban League:
Events, Programs, and Positions

1

Family Day: Celebrating Family and Community

August 16, 2000

August 26, 2000, will mark the eleventh annual presentation of Family Day by the Minneapolis Urban League. From noon to dusk, Plymouth Avenue (between Penn & Logan) will be transformed into an urban festival marketplace featuring food and merchandise vendors, live music of all types, games and rides for children, 3-on-3 basketball, and other contests for youth.

But Family Day is about much more than free entertainment on a hot Saturday in August. Family Day was created to promote family traditions and values, healthy and secure neighborhoods, economic development, and cohesiveness within inner city communities in Minneapolis. There are too many occasions for which the African American community comes together to grieve, to protest, or to resolve conflict. We gather to demand that a wrong be made right, to require that a voice be heard, to ensure that a problem be solved. Seldom do we meet to celebrate our victories, our strengths, or our accomplishments. Aside from Sunday services, our community doesn't have many chances to celebrate, to praise, or to bring joy.

We need to celebrate. We need to celebrate often. Our families are the strength of this community and the source of our joy. We all need to honor one another for families that are the center of our lives and the foundation of our community. Families come in many packages, bound together by mutual caring for one another. Families may include many members or few, may contain multiple generations, may or may not be related by blood, may be experiencing good times or bad times. What they have in common is a bond. We need to celebrate what that bond has given to each of us and what we pass on to our children.

Family Day was initiated by the Minneapolis Urban League in the summer of 1989 to recognize the strength and accomplishments of individuals and families who live in the core city. We come together to re-enforce hope, promote connectedness, and highlight achievement. A major focus of the day is on youth, emphasizing the importance of staying in school, graduating, and preparing for a career. We use this opportunity to present messages promoting healthy relationships, healthy lifestyles, and productive, nurturing families in a manner that appears more recreational than educational.

Family Day, along with Juneteenth and Rondo Days, give us all an occasion to be together in joy. It is important for each of us, and each of our children, to experience a great gathering of our community for the purpose of seeing friends and neighbors, participating as a family, and enjoying the activities of the day. Put Saturday, August 26, on your calendar for a memorable event.

The Minnesota Pipeline: From the Capitol to the Community

April 25, 2001

On April 20, Senator Paul Wellstone paid a visit to the Minneapolis Urban League offices in North Minneapolis to inaugurate a series of community conversations on current public policy. The series, entitled "**The Minnesota Pipeline:** *From the Capitol to the Community*," is intended to provide communities of color with a channel for an exchange of information with elected officials and appointed policy makers.

The term **pipeline** prompts an image of an important resource flowing uninterrupted from its source to its destination. **The Minnesota Pipeline** will connect people of color with important, timely information about national and local legislative decisions that directly affect their neighborhoods, communities, and families.

We were proud to welcome Senator Wellstone as our first speaker. He talked with us about education, standardized tests, and daycare. The discussion eventually turned to racial profiling. What was important was the dialogue that occurred between the senator and his audience.

The political powers that create and sustain public policies also dictate the frame and scope of our reality. It is important to offer resources such as **The Minnesota Pipeline** here in the community. We can watch CNN, read local and national papers, and listen to the news. While informative, none of those sources gives us an interpretation of how new or altered public policies will translate for African Americans and other people of color. What we are missing is a device that captures and passes along the true meaning of what we are seeing, hearing and reading. Less than six months ago, our attention was riveted upon the 2000 presidential election.   We need to harness that energy and that inquisitiveness to bring political leaders out to our neighborhoods to talk with us as equals. We need to have more opportunities to ask our political leaders to clarify what proposed legislation will mean for us. Many people do not know that some of the barriers they face and some of the challenges they must overcome are the result of legislation or public policy decisions.

Too often, statistics used for disease, unemployment, educational achievement, or standards of living do not reflect our reality. When a federal agency proclaims that the birth rate for teenagers is plummeting, it is actually skyrocketing in parts of Minneapolis. When the Star Tribune hails the low unemployment rate in Minnesota, we must find out what the rate is in Phillips or near North. When government programs are declared successful, we must demand to know if they are successful for us. I believe that we, as a community, are ready to engage in this conversation now. We need to explore every pathway to involve members of our community in the issues that dictate how they will live their lives. We must continue to do all that we can to increase the participation of people of color in public policy debate.

This is where the conversation begins. There is a particular sense of urgency now that demands activities such as **The Minnesota Pipeline**, and there are many ways to keep the pipeline open. Community organizations can provide the pumps, the valves, and the conduits that move information through the pipeline to the people.

April 2001 Minneapolis Urban League 25th Anniversary Banquet

May 3, 2001

On April 26, 2001, the Minneapolis Urban League celebrated 75 years of service to the Minneapolis community. President Clarence Hightower delivered this address at the event at the Hilton Minneapolis:

Seventy-five years ago, in 1926, the *Minneapolis Daily Star* was the newspaper of record. The paper cost a mere two cents. The headlines that graced the pages of the paper 75 years ago give us insight into the happenings and priorities of the day. For example:

- Auto Crashes Into Trolley
- 2000 Vigilantes Pledge to Fight a Moonshine Gang
- Whites Stabbed in Race Riots
- Church Burned, Colored Residents of New Jersey Town Deported
- First woman in history convenes Hennepin District Court in bailiff's absence.

Yes, my friends, 1926 was an eventful year. It was in that year, 1926, that President Calvin Coolidge told Congress that the country must provide "for the elimination of race prejudice and the extension to all elements of equal opportunity and equal protection under the law." Sadly, in 1926, twenty-three blacks were lynched. The year 1926 was the year that Negro History Week was introduced. And 1926 was the birth year of the Minneapolis Urban League.

This evening, we are here to celebrate the days, weeks, and months that have comprised the last 75 years of Minneapolis Urban League history. Through the years, the Minneapolis Urban League has made headlines of its own, sometimes loudly, sometimes softly, sometimes understood, sometimes misunderstood, sometimes appreciated, and sometimes unappreciated. Today, if we made headlines, the message would be, "Minneapolis Urban League--- Job Well Done!"

Today, we stand proudly and humbly on the shoulders of our ancestors and the many icons that have so richly added to the headlines, bylines, and skyline of this historic river city. So many people have paved the way for us to be here, leaders who have done so much with so little:

pioneers such as Gleason Glover, Gary Sudduth, Matthew Little, Nellie Stone Johnson, and Harry Davis, to name a few. All of you know that countless names could be added to this list. So to the mentioned and the unmentioned we say, " Thank you! Tonight is your anniversary!"

The Minneapolis Urban League was founded in 1926 to assist African Americans migrating from the southern part of our country to the country's most northern boundaries. It was born as a resting place, a center of social activity, a bastion of civil rights activism, and as an incubator for economic growth. Today, the Minneapolis Urban League reaches over 6,000 individuals and family members with direct services and approximately 20,000 individuals through various community-building events and activities. In many ways, that is good news. In some ways, that is bad news. It is good because all of us recognize the added value of an Urban League in Minneapolis. It is bad because, in some ways, little has changed in the past 75 years.

Today, African Americans in Minnesota:

> are ranked the highest in cases of Out-of-Home child placement in the country. In 1999, more African American children were placed in out-of-home care than every other ethnic group combined;
> are the highest in newly reported cases of HIV\AIDS; African American men and women with HIV/AIDS reflect 38% of the state's newly reported HIV/AIDS cases;
> represent the largest percentage of Minnesotans living in poverty;
> lead in every category identified by the Surgeon General as a health disparity, including diabetes, cancer, infant mortality, violence prevention, heart disease, and low birth rates;
> reflect the highest rate of teen pregnancy; the total number of African American pregnant teens, ages 15-17, is seven times that of white teens of the same age.

As we stand at this place tonight and look back 75 years to the Minneapolis Urban League that was located in a storefront, or look forward to the next 75 years to a League located in the Glover-Sudduth Center for Urban Affairs & Economic Development, we must understand that a great deal has been accomplished--- we have much to be proud of --- but there is still much to do.

On behalf of myself and my predecessors who have stood here before me, we thank you for your support of the past 75 years and we ask that you remain in partnership with us for the next 75 years. We are mindful that the Urban League didn't come this far because it has been so good or so perfect. Rather, the Urban League made it because of your help, sometimes pushing us and sometimes pulling us, but all the time supporting us.

And, quite honestly, we have made it thus far by the grace of God. A songwriter appropriately said, " We have come this far by faith." The Urban League, as a Movement, is one that is built on faith. We have faith that we will do the right thing at the right time with the right results. Thank you for believing in us.

Tonight, it is my hope that in another 75 years, our generations, the many generations that are represented in this room, will be looked upon favorably because we upheld and uplifted the dignity and tenacity of the founding members of the Urban League. It is my hope that, 75 years from now, when reading the headlines of today, our stewardship will be chronicled in newspapers, microfilm, and cyber space, but mostly in the hearts of those we serve.

During the next 75 years, we must ensure that the Minneapolis Urban League remains the *welcoming resting pl*ace that it was for so many of our brothers and sisters who migrated from the South. We must ensure that we remain *a center of social activity*, one that constantly builds a sense of community, one that ensures that even the least fortunate among us survive and flourish.

We must ensure that we remain *a bastion of civil rights activism* by refusing to falter in the face of adversity. While we may risk the disfavor of some of our supporters, we must realize that we have neither permanent political friends nor permanent political enemies. We have only depressing, disabling and debilitating issues that must be resolved.

And we must ensure that we remain *an incubator for economic activity*. We have an obligation to bring about the understanding that there are no second-class citizens in our midst, no residents without rights, and that there are enough resources in this nation to be divided and shared responsibly and reasonably.

What will the headlines read in another 75 years? What will our cumulative contribution be to a community that both needs and expects the best of our services? Will the headlines reveal an institution that faced and met some hard challenges, one that fought and won some critical battles, one that understood and addressed some vital issues? It is up to all of us to ensure that these **are** the headlines. That will be our cumulative contribution.

Happy 75th Anniversary, Minneapolis Urban League family! May God bless you all.

Glover-Sudduth Center for Economic Development and
Urban Affairs: $6.7-Million Capital Campaign

June 21, 2001

Throughout the past winter and spring, the construction project at the corner of Plymouth and Penn Avenues has generated a good deal of excitement and speculation. It has also generated a certain amount of skepticism. I have been asked probing questions about how the building was financed and what will happen in the building when it is finished.

The two-story building that will be completed on the corner of Plymouth and Penn at the end of September will be the Glover-Sudduth Center for Economic Development and Urban Affairs. The Glover-Sudduth Center will stand as a tribute to all of the people in this community and this state who have labored long and hard to advance the cause of civil rights and ensure equal treatment for all. Among those who labored are two civil rights leaders who were also CEOs of the Minneapolis Urban League, Gleason Glover and Gary Sudduth. The building will serve as a lasting tribute to their achievements.

The decision by the Minneapolis Urban League to develop a corner that had lain dormant for thirty years came as the result of a strategic planning process that began in 1997. The plan called for a consolidation of the Urban League's services into four streamlined divisions to be housed in space that was accessible, efficient and confidential. For the first time in its seventy-five year history, the Urban League undertook a $6.7 million capital campaign to provide better service to the community. Four new or remodeled buildings are involved in the capital campaign, two in South Minneapolis and two in North Minneapolis. The Glover-Sudduth Center is one of the four buildings.

The potential for this location and this Center is tremendous. The Glover-Sudduth Center will be a place for the entire community. Local entrepreneurs will be able to rent space in the business incubator. The coffee shop will open in the early morning before community residents head for work. Two major spaces could be used for community meetings, workshops, or forums. One primary space will be the home of a training program to prepare people to enter the workforce. Each year, training sessions ranging from two days to six weeks will give a thousand potential employees of all ages the opportunity to acquire the skills to seek and retain a job or complete computer training.

The unending battle against the diseases that devastate our community will be waged, in part, from the new Glover-Sudduth Center. Over 300 youth and adults are expected to participate in education programs teaching them how to change their behavior to avoid the risk of pregnancy or disease. Outreach workers will hit the streets of North and South Minneapolis to deliver the same prevention messages to another 3,000 people.

The $6.7 million capital campaign has been a success. We are within $300,000 of our goal. The response by all of our stakeholders has been overwhelming. Commitments from individuals, families, corporations, major foundations, and government entities have ranged from $100 to $1 million. Creative funding strategies have produced a healthy balance of private (55%) and public (45%) support. Private funding has come from over thirty foundations. Public support has come through the U.S. Department of Housing and Urban Development, State of Minnesota, Neighborhood Redevelopment Program and the City of Minneapolis.

I believe that the Minneapolis Urban League has been successful in this endeavor because of the expectation by all who have been directly involved that a great deal of good will come from the Glover-Sudduth Center as well as from our new Street Academy, Fresh Start Academy, and Client Services Center.

Minneapolis Urban League:
No Political Endorsements but Much Political Activity

August 8, 2001

Election season is almost upon us. The State Fair has begun. That means we're only weeks away from the primary. If it seems as though we just had an election, you're right. It's only been about seven months since we elected, or appointed, a president.

I'm often asked why the Urban League, which has vigorously proclaimed its stand on so many issues over the years, does not come out in favor of a political candidate or candidates. The answer is that showing political preference is outside the purview of a not-for-profit, human service organization such as the Minneapolis Urban League.

Human services differ from unions or commercial associations. As a non-profit organization, we are exempt from paying taxes under a special section of the Internal Revenue Code. This exemption makes us eligible to receive contributions from the public that are deductible on the donor's income tax.

The regulations covering our tax-exempt status prohibit non-profits, like the Urban League, from engaging in partisan politics. While we may grieve for those who have fallen and rejoice with those who have triumphed, we cannot endorse or support any candidate. (Needless to say, employees of non-profit organizations, including the Urban League, are free to support actively the candidate of their choice.)

Refraining from candidate endorsement stems from a principle more profound than fear of losing our status as a tax-exempt organization. Our work, in the long run, will be judged by solutions that no single election or elected official can produce.

The concept of helping people in need is not political in the context of partisan politics. People all across the political spectrum will argue that it is. But they are wrong. Our mission is far broader than party platforms. It transcends partisan politics. Our goal is to make it possible for African Americans and other people of color to compete on a par with all other Minnesotans. Accomplishing that goal is what drives our actions.

If there were reason to believe that, in the span of one politician's term or one politician's career, poverty would be eliminated, drugs would be gone from our streets, all new mothers would be over 21, and adequate housing would be available, then it might be in the best interest of human service organizations, like the Urban League, to identify with a particular candidate. But our interests are long-term--- longer than elected officials will serve, longer than cycles in the economy, longer than the promises politicians will make. As I have said before in this column, an organization like the Minneapolis Urban League has no permanent political friends or foes.

At the same time, it should be noted, we are in no way prohibited from actively pursuing issues or initiatives that appear on the ballot. The Urban League enthusiastically supported the Minneapolis Schools Referendum, in both 1996 and 2000, and urged others to do the same. We have just as actively called for an end to racial profiling.

A bill was introduced by the Minneapolis Urban League at the last legislative session proposing the creation of alternative support systems to ensure the graduation of first-generation college students. A lot of these students are African American and their graduation rate from Minnesota colleges and universities is worse than it is for high school. The bill didn't pass in 2001, but we'll be back next year.

Even during election season, nonprofit organizations need not remain on the sidelines. Our hands are by no means tied. For seventy-five years, the Minneapolis Urban League has conducted voter registration and Get-Out-the-Vote campaigns for every major election. We have conducted or co-sponsored candidate forums on a regular basis.

Traditionally, candidate forums tend to exclude inner city people. I believe it is important for candidates to come into our community and speak openly about what they stand for and what they plan to accomplish. Our audiences need the opportunity to make an informed decision come election day.

Like every other human service organization in the inner city, the Minneapolis Urban League desperately wants its constituents to learn to exercise their franchise, discharge their responsibilities as citizens, and participate fully in the political and civic life of the community. We all know what a difference it could make if the people who are the most in need were also the most politically involved.

Opening (September 22, 2001) of the Glover-Sudduth Center for Economic Development and Urban Affairs

September 17, 2001

On September 22, the Glover-Sudduth Center for Economic Development and Urban Affairs will open its doors for the first time. It will be an historic moment, not just for the Minneapolis Urban League, but for the African American community. While housing, light manufacturing, and service businesses have been built with public/private partnerships, the Glover-Sudduth Center is the first structure to rise up through the community on Plymouth Avenue since its destruction in 1968.

Over the past 75 years, the Minneapolis Urban League has played a critical role serving people of color struggling for the opportunity to make better lives for themselves and their families. Changing systems, both public and private, to improve the lives of African Americans and other people of color is the historic focus of the Urban League Movement. It is, nonetheless, abundantly clear that many African Americans and other persons of color, in Minneapolis as in other urban areas throughout the nation, face ongoing barriers to full social and economic equality.

With this reality in mind, the Minneapolis Urban League realized the need to reexamine our historic message and how our work was accomplished. The construction of this building is one phase of the execution of a long-range strategic plan by the Urban League. At its completion, new or remodeled facilities will exist throughout the central city to serve people through four divisions: Academic Education, Client Services, Economic Development, and Health Education.

The disparity in health outcomes for African Americans compared to both the majority population and other people of color is an acute problem. The Glover-Sudduth Center will offer programs for youth and adults in the prevention of pregnancy, sexually transmitted disease, drug abuse, and tobacco use, as well as support services for people living with HIV. Space is provided for both group work and confidential meeting space.

As the demand for skilled employees increases, people who are unemployed or under-employed need one-on-one assistance in preparing for the job market, securing training, finding a job, and keeping a job. Training is needed in developing a resume, participating in an interview, meeting expectations of the workplace, and dealing with cultural issues or harassment. Senior workers need special services to remain in the workplace.

Another finding of our market research was the need for an incubator for start-up businesses. A partnership with the Business Initiative Development Center (BIDC) will ensure that these businesses receive the consultation and technical assistance they need to succeed. With the business incubator proposed for the Glover-Sudduth Center, we expect to "grow" businesses owned and operated by ethnically diverse entrepreneurs who gain the support and knowledge to succeed as a direct result of occupancy in the Center. The first of these start-ups will be a coffee shop on the corner facing Plymouth and Penn.

A large, flexible space on the first level of the Glover-Sudduth Center will be used during the day for Employment and Training classes. In the evening this space will double as a community meeting room, for which the need in North Minneapolis is great. The Minneapolis Urban League acts as a common meeting ground for a multi-racial society where urban people can come together to solve problems. The availability of a gathering place--- as well as a space for meetings and conferences where neighborhood groups can meet to tackle critical issue--- will lead to a stronger sense of community empowerment in North Minneapolis.

A finished basement level provides the potential for future program expansion in areas such as employment training, services for African immigrants and refugees, and Northside program space for services based in South Minneapolis. Until that occurs, the lower level becomes another option for community use.

It is fitting that the Grand Opening of the Glover-Sudduth Center will occur on Urban League Family Day on September 22. Initiated in 1989, Family Day recognizes the strength and accomplishments of individuals and families who live in the core city. From noon to dusk, Plymouth Avenue (between Penn & Logan) will be transformed into a free, urban festival marketplace featuring food and merchandise vendors, entertainment, family activities, and community projects.

The goal of Family Day is to promote family traditions and values, healthy and secure neighborhoods, economic development, and cohesiveness within inner city communities in Minneapolis. The Glover-Sudduth Center was created to further that goal.

Advocacy for Arab Americans and Muslims

October 1, 2001

The Minneapolis Urban League offers its support and its resources to combat discrimination against Arab Americans and Muslims in the Minneapolis area. In the current situation, it is difficult to know what to do, how to be effective, and what help to offer.

The mission of the Minneapolis Urban League is to help people in need and to advocate for public policies that break down the barriers that inhibit people of color from achieving their full potential. Most of our resources go toward assisting those who are out of work or entering the job market for the first time, struggling in school, living with HIV, or facing a crisis in housing, in their family, or in the workplace.

Our advocacy role is just as important, perhaps more important, than the services we provide. Yet it tends to rise or fall in visibility depending upon the issues or events in our environment.

There is one element among all of the horrors of September 11 that African Americans can understand far better than anyone. The immediate threat to Arab Americans that followed the deadly destruction of the World Trade Center and the Pentagon did not surprise us. African Americans have lived with suspicion and accusations for four hundred years.

Three Arab Americans, perhaps more, have been murdered. People perceived to be Arab, but more likely perceived to be "foreign," have been removed from airplanes in seven cities around the country. Hundreds of incidents at mosques, in shops and restaurants, and on the street have been recorded. We need to stand up for Arab Americans who are now experiencing what we have known for so long.

We can begin by making this public statement of support. But what else should we be doing? We have an obligation to prevent the events of September 11, which have taken nearly 6,400 lives, from destroying the lives of thousands more citizens. That's where our mission takes us. How do we get there?

People from all over the world are being suspected of being Arab terrorists or their supporters simply because most Americans can't tell where people are from. Refugees and immigrants from East Africa are afraid to wear traditional garb out of fear of being harassed or beaten.

There's no doubt that we need to learn more about both Arabs and Muslims. Where do we go to learn? The answer may be to go to the source. Maybe we need to ask Arab Americans what they need from us.

Although our own struggle is far from over, we are thankful for the support of all the folks who have helped us along the way. Now it is our turn to be a voice for others in the fight against prejudice, discrimination, and hatred.

"Proud Legacy of Service to America":
Photo Exhibit at the Minneapolis Urban League

March 4, 2002

This week, the Minneapolis Urban League is hosting a moving and informative photo exhibit depicting the legacy of military service by African Americans in Minnesota. The exhibit opened on Sunday, February 26 with a touching ceremony of presentation of the colors, recognition of the veterans in the audience, and recollections by some of the men who appeared in the photos. It will remain open March 4 through March 8 from 8:30 a. m. to 6:00 p. m. at 2100 Plymouth Avenue North.

It is fitting that this exhibit should come at this time. The war that America fights now against terrorism may require new strategies and tactics, but the spirit we see in the faces of these men transcends any time period or theater of war. We are looking at heroes. Every African American young person should come to see the pride in their straight backs and in their clear eyes as they look out upon us. In spite of their own personal experiences, the heroes in these photos served their country out of a commitment to the things for which America ought to stand.

For me, this exhibit, "Proud Legacy of Service to America," brings forth mixed feelings about patriotism. We are all taught in first grade to say the Pledge of Allegiance and to sing "The Star Spangled Banner." The words of that pledge and the words of the national anthem have a different ring in the ears of African Americans. How much harder it has been for us to achieve "the land of the free" than it was for the author of the song. How much more we have wanted to see "liberty and justice for all."

Lt. Col. Charles Dryden, author of *A-Train, Memoirs of a Tuskegee Airman*, displays a similar ambivalence in reference to the lyrics of "America, the Beautiful." Dryden wrote , "Thine alabaster cities gleam / Undimmed by human tears . . . Would that it were true--- that no tears were ever shed anywhere, anytime in its history, caused by affronts to the dignity of its citizens of color, or by assaults upon their person. How lovely would my country be if its actions did not belie its brave words . . ."

Nevertheless, Dryden goes on to say, " I have fought in two wars for my America because I have loved its . . . principles."

Perhaps, because we have a deeper understanding of the values on which America claims to be founded, we have deeper feelings about what this country could be. I extend an invitation to each of you, and to each of your children, to come by the Urban League to see this important photo exhibit, "Proud Legacy of Service to America."

Annual Dinner 2002:
Kweisi Mfume and the Historical Roles of the
NAACP and the Minneapolis Urban League

April 8, 2002

April 18, 2002, marks the seventy-sixth time that the Minneapolis Urban League has hosted its Annual Dinner. Our League was founded in 1926 as an affiliate of the National Urban League, based in New York City. It began in Minneapolis as a small group of citizens, both black and white, struggling to bring change in opportunities for African Americans in jobs, housing, and education.

The 2002 Annual Dinner at the Minneapolis Hilton will reflect the strong, historic relationship between the major stakeholders of Minneapolis and the Minneapolis Urban League. The relationship has been one of innovation, creativity, and mutual benefit.

The highlight of the Annual Dinner is a speech given by a person who has played an important role in the creation of opportunity for African Americans and other people of color. This year, we are honored to have as our keynote speaker, sponsored by Target Corporation, the National President and Chief Executive Officer of the NAACP, Kweisi Mfume. A native of Baltimore, Maryland, Mr. Mfume graduated from Morgan State University and earned an M.A. from Johns Hopkins University. He was a member of the Baltimore City Council for seven years before winning a seat in Congress in 1986. As a member of the House of Representatives, Mfume consistently advocated for landmark minority business and civil rights legislation. He became President/CEO of the NAACP in 1996 after serving ten years in the United States Congress.

It is fitting that the President/CEO of the NAACP should address an Urban League gathering. Though each organization has a unique mission, our missions are complementary. The mission of the NAACP is advocacy for and defense of civil rights. The NAACP is the watchdog for civil rights at the national, regional and local level. It is one of the primary forces in the nation's capitol lobbying for civil rights and full political empowerment for African Americans.

The mission of the Minneapolis Urban League is one of advocacy and human service. While the Urban League has been at the forefront in the battle for the preservation of civil rights, it does not engage in legal action or lobbying. Our advocacy efforts are concentrated, most often, on specific local issues.

The Urban League focuses on the 10,000 people each year who look to us for help in finding a job, getting an education, preventing disease, or changing behavior. Thousands more depend on us to speak up when it comes to living wage jobs, affordable housing, quality education, or disparities in health status.

Together, the NAACP and the National Urban League are a powerful force on the national scene. Their long history of advocacy and services is recognized throughout the world. Please join us in welcoming Kweisi Mfume and representatives of Minnesota NAACP chapters on April 18. Call 612-302-3140 for tickets.

10

The Glover-Sudduth Life and History
Lecture Series: Mahmoud El-Kati

April 15, 2002

"The chief function of education is to create thinking human beings." W. E. B. DuBois said that. Recently, many of us had the chance to gain a deeper understanding of what that statement means. The Glover-Sudduth Life and History Lecture Series, presented over the past four weeks at the Minneapolis Urban League, has produced serious food for thought. Developed by Professor Mahmoud El-Kati, the four lectures covered important aspects of our history that never made it into the history books. It is fitting that the series was named after two champions of the Minneapolis Civil Rights Movement, Gleason Glover and Gary Sudduth.

The series began with an historical overview of the relationship of African Americans to the political system in America. This introductory lecture addressed two avenues of Black American participation in politics. The first avenue leads to various forms of protest: abolitionism, slave rebellions, petitions, social change movements, and demonstrations. The second avenue moves in the direction of electoral politics. Professor El-Kati used the example of the change among black voters from being overwhelmingly Republican to being overwhelmingly Democrat.

The lecture that followed addressed the reparations movement. Reparations refers to the demand for payment for damages by African Americans for the 250 years of free labor enjoyed by white Americans from 1615 to 1865. Professor El-Kati examined the people, places, issues, and struggles that are at the core of the fight for reparations.

Everyone could find the story of his or her own family in Professor El Kati's exploration of one of the greatest social changes in American history. When African Americans began to move from the South to the North, from farms to cities, from agrarian to industrial work, the states and cities of the north were forever altered. The concept of the ghetto and its place throughout history was discussed in the context of this migration.

The final lecture focused on the critical and creative role of the African American woman as an agent for social change. The black woman's contribution to shaping the politics of the African American community cannot be denied but, nevertheless, is often overlooked.

Our humble thanks go out to Mahmoud El-Kati for bringing us this extraordinary series of educational evenings. Mahmoud El-Kati is a lecturer and writer on the African American experience. He has had a number of his articles, essays, and reviews appear in a wide range of local, national, and international publications. He is currently lecturing in the History Department at Macalester College, where he teaches courses on the history of blacks in the United States. But more than that, he provides a sense of "still leadership" to all who listen.

We salute Mahmoud El-Kati as a legend among us. Those who attended his lecture series will treasure that moving experience and will value the opportunity he presented to grow as a thinking human being. Job well done!

April 2002 76th Annual Minneapolis Urban League Dinner: Kweisi Mfume and Scholarship Recipients

April 29, 2002

On April 18, 2002, over 1200 people attended the Minneapolis Urban League's 76th Annual Dinner. The keynote speaker that evening was Kweisi Mfume, National President and CEO of the NAACP. Mr. Mfume, a former U. S. Congressman and Chair of the National Black Caucus, fully engaged the audience with his vision and his challenge to all Americans.

In Mfume's view, America is a country that has the capacity to solve any problem. Issues of race and poverty exist today, not because America cannot resolve them, but because America has not been willing to take on the problem. He called upon each of us to be willing to open every subject for discussion, to put every issue on the table, and to examine every problem with an eye to finding solutions rather than points of difference. It is easy to see why Kweisi Mfume is the preeminent civil rights leader in the United States today. His words carried meaning for every person in the room.

Another highlight of the evening was the presentation of scholarships. African American students often face greater barriers to excellence and stronger peer pressure *not* to achieve than other students. We recognize what these students must overcome to succeed. Since the Urban League program began five years ago, over fifty young people have been awarded scholarships, sponsored by local companies, at our Annual Dinner. This year, fourteen winners were presented to the audience on videotape, which captured the young people talking about their ambitions and the influences in their lives. You would have been proud of each and every one of them.

Scholarship winners are not necessarily those with the highest GPA. School, community and church activities, employment and family responsibilities are also considered. A 500-word essay, written on a different topic each year, is another important factor. This year the topic was "How has your life changed since September 11?" The essays, judged by professional educators, displayed real insight into the priorities that we should all have.

On the evening of April 18, at our 76th Annual Dinner, we were treated to two examples of the best this country has to offer. First, a famous man talked about how things ought to be. Then, fourteen high school students, unknown to some of us now, showed us what they have the potential to become. You can't ask for more than that.

Thor and TCM: Contract to Construct
New Minneapolis Urban League Building

May 13, 2002

We've read or heard a lot recently about the ratio of majority to minority contractors employed on construction projects in Minneapolis. In case you haven't heard, the ratio is dismal especially when you consider the location of some of these projects in formerly black neighborhoods. The conventional wisdom is that there just aren't enough construction firms out there to participate in these projects. The question that must be asked is this: Is there a shortage of firms with the necessary skills, or is there a shortage of will to include minority contractors?

As we heard from Kweisi Mfume in his speech at the Urban League's Annual Dinner, America has the capacity to solve any problem it faces. Often, it does not have the will. This country, this state, this city each has the wherewithal to increase minority participation in building projects. It does not exhibit the commitment to make that happen. I know it's true because of my own experience.

In October of 2001, the Minneapolis Urban League opened the Glover-Sudduth Center for Economic Development and Urban Affairs. The building was constructed by a collaboration, developed specifically for this project, of the two largest African American general contractors in the state – Thor and TCM. The Glover-Sudduth Center was the first time that a collaboration of this kind was tried.

The partnership developed because the Minneapolis Urban League was committed to the value of minority firms making a significant contribution to a minority landmark. The decision was made early on that the building contract would include a minority participant. All of the potential bidders were notified of that decision prior to developing their proposals. TCM/Thor came in with the best bid, using not one but two African American firms.

Thor and TCM, in turn, insisted upon the participation of minorities and women subcontractors on the project. In the end, nearly 65% of the dollar value of subcontracts was awarded to firms owned by minorities (53%) or women (11.5%). That means that $2.6 million of a $4.1 million building stayed in our communities. At the Minneapolis Urban League, we are as proud of this statistic as we are of the structure itself.

Donald Crowther, one of the principals at TCM Construction, concurs with our assessment of the Glover-Sudduth Center as a landmark building, "I've never seen a project of this size achieve numbers like this. It has exceeded all of our expectations. We have demonstrated that involvement of minority firms on a high level can be achieved."

We have proven that it can be done. I recognize that the Glover-Sudduth Center is a small project by majority construction standards. I also recognize that if there is enough minority skill and talent out there for a $4 million building, there is enough for a $40 million project. It doesn't take more skill or talent for a $40 million building. It just takes more people and more time. But, more than that, it takes more "will" to get it done!

Praising Mercedes Burns, MUL Scholarship
Winners, And Others Who Do Graduate

May 27, 2002

It's spring, finally, and spring brings graduation. The proms are over and seniors are waiting for the big day. I have devoted a lot of space in this column to an examination of the failure of African American children in our schools. Too many African American students are absent each day; not enough of our students stay in the same school throughout their elementary or secondary careers. Too many African American students are suspended; too many drop out altogether.

A generation ago, 68% of the African Americans in Minneapolis were high school graduates compared with 76% of whites. Today, two white students graduate for every black student. This alarming fact represents the depth of the problem for our community when it comes to education.

But now is the time to praise those who do graduate. At the Urban League, we witnessed the amazing accomplishments of fourteen scholarship winners at our Annual Dinner. All were excellent students. Beyond that, they displayed a poise and maturity that only comes with confidence in who one is as a human being. We saw young people who envisioned a future in which they will be a mathematician, a biologist, an architect, a psychologist, a nurse, or involved in international business. We met young people who loved their life, who displayed a talent for poetry, singing, dancing, drama, drawing and every sport our high schools have to offer. When we witness the joy of young people who are proud of their accomplishments, proud of their families and their schools, it only makes it more painful to witness those who do not make it.

Recently, I received a letter from Mercedes Burns, winner of the Gleason Glover Memorial Scholarship, that I would like to share with you: "In all honesty, I (a south Minneapolis resident) had heard little about the work of the Urban League until I was presented with your scholarship opportunity. However, my mother and I were pleased to witness first-hand the fruit of the Urban League when we were invited to the annual fellowship dinner on April 18th. Through the music, video, and testimonies I encountered, I felt that I began to fully appreciate the majesty of this organization, whose sole goal is to enrich the lives of its city's citizens. There is much to admire in that work... High school has been a long journey for me, and just over the rise of a hill, I can see college, waiting to take me on yet another journey. I thank you and the Urban League for providing me with the means to take on this new journey at Macalester College and investing in the futures of myself and the people of Minneapolis."

A letter like that makes it all worthwhile. Not only does it make me think that the future of our community is in good hands, but it boosts my own energy for the work of the Minneapolis Urban League.

14

Representing the Minneapolis Urban
League on the MnSCU Board of Trustees

June 17, 2002

Last week, I was appointed by Governor Ventura to the Minnesota State Colleges and Universities (MnSCU) Board of Trustees. Six appointments were made to the fifteen-member board. I think it is important that the Minneapolis Urban League have a seat at this table.

The Minnesota State Colleges and Universities (MnSCU) system is the largest single provider of higher education in the state of Minnesota and includes technical colleges, community colleges, comprehensive community and technical colleges, and state universities. MnSCU's 34 institutions operate on 53 campuses in 46 communities around the state. There are about 225,000 students in credit-based courses each year.

In other words, the MnSCU Board of Trustees is responsible for all of public higher education in the state except the University of Minnesota, which has its own Board of Regents and multiple campuses. The MnSCU system produces 50 percent of all new computer information professionals in Minnesota, 50 percent of all new teachers, 80 percent of all new nurses, and 90 percent of all new law enforcement officers.

Recently, MnSCU Chancellor James McCormick set up an Advisory Committee, chaired by Vance Opperman and Glen Taylor, to advise him on strategic directions for the future of public higher education in Minnesota. The Advisory Committee published its report, Access to Success, in April of 2002. To no one's surprise, the report concluded that the state needs a higher education system that reaches out and invites a wider variety of people to participate and achieve.

Historically, MnSCU has been the most affordable higher education option in Minnesota. In a time of widespread tuition increases, we must note the organization's commitment to remain affordable. This is an educational bargain of which not enough of our people take advantage. Out of the entire MnSCU enrollment in Minnesota, only 18,000 are students of color. Immigrants and refugees make up a good portion of the 18,000. Not as many African Americans as you would expect are enrolled. I can attest to the benefits of this education. I graduated from Southwest State University in Marshall, Minnesota, in 1977 with a B.A. in Education.

We should keep in mind that education is a two-way street. It is the most important tool we, as a people, have to open the door to economic opportunity. On the other hand, higher education is the principal means that the state has to meet the challenge of economic, social, technological, and cultural change. The system is mutually beneficial.

As a Trustee, I intend to challenge the MnSCU system to develop marketing strategies that actively promote this educational resource to African Americans. MnSCU attracts students from many different countries, but very few African Americans from Minnesota, or throughout the U. S., can be found in Marshall, Mankato, or St. Cloud. At the same time, I want actively to promote this educational resource among our students. Much more can be done to acquaint parents, schools, and school counselors with the attractions of an education in the MnSCU group of institutions. Once again, other residents of Minnesota are seizing an opportunity that our people are missing out on. I want to alter that balance.

15

Visiting Families of Our Community in Their Homes

July 15, 2002

Next week, I will begin a series of visits to the homes of members of our community to educate myself on neighborhood issues and to share with them the work of the Minneapolis Urban League and our resources to help the community. This is a departure for us at the Urban League. Up to now, we have invited the community into our home on Plymouth Avenue, but we have not gone out into the neighborhoods to visit.

The Minneapolis Urban League brings elected officials and appointed office-holders to the Glover-Sudduth Center on a regular basis for discussion of issues that have a direct impact on our community. In recent months, we have hosted at least five meetings of representatives of the Somali and African American community who wanted to develop a better strategy for police-community relations to present to the Mayor and City Council. Their efforts have resulted in citywide public meetings on the subject.

On three nights this spring, we invited three African American Hennepin County Judges to participate in a Judges Roundtable to give our constituency a judge's eye view of how the judicial system works and what people of color, especially, need to know about the process.

In late June, Minneapolis Police Chief Robert Olson met at the Minneapolis Urban League with community leaders and members of our staff to look for ways to recruit more African Americans into the police force. If we are going to cite the shortage of officers of color as a problem in our city, then our community needs to be an agent of change.

It is important for residents of this city to understand the issues that influence their lives everyday. Gatherings such as those I just described are key to getting issues out on the table. But they lack one important feature. While there is always time allotted for questions at these events, there is never enough time to find out what is on the minds of our neighbors in both North and South Minneapolis.

I want to meet with our neighbors, in their homes, to exchange views on the needs of our community and to outline the things that the Urban League can do to help. I want to create an unhurried time for listening and dialogue that must be the basis for the solution to any problem. I want folks to hear, from me, how the Urban League can help to strengthen families, educate children, find jobs, and promote a healthy lifestyle.

At the same time, I want to hear from residents what they are doing, or are prepared to do, to strengthen their neighborhoods and their schools. Just as the police have the responsibility to protect and to serve, and judges have the responsibility to make an impartial decision on the facts, we, as citizens, have a responsibility to create the fabric in our neighborhoods that will protect us and hold us together.

As President of the Minneapolis Urban League, I have a responsibility to know what is going on in our community. There are some things I can learn by holding meetings at the Glover-Sudduth Center. There are other things that I can learn only by going into people's homes to listen to a group of neighbors discuss what is important to them.

If you would like to host a dialogue in your home or at your church, please contact Wesley Smith at the Urban League (612-302-3138 or wsmith@mul.org).

Minneapolis Urban League Participation
in Urban Gardens Project

September 30, 2002

An important event occurred on September 21, 2002. Not many people witnessed it, but that did not reduce its importance. Neighborhood organizations, city officials, and the Urban League gathered in a vacant lot on the corner of 35th and Bloomington in South Minneapolis to celebrate the founding of Urban Gardens, new townhomes that will be available for rent by low-income people in the spring of 2003. Four units will have four bedrooms; two units will have two bedrooms.

The Minneapolis Urban League and the Minneapolis Public Housing Authority (MPHA) have entered into an agreement to build replacement housing units in the inner city in accordance with the requirements of the Hollman Consent Decree (Hollman vs. Cisneros). The Powderhorn Park Neighborhood Association has committed $80,000 of its Neighborhood Revitalization Program (NRP) funding to get the development off the ground.

Affordable housing has become the top priority for city leaders, activist groups, foundations, the United Way, and a host of other interests. The City of Minneapolis currently has one of the lowest vacancy rates in the country among rental and owner occupied units. The shortage of properties for first time home-buyers is at an all-time high. City reports show a shortage of nearly 15,000 affordable housing units for extremely low-income renters and owners. Approximately 78 percent of renters and 61 percent of owners experience problems finding a place to live for which they can pay. Very limited housing availability encourages discrimination by landlords, lenders, and real estate agencies.

Six new units won't even touch vacancy rates in Minneapolis, but they represent a start. In the next two years there will be a total of 31 units. The partnership between MPHA and the Minneapolis Urban League offers hope to the families who will have affordable living quarters immediately and suggests a model of collaborative efforts in the future. Making meaningful progress in tackling an important issue often means taking the first steps toward incremental change. Then, in the future, additional steps can be taken and the strides can become longer. It is with this in mind that we embark on this important effort to address the issue of affordable housing in Minneapolis.

Assessing Minneapolis Urban League Success During 2002

March 3, 2003

At the beginning of each year, the Minneapolis Urban League assesses the progress it has made over the previous year. As I look back over 2002, I am pleased to say the Minneapolis Urban League had a solid year both in terms of its impact on the community and in its ability to provide direct service to our constituency.

As we entered 2002, the Urban League identified thirty objectives that we wanted to accomplish in the areas of helping people in need, influencing public policy, or strengthening our organization. We met 28 of our objectives, partially accomplished one more, and failed to make progress on another. First, we were able to increase our service level. Our four divisions--- Client Services, Academic Education, Economic Development and Health Education--- reached over 20,500 individuals last year. Nearly 9,000 people received individual assistance.

To ensure that people who seek our help are, indeed, able to change their lives, the Urban League Board of Directors launched a Continuous Improvement Initiative spearheaded by Program Committee Chair Ora Hokes. Throughout 2002-2003, all programs offered by the Minneapolis Urban League will undergo a comprehensive review conducted by independent consultants. This process, already employed by the Academic Education and Health Education divisions, is yielding truly insightful learning opportunities and has opened our minds to other ways of working.

Additionally, the Minneapolis Urban League embarked upon a partnership with the Minneapolis Public Housing Authority to develop 18 housing units for low-income residents in non-impacted areas of Minneapolis. The first phase of the project will open in May of this year. The 6-unit housing complex, located at 35th and Bloomington Avenue South, will be known as Urban Gardens.

In 2002, the Minneapolis Urban League increased its efforts to bring members of our community into the political process by working in a coalition to register over 1700 voters and engage nearly 700 in forums with policy makers, lawmakers, and elected officials. Our staff participated in hundreds of meetings over the year aimed at bringing about policy change in affordable housing, health disparities, or K-12 education. Staff members represent our organization on over a dozen boards and task forces that deal with K-12 education, health disparities, and access to technology.

I have also actively represented the Minneapolis Urban League in the broader community. In 2002, I served as president of the United Way Council of Agency Executives, a peer group of executives who lead 240 funded United Way agencies. I was also selected to a six-year term to serve as a trustee for the Minnesota State Colleges and Universities System (MNSCU). Finally, I was recently selected to serve as a board member for the Greater Minneapolis Convention and Visitors Association.

As I review the past year, I am proud to report that, with the opening of our new building in South Minneapolis, we have completed all four of the projects designated by our 75th Anniversary Campaign. New facilities to serve both North and South Minneapolis, coupled with academically oriented spaces for our schools, have given us the ability to serve more clients and to serve them better. To date, we have received $6,367,416 of the $6,414,839 pledged to the campaign.

In fact, Minneapolis Urban League maintained strong financial health throughout 2002, marking eight years with a balanced budget or a surplus and eight years with an unqualified audit. Over those years our staff has grown to 129 people. Our budget of $8.9 million in 2002 was supported by grants, contracts, and contributions.

As I reflect on 2002, by all accounts, it was a blessed year for the Minneapolis Urban League. I thank this important organization and the African American community for the opportunity to serve as its president.

18

MUL Preparation Site for AccountAbility Minnesota

July 14, 2003

Recently, the Minneapolis Urban League received a report from AccountAbility Minnesota, a volunteer organization that provides tax and accounting services for those in need. Accountability Minnesota was established in 1971 to provide pro bono accounting assistance to new, small businesses. After the Earned Income Tax Credit was introduced in the late 1970s, Accountability Minnesota expanded to offer free tax return preparation for low-income people. Other volunteer organizations offer similar programs across the state. Minneapolis Urban League received the AccountAbility report because we hosted two community tax preparation sites this past winter.

During the 2003 tax season, AccountAbility Minnesota helped 8,500 taxpayers receive $9.4 million in state and federal tax refunds. The service is available to individuals with an annual income of $25.00 or less per year and families with an annual income of $35,000 or less. Over 300 people came to the Urban League. At the Urban League site in South Minneapolis, tax returns were filed for $336,279 in refunds. In North Minneapolis, the number was $213,418. That averages out to about $1700 per taxpaying individual or family. Just as important, that's nearly $550,000 returned to this community.

Individual refunds are only part of the story. Families earning less that $35,000 per year, who do not prepare their tax return themselves, are likely to pay for tax preparation with a company that offers a Refund Anticipation Loan. Instead of collecting a fee at the time of service, the tax preparer calculates the expected refund, deducts his or her fees for the services provided and the interest that will be due on the loan, gives the balance of the anticipated refund to the taxpayer, and receives the entire refund when it arrives from the state or the IRS. This is a legitimate service but an expensive one. The Brookings Institute, in a nationwide study of this practice, found that Minnesotans paid $17 million in fees and interest on Refund Anticipation Loans in 2002.

Low-income taxpayers who do not use a tax preparation service end up filing their taxes themselves. Years ago, when people could understand the return, this was standard procedure for many families. Today, families risk getting a smaller refund because not all deductions were claimed or they risk serious error, such as failure to file the correct documentation, which could flag their return for future audit.

Bonnie Esposito, Executive Director of AccountAbility Minnesota, stresses the benefits of free taxpayer services: "In 2003, AccountAbility Minnesota was fortunate to have 390 volunteers who put in over 10,000 hours to help others do their taxes. Seventy percent of our volunteers are CPAs, accountants, tax professionals, or lawyers. The other 30% are accounting or law students, or people who are good with numbers and have experience doing their own taxes. Their work has an immediate payoff. We calculate that one volunteer hour saves $1,900 for low-income families."

Accountability Minnesota produces benefits for our community beyond free tax preparation. Families trust the organizations that are the host sites. They have confidence that they will receive all of the refund that is due to them. Those who receive a refund are likely to spend their money here in the community on a down payment on a home, a rental deposit, or to pay routine bills for food, clothing, or services.

"We couldn't do it without our community partners," says Esposito, "They are the key to reaching those in need of our program. Not only do they provide the host sites, they promote our services to their constituents."

After reading the report from AccountAbility Minnesota, I wanted to share the results with you and to congratulate the volunteers and staff on their contribution to our community.

19

Family Day Goes Forward After All

August 19, 2003

The 14th Annual Minneapolis Urban League Family Day Extravaganza, which took place on Saturday, August 16, is now part of the past, but I want to take this opportunity to thank Minneapolis residents and friends of the League for coming out to celebrate the occasion with us. I want to thank the area businesses, particularly those located in the Plymouth-Penn Shopping Center, for bearing with us as we tried to sort out their issues. To the many vendors who stuck with us throughout the whole ordeal, I extend my gratitude, as well. Let me also apologize for the on again-off again nature of the event. Although I regret the confusion it caused, I want you to know that the outpouring of support expressed in phone calls and visits to my office helped me to understand just how important the tradition of Family Day has become to this community.

It's impossible to gauge exactly how many people attended Family Day on Saturday, but I'd guess approximately 2500 people were around and about throughout the day. In light of all that has transpired, I am truly humbled by the fact that so many people chose to celebrate with us on a day that proved to be one of the hottest days of the year! If any of you caught the parade when it traveled down Oliver towards Plymouth Avenue, you know that a couple of the cars carrying parade participants (myself and MUL Board Chair John Green included) broke down due to overheated engines! So again, a huge thank you for your attendance. We don't know yet how well the 59 food, merchandise, and information vendors that set up shop for Family Day fared, but again, a huge thank you to the vendors for persevering.

The one negative was the heat. I'm told the temperature on Saturday reached 96 degrees!! Now, having reached the level of President and Chief Executive Officer, I'm in control of a lot of things, but one thing I can't control is the weather.

You should know that the staff of the Minneapolis Urban League, who did a tremendous job coordinating all facets of the day's activities, and of whom I am extremely proud, are anxious to begin planning for next year's Family Day event. They, together with our Board of Directors, will first take ample time assessing this year's event, making adjustments, and incorporating changes where necessary. That assessment will determine how soon the work to put Family Day 2004 into production must begin.

A lot of time and effort goes into the production of Family Day, but the Minneapolis Urban League believes that bringing together a community once a year to celebrate all that is positive and hopeful about families and family values goes a long way towards making that community stronger. As valued members of this community, you are worth our time and effort, and you can count on an even bigger, brighter, and better Family Day celebration in 2004.

Thanks again for your support.

20

Reflections on Five Years as President/CEO of MUL

September 5, 2003

On Sunday, August 31, I reached a milestone at the Minneapolis Urban League. For me, that day marked 5 years of serving as an Urban League President and Chief Executive Officer.

Whenever one reaches these kinds of milestones, she or he does so humbly; at the same time, though, it affords the opportunity to reflect on past strides and past difficulties. It also gives the person an opportunity to look forward. I am very excited about the prospect of looking forward, but allow me a few minutes to reflect on what brings me to today.

In 1998, after a brief introductory period with just time enough to get adjusted to my new surroundings, I and my new staff began structuring a management team. Together, we took a measured look at the internal structure of the agency, as would any new team of management. We found the basic structure to be sound and operating smoothly--- but more than that, we found a cadre of dedicated hardworking staff that is unsurpassed in this city--- a testament to the effectiveness of past leadership. Thanks Gleason and thanks Gary!

By 1999, with a smoothly running administration, we began to concentrate on the future. The budget at that time was just over $5 million. We had 90 employees and operated out of five sites, three of which the Urban League owned. There was a recently completed 10-year strategic plan in place, but for me, 10 years was too long--- so I looked forward 5 years. I envisioned an agency that could engage the community in a much broader sense. In other words, the Minneapolis Urban League would be a focal point of all economic growth, and would be a resource for the community from which information vital to community growth flowed.

In early 2000, the Urban League launched a major capital campaign effort, and we celebrated its success at our 75th Silver Anniversary Dinner in 2001. Our capital campaign was the catalyst for enabling the League to have an impact on economic development in Minneapolis. We raised over $6 million! Thanks for your support. We also entered into the development and ownership of affordable housing and look forward to having a significant impact on that area of concern for low-income Minneapolis residents. Finally, with a new department to deal directly with public and community advocacy, the Urban League has been instrumental in bringing priority legislative agendas forward and drawing the attention of key decision makers. We've also been successful in engaging community interest groups as collaborators or partners, to work pro-actively and productively on issues of common concern.

The League's budget reached $8 million by 2002, and our staff complement grew to 129. We now own five properties from which we deliver direct services, advocacy, and educational programming. Our headquarters facility, the Glover~Sudduth Center for Economic Development and Urban Affairs, shares space with small emerging businesses and provides community access to space for meetings and social gatherings. We've been astounded by the increasing demand for use of this space. Today, in light of widespread state and national budget cuts, we're focused on being fiscally responsible and programmatically sound. We've had to make some tough decisions, but our commitment to the mission and vision of the Urban League will not waver.

I know it may sound braggadocios to recount past achievements, but I'm proud to be at the helm of an agency that for 78 years has managed to remain viable--- has stayed the course for its core constituency. It has not always been easy. In fact, it's been very difficult at times. But through the grace of God, we are where we are! My foes and my detractors will say that my shortcomings outweigh my strides. Someone else might disagree. A songwriter summed it up best by grouping this collection of words together. They go something like this: "I have had some good days, and I have had some bad days. But when I look things over, I see that my good days outweigh my bad days. So I won't complain." To be sure, I have had my share of bad days. Many whom I counted on for support when I needed them most were nowhere to be found. But you know what, when I look things over, my good days outweigh my bad days and I won't complain.

After five years as President and CEO of the Minneapolis Urban League, I remain humble and thankful, steadfastly dedicated to providing advocacy, vision, and direct service to the community. I look forward to building effective relationships that will assist the Minneapolis Urban League and me in getting done the work that needs to be done.

Thanks!

21

2004 Black College Tour

March 26, 2004

By the time you read this, Minneapolis Urban League staff will be on the road with a busload of 32 students headed for a tour of historically black colleges and universities. Their eight-day journey marks the 18th annual Black College Tour for the Minneapolis Urban League. This group of students, from high schools located throughout the metro area, has demonstrated a potential to achieve a higher level of academic success, and a desire to see what a historically black college has to offer.

As a young kid growing up in Alton, Illinois, I wasn't familiar with the distinction of a black college. I didn't know why a black college deserved any more merit than any other college, so when it was time for me to consider where I would continue my education after high school, I didn't give much thought to the unique experience I could have by matriculating at a black college. But listening to Mr. John Green, Chair of the Minneapolis Urban League Board of Directors, speak to the students as they made their final preparations to leave on their tour made me reflect on what I'd missed out on.

Brother Green laid out all the reasons why every African American student should strive to walk the hallowed grounds of a historically black institute of learning. He recounted some of his own cherished experiences. He talked about the special treatment that comes from smaller class sizes, and the emphasis black colleges place on nonacademic elements of learning, such as good diction and personal grooming. He talked about all of the things outside of the basic college curriculum that a black college focuses on to better prepare its students for success in today's workforce.

No, I didn't attend a historically black institute of learning. But one thing I know now that I didn't know growing up is that major corporations target graduates of the most prestigious of HBCU's for developmentally lucrative internships because they know how well prepared those graduates are for the rigors of corporate America. So don't be surprised to learn that the brother or sister who you see anchoring the national news, or serving on the board of a Fortune Five Hundred company, or being interviewed on CNN for performing groundbreaking surgery, attended a historically black college.

Brother John Green, besides being one of the youngest chairs of an Urban League Board in the country, is himself a corporate professional at American Express Financial Advisors. He attended North Carolina A & T State University, and he uses his experiences to motivate young black students like the ones who are part of this year's tour. This year the tour goes east, to Washington, D. C.; Baltimore, Maryland; Norfolk and Petersburg, Virginia; and to Greensboro, Durham, Raleigh, and Winston Salem, North Carolina. They'll visit Bennett, Coppin State, Howard, Morgan State, Norfolk State, North Carolina A&T State, North Carolina Central, Shaw, Virginia State, and Winston-Salem State campuses. Every student on the tour, whether a first year student, sophomore, junior or senior, has been meticulously prepared to make an impression on the admissions staff at each college they visit. They've prepared research on each school, written essays, developed a resume, and completed a college application. With their individual Student Profiles in hand, they are a complete package and can often be accepted on the spot.

The young people that go on the Urban League's annual college tour will be in the good hands of eight volunteer chaperones. Some, like Richard Bell, are seasoned veterans of the tour, and they get great satisfaction out of the changes they see in the attitudes about education these young people bring back. Others, like Arivia Black, are young themselves, but have already taken up the mantel of responsibility for guiding their peers on a positive path and setting personal examples for them to look up to.

I believe that before we can instill in our youth a desire to seek out the unique experience that Brother Green talks about, we have to talk to them about what it meant historically for African Americans to gain an education in America. Dr. Josie Johnson gave an excellent commentary on that very subject in **Insight News**. She discussed how the justice system denied education for blacks. I encourage you to look up that article (3/8/04) and share it with a youngster whom you want to motivate.

Finally, say a prayer for our students as they travel the highways and the byways, that they return safe, sound, and encouraged.

22

Urban League Sunday

April 2, 2004

The Minneapolis Urban League has always prided itself on building coalitions. Our partnerships with community service agencies, city departments, grass roots organizations, and others has brought about many positive changes, and we look forward to continuing those cooperative relationships. But I'd like to discuss with you for just a little while the historic coalition uniting the Urban League and the religious community.

The African American church, past and present, serves as the cornerstone of the African American community. Consequently, it is out of the Church that the Urban League movement took form in the early 1900's. Wendell Jones, who was a postal clerk on Washington Avenue and was among the first to become a charter member of the Minneapolis-St. Paul Urban League in 1926, stated "At that time, there was no office, no paid staff, just a meeting in a church." That is a history shared by affiliates across the country. Therefore it is imperative and appropriate that the Urban League and the Church unite in addressing issues and concerns affecting the well-being of our community, reminding each of us of our common goals to provide spiritual, economic and socially relevant leadership.

The Urban League as a national movement has, for more than 25 years, designated one Sunday out of each year to pay tribute to our shared history. Urban League Sunday, as the tribute is called, will be celebrated in Minneapolis on April 18th. On that day, the Minneapolis Urban League will share information and testimony with church congregations of many denominations around the Twin Cities. Many of our own employees will serve as ambassadors, carrying a message of unity and commonality of purpose to their own place of worship or to a church of their choice on the 18th. Each of our Urban League ambassadors will be armed with information about League programs and services, as well as information about links to other vital resources in the community. Opportunities for getting job training and finding employment; alternative education for students K-12; and help finding affordable housing, emergency food, shelter, or clothing are the kinds of support services our ambassadors will give testimony about.

I believe it is totally appropriate for our folk to get this kind of information in the place where they feel most comfortable asking for help. As I've said, this is a historic bond that we have with the Church. Our work to support the basic human needs of our constituents only augments what the Church Mission does for its congregational membership, and we can work hand in hand in carrying that work out.

But going beyond basic needs, today African American churches all over America are beginning to trade ideas and take an increasingly aggressive stance when addressing a burgeoning set of educational, social, political, systemic, and economic problems. The Minneapolis Urban League has often partnered with the Coalition of Black Churches and African American Leadership Summit in the continuing struggle to enable African Americans and other people of color to cultivate and develop their individual and group potential on a par with all other Minnesotans.

Some years ago Vernon E. Jordan, Jr., former head of the National Urban League, stated in one of his keynote addresses that "to the degree that African American people have survived or will survive in the future, depends on the leadership of the Black church." What a true statement, and what a fitting theme to give to this year's Urban League Sunday in Minneapolis.

23

78th Annual Dinner

April 23, 2004

Just this past week the Minneapolis Urban League held its 78th Annual Dinner. For all of us at the League--- Board and staff--- planning this year's event was a challenge every step of the way. I'll admit I was nervous about the outcome. I was nervous because we had to change the date, and then we had to change the venue. I was nervous because we've all been trying to do business in a shaky economy, and I knew there were no deep pockets out there. I knew that for the Urban League, the idea of putting on an event of this magnitude would take resources that were scarce last year and are even scarcer this year.

Let me tell you why we had to persevere despite any niggling doubts about how the Dinner itself would fare. And let me be clear this is not a fund raising event for the Urban League. In fact, our biggest challenge is to have a successful event that doesn't cause our finances to suffer. As we strive at the Minneapolis Urban League to empower our people, it is fundamentally appropriate for us to give an accounting of our progress to-date. Our annual dinner is a once-a-year opportunity for us to share with our friends and stakeholders those benchmarks and achievements that represent progress. We look forward, therefore, to being able to celebrate another year of operating programs and providing services that have lifted up our constituents and have moved us forward toward the fulfillment of our mission of enabling African Americans and other people of color to reach their full potential on a par with all others.

And so on Thursday, April 15, we presented ourselves well, and we were well represented by many people who believe in the work that we do. We were pleased to have as our keynote speaker the League's own national President and CEO Mr. Marc Morial, who was making his first visit to Minneapolis. His passionate words about understanding the need to take preschool education much more seriously if we're to succeed as African Americans in this global and technological society no doubt left a lasting impression on his listeners. I know it motivated the staff of the Urban League to come back and push even harder for the support we need for our K-12 educational programming. We were grateful for the Governor's attendance and his greetings from the State of Minnesota, and we hope he took heed of Mr. Morial's message. We were glad that the Mayor could join us and share some of what the city intends to do to move Minneapolis forward. It was also a great feeling to have our City Council members present, expressing their support for the work of the Urban League and acknowledging the impact we have had on Minneapolis.

Another proud moment for me that evening was the video presentation of the League's "2004 Campaign for Achievement" scholarship award recipients. Twelve metro area students who are achieving academic success were awarded scholarships from area businesses, corporations, and foundations ranging from $2,000 to $3,000 to help them further their educational journey. It was exciting and rewarding to hear about their goals and aspirations.

But sincerely, folks, the most important part of the evening for me was just seeing so many of you there at the Convention Center, despite the venue change, and despite some of the financial hardships that I know we are all facing. I interpreted your presence as your individual demonstration of support for the Minneapolis Urban League, and that means a lot to me.

Thank you.

24

National Urban League Annual Conference: Thoughts on the National Urban League, the NAACP, and George W. Bush

July 30, 2004

As I write these remarks today, I am on my way to the National Urban League's Annual Conference, this year hosted by the original "Motor City," Detroit. I am excited about the prospect of being among 114 Urban League affiliates from across the nation and the over 15,000 people who will take part in discussions on politics, business, education, empowerment, entrepreneurship, and other areas of interest. I will take in everything with the knowledge that I am part of a movement that began some 90-plus years ago. For me the national conference is a reminder that decade after decade, the Urban League has guided the progress of African Americans in this country, with significant success. By emphasizing individual and group empowerment, we have advanced the ideal of equality and the protection of civil rights. That is, in fact, the basis of this year's conference theme: Empowerment: Building on the Civil Rights Movement.

Unfortunately, my excitement about traveling to Detroit, where the mayor is a young African American named Kwame Kilpatrick, and his mother, Carolyn Cheeks Kilpatrick, represents Michigan's 13th Congressional District, is marred by disappointment. I'm disappointed in what I see as an effort, fueled by the media, to pit the Urban League and the NAACP against one another.

If you've listened to the news lately you know that President George Bush declined an invitation to speak at the NAACP's convention in Philadelphia, Pennsylvania. The media reports that the President took offense at statements made by NAACP leadership--- statements that it views as partisan. I don't know if that is or is not the reason President Bush declined to appear at the NAACP's 95th Annual Convention. His official word was that he had a scheduling conflict, so if it's something other than that, then he should say so publicly. What I do know is that the NAACP, which has been around even longer than the Urban League, is absolutely worthy of an audience with the President of the United States. The NAACP is responsible for bringing about some of the most notable gains the civil rights movement has achieved, among them *Brown v. Board of Education*. If in fact the current administration would miss an opportunity to address this important organization because, as the media report, it disagrees with the current leadership, then I say it is their loss and, I would add, a grave political misstep, but that remains to be seen.

Let me state for the record that I am committed to ensuring that the Minneapolis Urban League's relationship with the NAACP remains strong. At different times in our histories the Urban League and the NAACP have both benefited from the same leadership: Roy Wilkins, Benjamin Hooks, Vernon Jordan. We share a common mission in our advocacy on behalf of people of color, a mission so important that we repel any efforts to "divide and conquer." Both organizations have garnered enough power and influence over almost 100 years of our intertwined histories that neither can be so easily marginalized. In the words of Smokey Robinson, "we've come too far to end it now."

25

Family Day "Gathering in the Park"

2005

After Juneteenth and the Minneapolis Aquatennial have come and gone, a lot of people in North Minneapolis look forward to Family Day. Family Day is a celebration that the Minneapolis Urban League first instituted back in 1989. It began as a way to bring our neighbors together in acknowledgment of and appreciation for families--- their struggles, their strengths, and their hopes for the future. That is still our premise 16 years later. We continue to strive to make it a day for families to enjoy one another's company, support neighborhood enterprise, and simply have fun in a safe environment with little or no expense attached.

On August 6, the Minneapolis Urban League will hold its 16th Annual Family Day celebration with all of the traditional elements people have come to expect. There will be a main stage to showcase local talent, plenty of children's games and activities, and a variety of clothing and food vendors. "Everybody loves a parade," and this year the parade, which has only been an element of Family Day for the past three or four years, will be larger than ever. Over 50 units, including floats, marching groups, local dignitaries, and community groups will participate. It will even have a Grand Marshall: Superintendent of Minneapolis Public Schools, Dr. Thandiwe Peebles!

Besides all that is familiar about Family Day, there are some new dynamics that I believe are exciting. One is that Family Day will be held at North Commons Park on 18th and James Avenue North in Minneapolis. Appropriately, we're calling this year's Family Day, "Gathering in the Park." The entire event will have a more intimate atmosphere and will be even more conducive to family activities. We'll be able to take advantage of the picnic tables, the wading pool, and the waterpark that North Commons Park has to offer. Another new element is that churches will be more involved in the overall atmosphere of Family Day than they have been in the past. True Vine, Greater Mount Vernon, New Salem, New Bethel, On Fire Ministries, Fellowship, and First Community all have their own outreach ministries, but we've invited them to join with us to make sure families have a meal while enjoying the day's activities. Each Church's Men's Ministry will cook and serve families that day.

At a time when gang activity and violent crime is so prevalent in our neighborhoods and too many families suffer from crime, abuse, and neglect, without anyone ever taking notice, Family Day serves as a welcome opportunity to focus on what's positive about our community. There is a wealth of resources in Minneapolis for families in need, but too often families find it difficult to tap into these resources, either because the resources are too scattered or because information is not effectively shared between agencies. On Family Day, many of these untapped sources of support are brought together. Families can speak directly to representatives of programs that can help them reconnect with a child who might be on the run or involved with a gang. They might need help finding the best school for their child or productive activities their child can get involved in. Someone might need help finding a job or locating health care services. All of this type of information will be shared at Family Day. Emerging entrepreneurs get the chance to introduce themselves to the community and generate business while at the same time helping our economy to grow. Folks can talk face to face with their elected officials to share ideas and ask questions about how they're being served as constituents.

In the end, Family Day is only one day out of the year; so what we hope for each year is that in the midst of all the fun and sharing, neighborhoods come just a little bit closer together. We hope that the African proverb, "It Takes a Village to Raise a Child" is a message that comes through clearly and reverberates long after the booths are taken down and the carnival rides are gone. On August 6 we look forward to making the Family Day "Gathering at the Park" a truly meaningful family affair.

327

26

Looking Toward the 2005 Minneapolis Urban League Annual Dinner: Changing Lives, Creating Futures, Connecting Communities

2005

In the tradition of the over 100 affiliates of the Urban League movement across the country, the Minneapolis Urban League will hold a formal event to celebrate its accomplishments over the past year with more than 1,000 of our community and corporate stakeholders and friends. That event, our 79th Annual Dinner, will be held on April 7, 2005, at the Hilton Hotel in downtown Minneapolis. The evening promises to be an exciting mixture of entertainment, commentary and reflection.

We begin planning for this annual event as early as September of the previous year. That's when we initiate our search to identify the person who will bring the keynote address, which is the highlight of the evening. As we began thinking about that last year, we knew we wanted a speaker who was dynamic--- who could ignite something exciting and thought-provoking in the consciousness and the conscience of those in attendance. We wanted someone who's effect on the hearts and minds of those in attendance would gain momentum, lasting long after the dinner was over. That way, we can tap into the motivated spirit that comes in the wake of an event such as this and use it to build new relationships, strengthen our support base, and prepare for the work ahead.

Our speaker this year will be Reverend Al Sharpton, a man with an indomitable spirit, an abundance of positive energy, and a dynamic personality. As you know, he ran for the presidency of the United States and, though his bid was not successful, people from all over the world quickly learned that he had keen insight and depth of knowledge about a broad range of subjects important to a world leader. Currently president of the National Action Network, an organization based in New York whose mission is to be the voice of empowerment for the disenfranchised throughout America, Rev. Sharpton remains at the forefront of civil rights issues. As Rev. Jesse Jackson once said: "When an injustice has occurred, the victims don't look for the public official with the most credentials, or the preacher with the largest church. They just call Rev. Al, and they know that he'll do something about it." However, after his powerful run for president, he can no longer be thought of as just a civil rights leader. I believe those in attendance at the dinner on April 7 will be glad to have had the chance to be motivated by Rev. Sharpton.

That night we will also be honoring a good friend of the Minneapolis Urban League. David Nasby, who spent 25 years at General Mills (most recently as its Director of Community Action) helping to direct resources to community agencies for important program initiatives, spent even more years as a volunteer. He serves on the boards of organizations whose missions include community empowerment, youth achievement, economic development, and personal growth. Many of you may not know that he was the first Executive Director of The City, Inc. (1970-1979). Though retired from General Mills, his volunteer work continues. We want to recognize his contributions to the Minneapolis Urban League and to other nonprofit organizations as well.

We will also be giving special recognition that evening to two groups who have taken on the task of actively formulating positive interventions for African American men. The first group's formation stems from the Million Man March on Washington held October 16, 1995. Building on the pledge that participants took on that national day of atonement to practice and promote personal principles for improving their lives and the lives of their wives, children and families, the Men of March has been an influential force on African American men in Minneapolis. The organization conducts programs and events that promote its most important themes, and its members serve as role models for young African American males who are seeking direction and purpose in their lives. The other group is the African American Men's Project. Funded by Hennepin County and directed by well-known community advocate Shane Price, this research-based organization has produced a comprehensive road map for addressing the unique circumstances that shape the lives and well-being of African American men. The African American Men's Project, in partnership with community organizations like Sabathani, Pilot City, the Urban League, and area churches, are leading a charge within the Greater Minneapolis area to help men living in crisis choose a new direction for their lives. The significance of both of these groups is phenomenal, and they deserve our praise and recognition.

Finally, as of today, we have a commitment of 10 scholarships (hopefully more by the day of the event) to be awarded to youth who are achieving academic success and are seeking to further their education at institutes of higher learning. This is also a highlight of the evening, because the corporate sponsors of these scholarships are often present, and our guests get an opportunity to hear from the award winners about their aspirations via video telecast.

Those who are with us for our 79th Annual Dinner will be greeted by some of the most powerful voices in city and state government. Governor Tim Pawlenty has been invited to bring greetings from the State of Minnesota, and we hope that Mayor Rybak will be on hand to bring greetings from our city. The newest president of the Urban League Guild, Ms. Lucretia Sudduth-Woods, will be present, as will several Guild members who always do an outstanding job of supporting Urban League programs and events. Rev. Jerry McAfee, pastor of New Salem Missionary Baptist Church, will be bringing a powerful invocation and benediction to properly open and close the dinner. Serving as M.C. will be the always-distinguished Don Shelby, news anchor for WCCO TV.

For everyone who has supported the Urban League over the 79 years we've been honored to serve the Minneapolis community, let me say "thank you" for enabling us to continue our work toward the fulfillment of our mission. I'm not just referring to monetary support--- your moral support is equally important. We are an organization committed to Changing Lives, Creating Futures, and Connecting Communities--- and without you we could not succeed.

If you want to join us at our Annual Dinner and you are someone who didn't get a formal invitation, give our office a call at (612) 302-3102 for information about tickets and times. If you already have a ticket reserved, count yourself fortunate because excitement is building and tickets are going fast.

2005 Annual Minneapolis Urban League Dinner:
Saying Thank You to the Friends of the Urban League

2005

The Minneapolis Urban League recently celebrated 79 years of service to the community at our Annual Dinner, held this past April 7, and I want to take this opportunity to thank everyone who joined us. If you missed the occasion, I'm sure somebody told you something about what took place that evening.

So many people have come to me and commented that this year's dinner--- this celebration of the Urban League--- was one of the best events they've attended. I am humbled by these comments, but I want to acknowledge the 1,300 people who showed up to say with their presence that "we care" about what happens to the residents of the city of Minneapolis. The hundreds of people who took out time to celebrate with us represent an even broader group of members, stakeholders, and friends whose support of the Urban League helps us to carry out our mission and gives us the motivation to change lives, create futures, and connect communities.

Clearly one of the highlights of the evening was the challenge issued by Rev. Sharpton for folks to do more than just "stop on by" for an occasion, but to contemplate what each of us can do, individually, to help someone who may be facing challenges in her or his life. He reminded us about the admonition in the book of Matthew that we will all one day be judged based on what we do for "the least of these." His delivery was much more eloquent than I am able to recall, but suffice it to say that his words that evening left an impression.

On the night of our 79th Annual Dinner, we paid tribute to the African American Men's Project. AAMP is a research project commissioned by Hennepin County whose work is having a major impact on a population of African American men who face daily challenges to successful integration into society.

We also recognized the contributions that David Nasby, long-time Vice President with General Mills, made to strengthening many of Minneapolis's diverse communities. Many people were surprised to learn that Mr. Nasby was the founding director of The City, Inc.

I will remember with pride the sight of the 13 students who stood up to receive resounding applause for their academic achievements and aspirations. Each one was awarded a corporate-sponsored scholarship ranging from $2,000 to $2,500. Our corporate sponsors understand the importance of making a contribution to a college education that can one day pay them back a hundred-fold. I commend them for their foresight.

Finally, let me mention that the dinner marked the public release of the Minneapolis Urban League's first major publication, *The State of African Americans in Minnesota 2004*. Each guest was given a copy as our way of saying, "Thank you for supporting us tonight, but your continued support is needed." You will be hearing from me soon in subsequent *Insight News* "Views" about how the Minneapolis Urban League plans to use *The State of African Americans in Minnesota 2004* to proactively address the inequities and disparities the book outlines.

Again, the outpouring of support that our 79th Annual Dinner received leaves me humbled and honored to serve as President of the Minneapolis Urban League, but I offer the following heartfelt promise: "We won't rest on our laurels!"

Chapter Twelve

The Lighter Side

1

Predictions for 2002 Final Four Basketball Tournament

April 1, 2002

Each week, my Urban Views column addresses the weighty matters facing our community. Our mission at the Minneapolis Urban League is to remain vigilant in our exposure of inequality and vigorous in our condemnation of bigotry. We strive continually to bring about change in our major institutions and service systems.

Now, I think it's time that I let you in on a little secret: What we really talk about at the Urban League is The Final Four.

I realize that I have not shared with readers of this column the very thing they are probably most anxious to learn: my picks for the winners of the NCAA Men's and Women's Basketball Tournaments. I do apologize for this oversight. I should have done this earlier.

You should know that the rationale for the choices I have made is based on observing my 15-year-old daughter's mastery of the game, coupled with finely honed instincts for spotting a winner developed over the years.

By the time you read this, all but the final game will be over. Please remember that I submitted this to *Insight News* last week. Beginning on Saturday, March 30, at 5 p. m., Indiana plays Oklahoma. At approximately 7 p. m. that evening, Oklahoma will advance to the finals. I know Oklahoma will win, because they play defense like my daughter, Ashley. They are aggressive, they stick to their opponents like glue, and they get in the passing lane and make the opponent earn every basket. But, deep down, the real reason I'm predicting an Oklahoma win is that Ashley likes the color of their jerseys.

At 7:45 p. m., Maryland will face Kansas. Maryland will beat Kansas because they have point guard Juan Dixon. He reminds me of Mia

333

Johnson of North High. Mia can break an opponent down offensively and leave her standing in her own footsteps. But the real reason I know Maryland will win is this: Brett McNeil from North High picked Kansas. Enough said.

When we get to Monday night, Maryland will win over Oklahoma. Angela Davis of Channel 5 News graduated from Maryland. She told me they were the best. Who could doubt Angela Davis?

The NCAA Women's Tournament is going on at the same time. I have a special talent for calling these games. By 8 p. m. on Friday, March 29, the Duke women will have defeated Oklahoma. Since I picked the Oklahoma men's team to move up to the finals, I can't predict a win for the women, too. That wouldn't be fair to all of the other talented, hardworking NCAA teams. Besides, the Duke men have already lost.

The next game, Connecticut versus Tennessee, is easy. Connecticut is simply the best team in the country. What causes them to triumph over all of their opponents is that mascot. They have a really, really cute mascot.

There you have it. Connecticut will be crowned champs for the women; Maryland for the men. Call me Tuesday to let me know how I did.

Predictions for the 2004 NBA Playoffs

May 28, 2004

We've been hearing a lot of bad news lately, like how the state legislation didn't get much accomplished during its latest session, how the state is losing jobs and continuing a huge deficit. Schools are doing a little bit better, but not when it comes to African American children. But amid all the bad news, there is some good news--- of an entirely different sort.

The good news is in the form of the NBA playoffs. The news is not so good for the Timberwolves, however, because the series is going back to Los Angeles for Game 6 and will not return for Game 7. I predict the Lakers in 6.

On the East Coast, the Pistons will beat the Indiana Pacers, for two reasons. Reason number one is grounded in our common knowledge that age has an impact on a person's mobility: I never thought that I would say this, but Reggie Miller is getting old! The second reason I predict the Pistons will beat the Pacers is that the Pistons have the best defense in the League. Because of that simple fact, I predict the series will go to Detroit next Tuesday for Game 6 and it won't leave the Motown city. This presents a match up for the Los Angeles Lakers and the Detroit Pistons.

I am picking Detroit over L.A. because of "Wallace and Wallace": the duo of Ben Wallace and Rashid Wallace. They both have figured out how to play defense reminiscent of the days when Bill Russell worked his artistry with the Celtics.

Now, I know that the next pick is too easy, so let me predict how long the series will go. The series will go to Game 7. Game 7, as I said earlier, will be in Detroit. Detroit will beat the Lakers 76-68. Shaquille O'Neal will hit a meager 4 for 16 from the foul line. His poor free-throw shooting will cause team dissension, and Kobe will jump ship and play someplace else in 2005.

I realize I'm upsetting people in two quarters with my prediction, but it can't be helped. The loyal Timberwolves fans will be upset for obvious reasons, and I'm really sorry about that. All of those on the Northside who remember Devon George when he used to be a bad boy for Kato will be upset. If you get an opportunity to see this, Devon, I just want to tell you it's not personal, man. Shaq just can't shoot a free throw.

Chapter Thirteen

Concluding Thoughts: Claiming the Constitution

> There is hope for a people when their laws are righteous, whether for the moment they conform to their requirements or not.
>
> Frederick Douglass, 1883

For the social contract connecting citizens and institutions to be effective, both parties to the agreement have to act upon their obligations. Citizens must be mindful of the behaviors that affect the quality of their own lives and those of their fellow citizens, with whom they have joined in the social contract.   Institutions created for the sustenance and advancement of the common good must be accountable for the quality of their service to the people.

Citizens must cultivate those habits of mind and action that contribute to their personal and common welfare. They must recognize the importance of an excellent education and make sure that they do all that they can to inculcate in young people a respect for education and educators. Citizens must be the first guardians of their own health, taking care with the substances that they ingest into their bodies, understanding the importance of diet and exercise, and exercising caution with the habits that they display when they get into cars and engage in other acts that affect the safety of themselves and others. The community of human beings pledged to each other in the social contract must recognize the responsibility that parents and all caring adults have for the nurturance of the young. Women and men who give children the precious gift of life must understand that their most important duty, superseding all desires for personal satisfaction, lies with the raising of their progeny. And we must cultivate in ourselves and our children a concern for the welfare of those less fortunate, a sense of responsibility for being the keeper of our brothers and sisters in the human family, and a respect for the potential that lies within all human beings: We must heed the dictum, "Don't throw away any bricks." We must honestly evaluate the state of our families, working to build on manifest strengths while effectively addressing observed deficiencies. We should live our lives with a sense of gratitude for those who have helped us along the way.

336

Those of us in the human community joined in the social contract serve ourselves best when we are forward looking and optimistic, regarding the proverbial glass as half full, even in times of trouble. For our democracy to function as it should, it is incumbent upon all of us as citizens to take an active interest in politics and governance. We all bear a responsibility for the way in which our fellow human beings are housed, clothed, and fed. We must have both grassroots participation in constructing the policies that affect us and effective leadership for the articulation of community concerns. As I call upon people of the community to be active and exemplary citizens, I am animated by the sentiments expressed so eloquently by one of the greatest leaders to have sprung from the African American and the national community:

> A nation is formed by the willingness of each of us to
> share responsibility for upholding the common good.
> A government is invigorated when each of us is
> willing to participate in the shaping of its future...
> Let each person do his or her part. If one citizen is
> unwilling to participate, we all suffer. For the
> American idea, though shared by all, is realized in
> each one of us.

Congressperson Barbara Jordan, 1976

Institutions of commercial enterprise and public governance have in turn a solemn set of obligations as parties to the social contract. Police have the responsibility to protect and respect all citizens equally; they must not be guided by considerations of race and ethnicity when they respond to calls for assistance, stop and search people riding in and driving vehicles, or arrest individuals upon suspicion of criminal conduct. Our courts must deliver judgments and impose sentences equitably, and our systems of correction must function so as to discourage recidivism: Those who create and sustain our institutions of criminal justice and corrections, and the larger society served by these institutions, must ask and seek answers to hard questions as to why African Americans and other people of color occupy such outsized proportions of our prison population. Professionals who operate our family and child welfare system must be aware of the disproportionate rates of out-of-home placement for African American children and examine the attitudes that lead to such a situation. The leaders of the city of Minneapolis must do a much better job of cultivating the talents of African Americans and other people of color in their midst, grooming them for positions of high responsibility when the

337

time for new leadership arises.   Professional educators with the Minneapolis Public Schools must address as an issue of paramount concern the daunting achievement gap separating children of color from their white counterparts.   Officials at the University of Minnesota should ask themselves why graduation rates for their students of color lag so significantly behind those of white students;   they might wonder if the answer is related to any explanation that might be offered as to why their students of color see so few University officials who look like themselves, and why they witness such differential treatment of those people of color who do rise high in the public profile.

These issues are contemporary manifestations in Minneapolis and Minnesota that reflect national circumstances grounded in the history of the United States. Full-fledged citizenship for African Americans and other people of color has necessitated hard struggle at every major historical stage, and the struggle continues to this day. "We the People" of constitutional fame included only marginally, by at best a 60% ("three-fifths") calculation of worth, people of African provenance. Leaders of the Reconstruction following the Civil War literally made amends for this situation with three great addenda to the Constitution, but Supreme Court Justices of the United States soon set about undermining the very document they were sworn to uphold and interpret fairly. With the highest court in the land throwing its weight behind formal segregation in the South, and with power holders variously ignoring or conspiring in racist housing and hiring practices in the North, African Americans and other people of color had to devise fresh strategies for achieving goals actively sought by black leaders from the antebellum era forward:

> We are natives of this country... Not a few of our fathers suffered and bled to purchase its independence... We have toiled to cultivate it and raise it to its present prosperous condition. We ask only to share equal privileges..., to share he fruits of our labor.

> Reverend Peter Williams, Jr., 1830

Let this book be my call to the community for action flowing from high moral values, strong social consciousness, and a level of citizenship that meets the standards of Barbara Jordan. Let this book be my demand for an institutional response based on respect for democracy, equitable treatment of all people regardless of race or ethnicity, and a level of justice that dignifies the labor and sacrifice cited by the Reverend Peter Williams. Let this book be my assertion that the time is now for uniting

338

people of the human community with those institutions that serve them, for matching high ideals with proper policies and processes, and for establishing a record of deeds that justifies the hope in righteous laws expressed by Frederick Douglass. And let this book be my pledge to offer my personal labor and the service of the great Minneapolis Urban League that I lead as a bridge uniting people and institutions inspired by the mutual goal of "claiming the Constitution."